BLACK PERFORMANCE AND CULTURAL CRITICISM
Valerie Lee and E. Patrick Johnson, Series Editors

# When the Devil Knocks

The Congo Tradition and the Politics of
Blackness in Twentieth-Century Panama

**Renée Alexander Craft**

THE OHIO STATE UNIVERSITY PRESS
COLUMBUS

Library of Congress Cataloging-in-Publication Control Number: 2014027043.
Further data available online at catalog.loc.gov.

ISBN 978-0-8142-1270-7 (cloth : alk. paper)
ISBN 978-0-8142-9375-1 (cd-rom)

Cover design by Juliet Williams
Text design by Juliet Williams
Type set in Adobe Minion Pro


♾ The paper used in this publication meets the minimum requirements of the American
National Standard for Information Sciences—Permanence of Paper for Printed Library
Materials. ANSI Z39.48-1992.

9  8  7  6  5  4  3  2  1

*Dedicated to*
*the Congo community of Portobelo, Panama*


*In loving memory of*
*Dwight Conquergood*
*and*
*Celedonio Molinar Ávila*

# CONTENTS

List of Photos and Illustrations viii

Acknowledgments xi

PROLOGUE   Playing (with the) Devil 1

INTRODUCTION   Between the Devil and the Deep Blue Sea 5

CHAPTER 1   "Una Raza, Dos Etnias": The Politics of Be(com)ing "Afropanameño" 29

CHAPTER 2   Christ, the Devil, and the Terrain of Blackness 57

CHAPTER 3   Baptizing the Devil: Circum-Local Transmission and Translation of Culture 109

CHAPTER 4   "¡Los gringos vienen!" / "The gringos are coming!": Race, Gender, and Tourism 137

CHAPTER 5   Dancing with the Devil at the Crossroads: Performance Ethnography and Staging Thresholds of Difference 157

EPILOGUE   Dialogical Performance, Critical Ethnography, and the "Digital Present" 193

Notes 201

References 212

Index 227

# LIST OF PHOTOS AND ILLUSTRATATIONS

1.1    Preparing for Congo Carnival    28

2.1    Photo of Portobelo taken from El Mirador    56

2.2    Portobelo, Panama 2012    58

2.3    View of Portobelo Bay from local fort    60

2.4    Congo couple dancing at local event    62

2.5    Congo palenque/palacio    66

2.6    Pajarito performing during local Congo event    67

2.7    Congo Queen and King    68

2.8    Congo King and Queen    69

2.9    Yaneca Esquina dressed in male Congo costume    70

2.10    Pajarito's costume    73

2.11    "Devil's Den" with Raul and Carlos    74

2.12    Celedonio's Diablo Mayor costume    75

2.13    Archangel and Ánimas    77

2.14    Congo drummers, primary singer, and chorus    78

2.15    Photo of symbolic princess    83

2.16    Collecting "Congo tax" near the road    85

2.17    Congos waiting outside church on Ash Wednesday                          96

2.18    Celedonio getting dressed                                              97

2.19    Devils gathered in Celedonio's den/living room                         98

2.20    Photo of Celedonio                                                     99

2.21    Carnival Devil in the Street                                          100

2.22    Photo of Raul                                                         101

2.23    Peaceful devil                                                        102


3.1     Blessing the Devil 2013                                               108

3.2     Devil mask from El Festival de los Diablos y Congos                   121

3.3     Devils participating in El Festival de los Diablos y Congos           123

3.4     Partial view of El Festival de los Diablos y Congos spectators        124

3.5     Celedonio retires                                                     127

3.6     Celedonio's mask and shoes                                            129


4.1     Congo women awaiting a tourist presentation                          136

4.2     Local Congo performers relaxing after Carnival season performance     139

4.3     Congo female practitioners preparing to give a tourist presentation   141

4.4     Speaking in Congo                                                     144

4.5     Cruise ships in Portobelo                                            147

4.6     Tourists gathering for presentation                                  149

4.7     Elsa Molinar de la Fuentes dancing Congo with her grandson           150

4.8     Congos posing for pictures after tourist presentation                153


5.1     Carnival "Diablito"                                                  156

5.2     Entrance to "I'll Fly Away"                                          174

5.3     View from the back of "I'll Fly Away," looking out                   175

5.4     Brown Congo Queen with blond rope hair and painted blue eyes         176

5.5    Brown Congo Queen with mirror fragments in her crown          176

5.6    Blue Devil Queen with pink lips and green eyebrows          177

5.7    Red and black Devil mask with toothpick teeth          177

5.8    Clay, green, yellow, and pink Devil mask          178

5.9    "El espíritu de los ancestros de los congos"          179

5.10    Close-up of Congo hat hung on fort wall          180

5.11    Close-up of Congo jacket with amulets and talismans          180

5.12    Moraitho and Hector's "Untitled" installation          181

5.13    Close-up of Moraitho's artwork          181

5.14    Jerónimo and Tito's "Untitled" Devil installation          183

5.15    Side wall of "Untitled" el Diablo installation          183

5.16    "Pajarito" on his recycled pedestal          184

5.17    "El monumento de homenaje a los espíritus de los congos"          185

5.18    Adinkra stone border and mirror footprints          185

# ACKNOWLEDGMENTS

To the Congo community of Portobelo, Panama: Les agradezco por abrir sus hogares y sus vidas a mí. Ustedes han sido generosos sin medida. Son los mejores colaboradoes, maestros, y amigos que alguien pudiera desear. Somos del uno al otro. Quiero ofrecer un agradecimiento especial a los artistas actuales y anteriores de Taller Portobele, incluyendo: Virgilio "Yaneca" Esquina, Virgilio "Tito" Esquina, Reynaldo "Rey" Esquina, Gustavo Esquina de la Espada, Ariel Jiménez, José "Moraitho" Angúlo, Manuel "Tatu" Golden, and Jerónimo "Jero" Chiari. Son mi familia.

Thank you to an extraordinarily brilliant group of U.S.- and Panama-based scholar-artist-activists who have been instrumental in helping me to develop my voice and praxis. To D. Soyini Madison, Dwight Conquergood, E. Patrick Johnson, Arturo Lindsay, and Sandra Eleta: You have been my buoy and my lighthouse, my "homeplace" and my bridge. Thank you for your wisdom, vision, rigor, and grace. Mostly, though, thank you for your beautiful friendship and your faith. I love you. Dwight, the cord was cut but remains unbroken. I still leave a window open for you and an empty chair.

To Melva de Goodin Lowe, Gerardo Maloney, Roberto Enrique King, and Ileana Solís Palma: Thank you for helping me nuance my understanding of Blackness and Black performance traditions in Panama and for being so generous with your wisdom, support, and time. This book stands on the foundation that you built. You continue to teach and inspire me.

Thank you to all of my wonderful colleagues at the University of North Carolina at Chapel Hill, especially those in my home department of Communication Studies as well as those in the Curriculum of Global Studies, the Department of African, African American, and Diaspora Studies, the Institute of African American Research, the Institute for the Study of the Americas, the Sonja Haynes Stone Center for Black Culture and History, and those affiliated with the Carolina Digital Humanities Initiative. I would especially like to thank Della Pollock, Lawrence Grossberg, Lawrence Rosenfeld, Dennis Mumby, and Patricia Parker for your wisdom, guidance, and generous support throughout the development of this manuscript. Sarah Dempsey, Sarah Sharma, Joseph Megel, Tony Perucci, and Ken Hillis: Thank you for your support, insight, laughter, and care throughout this research process.

To Harry Amana, Charlene Register, Harold Woodard, Reginald Hildebrand, and Genna Rae McNeil: Witnessing the ways that you and D. Soyini Madison chose to embody teacher, scholar, mentor, and activist during my undergraduate years oriented me toward our profession. Your brilliance struck a match within me and your commitment to the principles and praxis on which scholars like you founded African American studies programs has nurtured it from those early embers onward. Thank you for your belief, your encouragement, and for lighting the way.

Thank you to an amazing group of burgeoning scholars who taught me as much or more than I taught them, including Kashif Powell, Marie Garlock, Chris Courtheyn, Jade Davis, Pavithra Abhirami, Seana Monley Rodriguez, Helen Orr, Christina Davidson, Eric Sorensen, Armond Towns, Brittany Chavez, and Elizabeth Melton. I appreciate your amazing minds, your critical attention, and your commitment to making your work matter within and beyond the academy. Your process of becoming continues to fuel mine.

This manuscript owes a great debt of gratitude to readers who offered critical feedback during its various stages of development. To E. Patrick Johnson, Margaret Drewal, Michael Hanchard, Elin Diamond, Diana Taylor, Deborah Thomas, John Jackson, Lisa Merrill, Toshi Sakai, Sheila Walker, Tanya Golash-Boza, and Ramón H. Rivera-Servera as well as to the anonymous readers who offered thoughtful responses to this publication: thank you for your careful attention and generous feedback. Your comments made this work stronger and better. To Cheryl Odeleye: Thank you for your keen editorial eye and your loving patience. You were the best book doula that I could have imaged. Thank you for laboring with me. I am abundantly grateful.

Thank you to The Ohio State University Press, especially Malcolm Litchfield, Lindsay A. Martin, Tara Cyphers, and the editors of the Black Performance and Cultural Criticism series, E. Patrick Johnson and Valerie Lee, for your patience, faith, confidence, and support. Thank you as well to the staff of copyeditors, designers, marketers, and other such magicians. I could not have asked for a smoother process.

I am blessed to be a part of an amazingly supportive and *fierce* circle of visual and performance artists, writers, educators, and activists who honor the values of collective struggle and progress, which are at the core of this project. To Oronike Odeleye, Torkwase Dyson, Pamela Sunstrum, Crystal Wiley Cene, Michelle L. Thomas, Olufunke Moses, Mshaï S. Mwangola, Meida McNeal, Queen Mother Earth Meccasia Zabriskie, Billye Sankofa Waters, Fahamu Pecou, Michelle Lanier, Joseph Megel, Elisabeth Lewis Conley, Jeffrey McCune, S. Tina Greene, Öykü Potuolğu-Cook, and Toni Salizar-Parker: You have taught me through your words and actions that we must not stand on stage as solitary beings basking in borrowed light. No lasting good will come of it. We must instead be light-bearers, letting the collective amplify the light of the individual and allowing the shared responsibility and glow of it to change us. Oronike, Portobelo has directed our lives, activism, art, and imagination since we first encountered it in 2000. Thank you for sharing your brilliant mind, expansive vision, wicked wit, and boundless care with me. Most importantly, thank you for your love and for your friendship. This project would not exist in its current form without you, and neither would I.

I am grateful beyond measure to my family: my parents, Hazeline and Raymond Alexander; my sister-in-law, Joann Craft; brother-in-law, Samuel Craft; Aunt Shirley and Uncle James "Pete" Patterson; and my amazing and talented husband, Howard L. Craft. You nourished me, wrapped me in your loving arms, took care of our baby so that I could write, and are the best support circle any human could ask for. I am blessed to have you and I love you dearly. Howard, thank you for not only offering your unwavering support of my travel and writing, but for packing your bag, grabbing your passport, and joining me whenever possible. Bakari, you are my greatest inspiration and my deepest joy. Thank you for giving my work new meaning and for knocking on my door to tell me to stop.

I am grateful for the funding support this project received over its fourteen-year process of development including a Fulbright Fellowship, Northwestern University Latin American/Caribbean Studies Summer Research Grant, Northwestern University Graduate Research Grant, UNC Carolina Postdoctoral Fellowship for Faculty Diversity, University of North Carolina at Chapel Hill Junior Faculty Development Award, UNC University Research Council Small Grant, an Institute of African American Research Small Grant, and a Spelman Collage Ahijada Fellowship. Although not awarded directly for this project, the University of North Carolina at Chapel Hill's Digital

Innovations Lab/Institute for the Arts and Humanities Fellowship offered me the ability to digitize and completely transcribe and translate important interviews without which this manuscript would not have been possible in its current form. To Robert Allen, Pam Lach, and Stephanie Barnwell: Thank you for helping me to expand this project into the digital humanities. Working with you has broadened my horizons and helped me create new thresholds through which communities may engage with this work. Pam, thank you for helping me build a wonderful bridge between this book and Digital Portobelo (digitalportobelo.org). To Charlotte Fryar, Sandra Davidson, and Mishio Yamanaka: Thank you for helping me to digitize my work and for processing my transcriptions. To Lindsay Foster Thomas, Andrew Synowiez, Rachel Cotterman, and Roni Nicole: Thank you for using your talents at audio and video processing and photography to enrich this project.

An earlier version of chapter 1, "Una Raza, Dos Etnias": The Politics of Be(com)ing "Afropanameño," was published in *Transforming Anthropology,* 16.1 (2008) 20–31. An earlier version of chapter 4, "¡Los gringos vienen!" / "The gringos are coming!": Race, Gender, and Tourism, was published as "'Los Gringos Vienen!' (The Gringos Are Coming!): Female Respectability and the Politics of Congo Tourist Presentations in Portobelo, Panama" in *Latin American and Caribbean Ethnic Studies* 3.2 (2008): 123–49.

# Playing (with the) Devil

| | |
|---|---|
| *Ayer soñé con un hombre* | Last night I dreamed of a man |
| *De dientes de oro* | With teeth of gold |
| *Y me quiso lleva* | Who wanted to carry me away |
| *Ay, ¿sabes quien es?* | Oh, Do you know who it was? |
| *El Diablo Tun-Tun* | The Devil knocks |

—from "The Devil Knocks," a song from the Congo Carnival
tradition of Panama

I met the Devil dressed in white on his way home from mass in Portobelo, Panama. Celedonio Molinar Ávila (1916–2005) was the most renowned Major Devil in an Afro-Latin Carnival tradition whose practitioners call themselves and their cultural performance "Congo." An active member of the Catholic Church who regularly assisted local priests with communion, Celedonio[1] confounded my assumptions of "devil." By the time I met him, children and elders alike had told me stories about being chased through the streets by his legendary embodiment of a Devil character that could jump from roof to roof and corner you at the end of an alley before you firmly committed to going down it, and of secret rituals that made him stronger and faster as "Devil" than he was as "man." Parents warned naughty children not about Satan coming to get them, but about Celedonio's embodiment of El Diablo Mayor.

Although my logical mind knew that the Major Devil was simply a character in a Panamanian Afro-Latin Carnival tradition and that Celedonio was the renowned practitioner who had played the role in Portobelo for the better part of the twentieth century, the mystical stories about him led my imagina-

1

tion down a rabbit hole. Was he sinister? Did he possess mysterious powers? Was he dangerous? Were the stories really real?

The role that the Devil character plays in the Congo tradition is a performance—a framed event, set aside in space and time, with its own script, costuming, props, and movement vocabulary. Yet, well-played roles often leak from the space of staged performance into everyday life. The sociocultural identity most associated with Don Celedonio in local imaginaries was that of Major Devil. He was never *only* that. After all, he was a devout Catholic, a respected Boy Scout leader, a family man, a "race man," and an honored community elder. But he was always *also* "devil." There were moments, then, when townspeople and visitors, like me, engaged him as Major Devil when he was moving about the world out of character and outside of Carnival season.

As I stood unnecessarily tense on Celedonio's porch waiting to meet the "devil," I met the "man." He was a copper-colored elder of slender build with deep lines on his hands and face that gave him a look of authority and endurance. He walked with a military gait—chest pushed forward, back board-straight, and head held high on square shoulders. At five-foot-four, I was as tall as or taller than he was. Yet, he cast the bigger shadow. My father has a saying to describe people of commanding presence: "He owns every inch of the ground he stands on." Even at 85, Celedonio most certainly did.

During that first interview with Celedonio, I asked basic questions about the meaning and significance of the Congo tradition as well as the Devil character's role within it. I also asked about how the man became the myth—about the levels of transformation Celedonio employed in order to enact such a legendary embodiment. He offered a metaphysical response that I did not understand immediately or in reflection until I engaged it through performance-based theories and praxis. It was a performance-centered[2] approach to critical ethnography that best helped me understand Celedonio's Devil performance not only as an act of community and an expression of culture but also as an act of *faith*. It was performance that helped me to make sense of perceived contradictions within the Congo tradition and to locate it at the center of the Afro-Latin community of Portobelo, Panama's sociocultural identity.

My critical inquiry into the Congo tradition and its relationship to contemporary constructions of "Blackness" in Panama coalesces into three scenes of action: identity performance, cultural performance, and ritual performance. On the page, these categories line up in a neat row, honoring the deliberate spacing that grammatical structures are made to impose. On the ground, however, they do not line up so tidily. They merge, blend, mask, and change places. They anti-structure. That is to say, they "carnival"; they "Congo."

# The Congo Tradition: A Brief Synopsis

Congo Carnival traditions in Panama celebrate the resistance of Cimarrones, formerly enslaved Africans during the Spanish colonial period who escaped to the hills and rain forests of the Americas to establish independent communities.[3] Los Cimarrones assisted English privateers like Francis Drake and pirates like Henry Morgan to successfully sabotage Spanish colonial trade practices. Using these partnerships as leverage, the Cimarrones were able to negotiate with the Spanish to gain their freedom.[4] Once successful, they were no longer "Cimarrones," meaning "wild" or "runaways." They were free Blacks, free "Congos."

Origin narratives surrounding the name "Congo" suggest that it originally functioned as a generic nomenclature, similar to "Negro," that Spanish colonists used to refer to Africans and their descendants, and that a significant number of enslaved people initially might have been transplanted from the former Kongo kingdoms of Central and Western Africa.[5] While "Congo" was once an explicit ethnoracial term, contemporary practitioners use it to mark a cultural performance traditionally enacted by Afro-Colonial communities as a celebration of their history and culture in Panama.

"Playing Congo"[6] allows practitioners to celebrate and share their history and traditions through a set of ritual performances nested within larger cultural ones.[7] The main drama of the Congo tradition takes place on the Tuesday and Wednesday before the beginning of Lent, the forty days from Ash Wednesday until Easter.[8]

The Congo drama is a mythic battle between good and evil that pits Congos (self-liberated free Blacks) against Devils (brutal enslavers). Like most Carnival traditions throughout the Americas, Congo traditions in Panama rely on a hierarchy of characters. The primary characters include Merced (the Queen),[9] Juan de Dioso (the King), Pajarito (the Prince, whose name means "little bird"), Menina (the Princess), Diablo Mayor (the Major Devil), Diablo Segundo (the Secondary Devil), a host of minor Devils, a Priest, one Angel and six souls, a Cantalante or revellín (primary singer), a female chorus, three male drummers, and a multitude of male and female Congo dancers. Through the Congo drama and the language of the Congo dialect, the characters parody the Catholic Church and the Spanish Crown to create an embodied critique of the institution of slavery and its primary agents. Parody, manifested in reversals of meaning as well as reversals of clothing, is a central element of the drama.

Spanish colonialists appropriated the Christian devil as a weapon to wield against enslaved communities. Oral history suggests that they sometimes used the threat "The devil will get you" to dissuade rebellion and discourage escape. Congo practitioners recognized their enslavers as the embodiment of that threat and repurposed the trope of "devil" as parody. In doing so, they created a narrative that casts enslavers as whip-wielding Devils to be captured, baptized, and sold by communities of self-liberated Blacks powerful enough to do so. They created a narrative that celebrated the history and spirit of cimarronaje—of self-determination, resistance to enslavement, communalism, and freedom.

The Congo drama, also referred to locally as "the Congo game," does not end until the main Devil, El Diablo Mayor, is de-masked, de-whipped, baptized, and symbolically sold. The ethos of Black rebellion, resistance, and reappropriation, which frames Panamanian Congo traditions in global imaginaries, stems from the cultural context of playing with the devil and *winning*.

# Between the Devil and the Deep Blue Sea

Panama is a study in contradiction: it often rains while the sun is shining.

    —Arturo Lindsay

Our experience of life is contingent upon the expressive traditions and performative resources of our community.

    —Dwight Conquergood, "Between Experience and Expression:
      The Performed Myth"

Power is constitutive of the story . . . Power does not enter the story once and for all, but at different times and from different angles.

    —Michel-Rolph Trouillot, *Silencing the Past*

In May 2001, during my second trip to Portobelo, Panama,[1] I stood on the balcony above Taller Portobelo, a workshop and gallery run by visual artists who participate in a local Carnival performance tradition called "Congo," and witnessed my first local El Día de la Etnia Negra celebration. Instituted into law on May 30, 2000, El Día de la Etnia Negra (The Day of Black Ethnicity) is an annual civic recognition of the culture and contributions of people of African descent to the Republic of Panama (Asamblea 2000). The commemoration is a contemporary site of Black identity discourse within the country that opens a space for racial and ethnic dialogues at national and local levels. It is historic not only because it is the first time that Panama has recognized "Afro-

Panamanian" history and culture at the level of the State, but also because it is the first form of legalized redress that places the contributions of Afro-Colonials and West Indians side by side as uniquely *Panamanian* and *Black*. The term "Afro-Colonial" refers to African-descended populations that arrived on the isthmus as enslaved laborers during the early-sixteenth-century colonial period in Panama. "West Indian" refers to African descendants who arrived in the nineteenth and twentieth centuries as neocolonial laborers for the banana plantations, Panama Railroad, and Panama Canal.

Significantly, the law that created El Día de la Etnia Negra, Ley No. 9, stipulating that the Ministry of Education and the Institutes of Tourism and Culture organize relevant activities to commemorate the holiday, and that all schools and public institutions celebrate it as a civic proclamation of "*Black* ethnicity" contributions to the culture and development of Panama, was enacted on May 30 (Van Gronigen-Warren and Lowe de Goodin 2001, 83).[2] May 30 coincides with the date in 1820 when King Fernando VII of Spain abolished slavery in Spain and its colonies, including Panama.

As I stood on the balcony, I heard the rhythmic chanting of young voices long before I saw their bodies. Guided by their teachers, brown schoolchildren in white tops and navy blue bottoms marched down a cobblestone Portobelo road carrying banners and raising chants for better *etnia negra* representation in their textbooks and in their government as well as greater resources allotted to *etnia negra* communities. Intermingled with the uniformed children were those wearing "Congo" costumes—little girls with long multicolored skirts, white blouses, and flowers in their hair, and young boys with charcoaled faces,[3] embellished conical hats, and pants turned inside out. Because the law mandated that all schools observe El Día de la Etnia Negra, and because it was then too early in my fieldwork to grasp the complexity of ethnoracial identities in Panama, I did not know whether or not Portobeleños considered theirs principally an *etnia negra* community or a *mestiza* (mixed race) community. Were these Portobeleño children, especially those costumed as Congo, chanting for their own necessities, showing solidarity with other *etnia negra* communities, responding to a legal mandate, or some combination? These questions were further complicated as I spoke with friends in Panama City of West Indian descent who questioned my work with the Congos of Portobelo, especially in the area of *Black* identity. The most common critique was that Congos are not "political" and do not even consider themselves "Black." More than once I was told, "They just dance. If you want to understand Black identity in Panama, you need to spend time [here] on the Pacific coast with us."

On May 30, 2003, I interviewed Elsa Molinar de la Fuentes, a Congo ritual specialist and the daughter of Celedonio Molinar Ávila, a renowned elder in the tradition, about whether the community had always embraced an *etnia negra* identity or not. She responded, "*Anteriormente, la gente no supieron nuestra identidad; nosotros no aceptamos nuestra identidad. Decíamos 'café con leche' o 'morena,' pero no 'negra.' Ahora, no. Somos afropanameños* [Previously, the people did not know our identity; we did not accept our identity. We said 'coffee with milk' or 'brown-skinned,' but not 'black.' Now, no. We are Afro-Panamanians]."[4]

With these various experiences in mind, I wondered: How and why did an African-descended community whose performance traditions celebrate their unique Black cultural heritage in Panama choose not to self-identify with sociopolitical constructions of Blackness during various moments of the twentieth century? What is the relationship between the Congo Carnival traditions of Panama and the history of twentieth-century Panamanian *etnia negra* culture, politics, and representation? On what basis and through what means have Afro-Colonials and West Indians negotiated their relationship with each other in the twentieth century? How have Congo articulations of the meaning and purpose of their tradition fit alongside those imposed on them by other ethnic nationals and the State?

*When the Devil Knocks* is a performance-centered critical ethnography that focuses on the stories one community tells about itself through its primary cultural performance—Congo. These stories are about self-liberated Africans' triumph over enslavement, parody of the Spanish Crown and Catholic Church, values of communalism and self-determination, and hard-won victories toward national inclusion and belonging. Whereas existing research on Panamanian Congo traditions examines aspects of its rituals, dance, music, dialect, and iconography in order to establish a more generalizable "script" of Congo ritual performances within unexamined "Black" ethnoracial categories,[5] *When the Devil Knocks* takes the shifting terrain of twentieth-century Panamanian "Blackness" as an object of analysis. Further, it engages the contentious fault lines between the tradition's more *scripted* "official consciousness" and its *lived* "practical consciousness"—between the repeatable narrative that practitioners tell about the tradition and what they actually do (Williams 1977, 130). With attention to the Congo tradition's transition from marginal ethnic performance at the dawn of the twentieth century to national folklore at its twilight, *When the Devil Knocks* presents a partial history of the tradition as it exists in the living memory of Portobelo practitioners alongside a critical analysis of contemporary Congo practice as a performance of

African Diaspora identity and culture within a Panamanian sociohistorical frame.

Although it inhabits the overlapping geographical categories of North America, Central America, Latin America, and the Caribbean, Panama represents an underresearched site of African Diaspora identity, culture, and performance, especially within the U.S. academic community. Moreover, the town of Portobelo stands as a rich case study for Congo performance not only because it is believed to be the probable birthplace of the tradition in Panama (Smith 1976, 64), but also because it is one of the few Afro-Colonial communities in the Republic with sustained global engagement for trade and/or tourism. In the last decade, festivals related to Congo performance have created an even stronger link between Congo culture and Portobelo in the public imaginary. These factors make the town a unique location in which to analyze the Congo tradition and its evolving relationship to Panamanian Blackness.

## Afro-Panamanian

The term "Afro-Panamanian" entered into popular usage in Panama in the waning decades of the twentieth century as an unofficial unifying designation for *afrocoloniales* (Afro-Colonials) and *afroantillanos* (Afro-Antilleans/ West Indians). Afro-Colonials, represented by the Congo tradition, have roots anchored over five hundred years deep in Panama and entered the twentieth century as Spanish-speaking native Panamanians. In contrast, West Indians have roots reaching just beyond one hundred sixty years and entered the twentieth century predominantly as English-speaking immigrants (J. Arroyo 1995, 157).[6]

The creation of the Panama Canal imported U.S. Jim Crow racialized socioeconomic structures and social biases through the conduit of English-speaking agents and helped to create a Panamanian nationalism aimed against the United States and other non-hispanicized Canal laborers. This brand of nationalism embraced Afro-Colonials like the Congo as compatriots, but demonized West Indians associated with the Canal, even those whose legal citizenship was Panamanian, as undesirable or prohibited immigrants (Constitución 1941). West Indians were treated as a "racial" category that existed outside of what it meant to be Panamanian, while Afro-Colonials were treated as a Panamanian "ethnicity." "Black" became the marker of West Indian identity, of "otherness," while Afro-Colonials were ethnically demarcated as "mestiza."[7] This damaging wound, which bifurcated African descendants in Panama, did not begin to heal until after the 1977 Panama Canal Treaty[8] began a process that dismantled the U.S.-controlled Canal Zone, which initiated greater West Indian integration into Panamanian society.

## Methodology: A Performance-Centered Approach

### DIALOGICAL PERFORMANCE AND PERFORMATIVE WRITING

In his preeminent essay "Performance Studies, Interventions and Radical Research," the performance theorist and critical ethnographer Dwight Conquergood (2002) calls for "an ethnography of the ears and heart," where knowledge must be "*located*," "*engaged*," and "forged from *solidarity with, not separation from,* the people" (149; italics in the original). He theorizes this standpoint as "dialogical performance." As Conquergood (1985a) asserts, "This performative stance struggles to bring together different voices, world views, value systems, and beliefs so that they can have a conversation with one another. The aim of dialogical performance is to bring self and Other together so that they can question, debate, and challenge one another" (9). *When the Devil Knocks* is guided by a layered praxis of dialogical performance. From fieldwork to "homework" and (re)presentation, it informs my methods of critical inquiry, documentation, and dissemination. As a mode of critical analysis, dialogical performance serves as both an engaged praxis to increase understandings across various boundaries of "otherness" as well as a method of meta-analysis (Madison 2005, 167–68; E. Johnson 2003a, 8). Dialogical performance also serves as the bedrock for my use of staged, embodied performances as a means to rehearse my interpretations with community members, local ritual specialists, and scholars in order to check, revise, and clarify them. It represents the broad area of convergence between my praxis of critical and performance ethnography.

As a modality of documentation, performative writing yearns, as Ruth Behar (1997) argues, "to try to write ethnography in a vulnerable way" (21). This approach is an impetus to stage in print a dynamic echo of dialogical performance's complex face-to-face, affective, coperformative encounters. As Della Pollock (1998b) theorizes, performative writing "collapses distinctions by which creative and critical writing are typically isolated" (80). It reckons with the space of difference between researcher/researched, writer/reader, here/there not by attempting to render experience into language objectively or by seeking to completely reconstitute its sensual presence through text, but by marking itself as a finger pointing at the moon. It takes up a position from which to point; it is bounded by the limits of its stretching body among the other co-present bodies; and it "enters into the arena of contest to which it appeals with the affective investment of one who has been there and will be there at the end, who has a stake in the outcomes of the exchange" (96).

## CRITICAL/PERFORMANCE ETHNOGRAPHY

Throughout this book, I employ the hybrid term critical/performance ethnography to name my methodological praxis. I do so not because they are interchangeable. They are not. At their best, however, they overlap significantly and are highly complementary. Both are rooted in a feminist commitment to the body as a site of knowledge production, consumption, curation, and (re)production. My theoretical orientation to the body is guided by Elizabeth Grosz's (1994) concept of the "lived body" (xii), Judith Butler's (1990) formulation of the body as a "historical situation" (272), and Michel Foucault's (1977) contention that the body is bound within the various "political fields" in which it exists (25–26).

Using dialogical performance to collapse the mind/body, theory/practice, observer/observed, seeker of knowledge/possessor of knowledge splits by implicating the entire thinking, feeling, reflexive, co-present researcher on delicate thresholds of understanding with other equally co-present agents and subjects, critical ethnography is "committed to unveiling the political stakes that anchor cultural practices—research and scholarly practices no less than the everyday" (Conquergood 1991, 179). It is committed to 1) bodily presence; 2) tracking the complex local, national, and global contexts in which bodies *mean* and *matter;* and 3) unveiling the germane coterminous political economies in which "we" exercise meaning.

My use of critical ethnography is strongly informed by the work of Dwight Conquergood, D. Soyini Madison, Judith Hamera, E. Patrick Johnson, John and Jean Comaroff, Purnima Mankekar, Micaela di Leonardo, John Jackson, Deborah Thomas, Arturo Escabar, Anna Tsing, Roger Lancaster, and Deborah Poole. The works of Michel Foucault, Mikhail Bakhtin, Michel de Certeau, bell hooks, Marta E. Savigliano, Zora Neale Hurston, Henry Louis Gates Jr., Margaret Thompson Drewal, and David Guss offer theories of power, resistance, and agency (including, but not limited to, cultural performances as sites of agency and "homeplace" paradigms through which cultures theorize themselves) that I find crucial in understanding the "critical" of critical ethnography.

In accord with Conquergood (2013), I argue that one of the most politically crucial interventions that "performance studies allied scholars" are making to the field of critical ethnography is creating "performance as a supplement to, not a substitute for, their written research" (41). Indebted to the performance ethnographic work of D. Soyini Madison, E. Patrick Johnson, Norman Denzin, Omi Osun Joni L. Jones, and Bryant Keith Alexander as well as the work of artist scholars Arturo Lindsay, Guillermo Gómez-Peña, Coco Fusco, and Adrian Piper, *When the Devil Knocks* uses both embodied performance and performance installation art "as a way of knowing and as a way of showing" (14; Kemp 1998, 116).

Eight months after my initial field research, I began complementing written scholarship with critically engaged performance in order to create a dialectic between indigenous and external analysis of the tradition. From 2000 and 2004, I created one solo performance, one ensemble performance, and three performance installations. D. Soyini Madison (2005) refers to the staging of dialogical performance as the "performance of possibilities" that "aim[s] to present and represent subjects as made by and makers of meaning, symbols, and history in their full sensory and social dimensions" (173). The first solo piece, entitled *La historia de los congos de Portobelo: Translating History Through the Body,* focused on the primary Congo characters and their sociohistorical contexts. *Dancing with the Devil at the Crossroads* was an ensemble performance that interwove the stories of Celedonio Molinar Ávila, renowned Congo Devil, and his contemporary peer, legendary blues musician Robert Johnson, to highlight similarities and differences in the two traditions' ideologies of "devil" and "crossroads." Each of the performance installation projects—*Making the Sign of the Cross, Mojonga: A Performative Altar to Former Congo Queens,* and *El museo congo*—was exhibited publicly in Portobelo. My use of dialogical performance allowed me to hold up my interpretations of the tradition for public view in order to allow the work to benefit from the community's input, critique, and feedback. The process of developing and sharing these projects evinced new questions related to race, identity, belonging, and exclusion with regard to the Congo tradition. Each of my performances and installations was followed by formal or informal "talk-back" sessions that facilitated dialogues between the audiences and me.

Entering this project, I had four primary assumptions regarding Congo traditions in Panama: 1) they represent one type of Panamanian "Black" identity performance; 2) Congo traditions have survived because successive generations of practitioners continue to find value in them, 3) "the" Congo tradition does not exist; rather, many related Congo traditions exist; and 4) the traditions re-present a site of resistance that has changed over time.

## Field Research: On Dialogical Performance and Coperformance

My principal method of field research blends Conquergood's reformulation of "performance-observation" as "coperformative witnessing" (2002) with Johannes Fabian's (1983) theory of ethnographic "awareness." The difference between the two in my praxis of field research is akin to the necessary shifts between "hard focus" and "soft focus."

"Witnessing" suggests a heightened state of awareness, which may be honed toward a specific encounter but which may be difficult to maintain throughout one's field experience. I regularly engage with Congo Carnival performances in Portobelo as an invited participant in the chorus, as a dancer, and as an audience member. The community and I actively *witness* one another, comment on various practitioners' proficiencies, and document the moment through photography and video (especially with the popularity and increasing affordability of smartphones). These set-apart "staged" moments, which Victor Turner (1982) refers to as "cultural performance, including ritual, ceremony, carnival, theatre, and poetry" (13), sharpen the ethnographer's attention to a discrete event while offering the communities within which she works a framed opportunity to watch the watcher watch.

In addition to these "staged" moments, coperformative witnessing also aptly names the ways the community and I attend to one another within the early days of each field research encounter. When I first re-enter the community after a moderate absence, even mundane acts like shopping, walking, and sitting on a park bench are all slow, deliberate processes of both being in and taking in the space anew. If I return during the dry/Carnival season, for example, I am alert to the sweet smell of *cocadas* (coconut candy); the heat of the sun and cool of the bay breeze on my skin; the taste of fried fish, red beans, and coconut rice; the sound of salsa, merengue, hip-hop, and reggaeton mingled with the sound of construction; and the sight of familiar faces against the background of brightly colored buildings on cobblestone streets. Likewise, the novelty of my presence causes friends and collaborators to pause their daily routine in order to greet me and to size up whether I have grown too fat or too thin in our time apart. We ask one another questions about our health, our families, and shared friends in Panama and the United States. Those I have not yet met let their eyes linger on me as an anomaly, a stranger. These back-in-town/new-in-town encounters, therefore, evince a more acute "hard focus" that also falls within the realm of "witnessing."

Once the novelty of each new visit wears off, however, the community and I attend to one another with a more "soft focus" in the midst of managing the business of our daily lives. This is also true in the space of ritual performance after prolonged experience and exposure. As a researcher who has witnessed multiple iterations of Congo performance over the course of more than a decade, there are elements that I now experience in the taken-for-granted way in which routine becomes ritualized on/in the body. These are "soft-focus" moments of what I would deem "coperformative awareness." "Awareness," Fabian (1983) argues, "if we may thus designate the first stirrings of knowledge beyond the registering of tactile impressions, is fundamentally based on hearing meaningful sounds produced by self *and* others" (162; italics in the original).

The space of "awareness" snaps back into that of "witnessing" when there is a breach in the social or cultural norm. I have experienced this, for example, when someone new (to me) dons a Congo costume or when a character significantly alters an established "script." Guided by a dialectic of coperformative witnessing as well as coperformative awareness, *When the Devil Knocks* implicates the entire thinking, feeling, experiencing, reflexive, co-present researcher on tenuous thresholds of understanding with other equally co-present agents and subjects.

In addition to coperformance, my ethnographic process incorporates formal and informal interviews, oral histories, relevant archival research, historiography, and newer methods that engage art and performance as experiential ways of gathering and sharing ethnographic data. I have conducted over thirty in-depth interviews with intergenerational Congo practitioners; witnessed and participated in the Portobelo Congo tradition both within the town and with the group as it traveled to other cities and townships; engaged in archival research in personal archives in Portobelo and in public archives in Panama City (such as the National Library, Panama Canal Authority Library, the National Archives, and the libraries of the two main tourism bureaus); and witnessed nationalist celebrations involving different Congo communities, including celebrations surrounding the 2003 Centennial. In addition, I have staged three performance projects and am in the process of creating a Portobelo-centered collaborative digital repository and cultural preservation initiative (digitalportobelo.org) as part of my critical/performance ethnographic process.


## A COLLABORATIVE WORKSHOP APPROACH

Similar to Elizabeth McAlister's (2002) articulation in *Rara!: Vodou, Power, and Performance in Haiti and Its Diaspora,* my prolonged field experiences

in Portobelo have not been those of a seemingly "lone" ethnographer working in sustained separation from "homeplace" relationships and contexts.
My analytical processes as well as my embodied experiences in Portobelo
have always flowed through my relationships with small, local, and transnational African/Black Diaspora cultural arts organizations and institutions.
These include Taller Portobelo, the painting workshop of the Congo artists;
the Spelman College Summer Art Colony, a three-week program that creates collaborative opportunities for Spelman students as well as for emerg-
ing and established U.S. artists/scholars to live and work alongside Congo
artists in Portobelo; and Creative Currents: Art + Culture + Collaboration
(formerly Taller Portobelo Norte), an international collaborative of artists and
scholars, founded in 2001 by Spelman College Summer Art Colony alumna
Oronike Odeleye, that focuses on the history, art, and culture of the African/
Black Diaspora. *When the Devil Knocks* has benefited from my ability to work
in Portobelo through these overlapping organizations that actively engage
in the use of performance and art-making as processes of cultural preservation, analysis, and community empowerment. These processes align with
Conquergood's (2002) conception of performance studies as artistry, analysis,
and activism. The Congo tradition itself reflects these commitments. Working within these various collaborative workshop models, which I will detail
below, has anchored my "staged" practices of dialogical performance within
communities actively engaged in critical dialogues around the Congo tradition and the sociopolitical realities of everyday life in Portobelo.

## TALLER PORTOBELO WOMEN'S COOPERATIVE

Under the banner of El Grupo Portobelo, the acclaimed Panamanian photographer Sandra Eleta and a group of Panamanian artists began collaborating
with members of the local Portobelo community in the 1970s to create visual
and performance art celebrating the culture, history, and natural beauty of
the area as well as to "engage in critical discussions about art and aesthetics,
and exchange creative ideas" (Lindsay 2005, 3). With the help of the artist
Juan Delvera, El Grupo Portobelo evolved into a successful women's clothing cooperative called Taller Portobelo that made and manufactured original
clothing through the creativity and labor generated by the collaboration. In
addition to "producing clothing with beautiful geometric designs, as well as
naturalistic forms in brilliant colors reflecting the rich flora and fauna of the
region" (3) for national and international consumption, the workshop also
served the local function of making the elaborate robes for El Cristo Negro/

El Nazareno, a life-sized wooden Christ figure for which the area is known, and generating income for its local female participants. Eleta's act of collaborating with national artists in the space of Portobelo mobilized the resources, name recognition, and influence of those artists to allow local women interested in the project another avenue for creative expression and economic empowerment. The woman-centered textile arts space of Taller Portobelo existed for nearly eleven years.

In the 1950s the professor, activist, folklorist, and Portobelo-native Felicia Santizo (1893–1963) succeeded in bringing the margin to the center when she organized a public performance of Congo dance at the University of Panamá, which was pivotal in framing Congo performance as Panamanian folklore. Eleta's sustained cultural engagement with the Congo community of Portobelo, however, including her delicate and reverent photo essay of the people of Portobelo, *Portobelo: Fotografía de Panama,* as well as her founding of the Portobelo Foundation, "brought the attention of the center [. . .] the privilege of the state, the corporate world, and the arts community [. . .] to the margin," explained Lindsay when I interviewed him on May 21, 2003. Doing so expanded support for the Portobelo Congo community's cultural preservation efforts.

## TALLER PORTOBELO PAINTING WORKSHOP

After experiencing the 1989 U.S. invasion of Panama from the geographic and cultural distance of the United States, Lindsay returned to the country of his birth to reconnect with loved ones as well as to refocus his scholarship there. When I interviewed him on September 16, 2013, he explained his decision: "I made a promise when I was twelve years old when I left Panama that I was going to return to make a contribution [. . .] I couldn't undo the invasion, but what I could do at least was try to help Panama in the healing. [. . .] Because of the research I was doing in African retentions, rediscoveries, and reinventions, I began to have a greater interest in the Congos." Arturo's research quickly led him to Portobelo, Eleta, and distinguished Congo practitioner Virgilio "Yaneca" Esquina. The invasion devastated parts of the country's infrastructure and economy. Describing the situation, Lindsay (2003) wrote:

> The United States' invasion of Panama in December 1989, on the pretext of extricating General Manuel Noriega, intentionally destroyed [Panama's] National Guard and resulted in the eradication of law and order. Drugs that once passed through Panama to feed the habits of street addicts and

yuppies in the United States and Europe, while making Colombian and United States drug lords and businessmen wealthy, were now staying in Panama. (145)

Having been invited by Eleta to a meeting to brainstorm ways of countering the growing drug epidemic in Portobelo, Lindsay reasoned that poverty more than drugs was the problem and proposed a "painter's workshop that could serve to both preserve Congo traditions and to provide much needed hard currency [for the town]" (146). At the time, Esquina had begun working alongside Lindsay to expand his creative repertoire. He had been painting Congo *bastones* (walking canes) for years as part of Congo cultural expression and, having witnessed Arturo's visual arts practice, began painting on canvas. In 1996 Lindsay and Esquina joined Eleta to act on Lindsay's proposal and Taller Portobelo was reborn as a studio and gallery space for self-taught local artists.

## SPELMAN COLLEGE SUMMER ART COLONY

As part of the Taller's mission and in an effort to offer international student and professional artists an opportunity to live and work in Portobelo, Lindsay established the Spelman College Summer Art Colony in 1997 as well as the Spelman College International Artist-in-Residence Program, which allows Congo artists to live and work in Atlanta (Lindsay, 2000a). The Congo art created by Taller artists and Congo-inspired art created by visiting international artists appeared for the first time publicly in Panama City at the conclusion of the first Spelman Art Colony.

Taller Portobelo and the Spelman College programs have benefited the local Portobelo economy and bolstered the community's sense of pride regarding its Congo tradition. In 2000 Yaneca's son, the Congo artist Virgilio "Tito" Jimenez, won second place for his painting in a prestigious national art competition. He used his $5,000 prize to replace his mother's leaky roof and to help with his family's needs before taking any money for himself. In 2003 Cable and Wireless, the country's largest communications company, exhibited the Taller's Congo work in Panama City, where most pieces sold for $300 or more. The Spelman Artist-in-Residency Program has enabled Portobelo artists to get U.S. visas, which are often difficult to obtain, especially for poorer citizens. When I interviewed him in 2003, Lindsay explained: "I wanted to create a bridge where people could go back and forth. You know, I'm not going to impact an entire nation, but whatever little piece of something I could do, that's what I wanted to do." Participation with the two organizations that Lindsay founded as well as engaging his research introduced me to the Congo tradition and served as a springboard for my research.

I encountered Portobelo for the first time in 1998 through a lecture and slide presentation at the University of North Carolina at Chapel Hill that focused on Lindsay's work in Panama. At the time, I was a master's student working at the Institute of African American Research with one of Lindsay's former students and a participant in the inaugural Spelman College Summer Arts Colony, Michelle Lanier. Her discussions about the Spelman program and Lindsay's work led me to attend his talk. Lindsay's presentation ignited my critical curiosity about the Congo community of Portobelo and the complexities of hemispheric Blackness, which I had yet to engage outside of a U.S. context.

After witnessing his presentation in 1998, I traveled to Portobelo as part of the 2000 Spelman College Summer Art Colony in order to lay the groundwork for my ethnographic research on the Congo tradition. Although my first analytical exposure to conceptual and installation art came through my performance-centered master's research focused on the artist Adrian Piper, my first experience of installation art as a practitioner came through my experiences with the Art Colony, especially via Lindsay's work. During my initial field research, Lindsay participated in an installation exhibit in "the ruins of Santo Domingo monastery, popularly known as the 'Arco Chato' in the colonial section of the city" (Lindsay 2003, 153). Suspending a "dugout canoe [he] purchased from a local fisherman in Portobelo" above an altar of candles and sacred objects inside a Congo-inspired *palacio* (palace) wrapped with gauze, Lindsay created an altar to African spirits of the Middle Passage and to the spirits of tortured Cimarron spirits. Not only was the artwork itself powerful and meaningful, but also Lindsay's process aligned with Conquergood's conceptualization of dialogical performance in that it intentionally created a space for discourse, debate, and community-building. As in all of his art projects in Portobelo, Lindsay worked both inside the Taller and in an open-air studio formerly located in the building adjacent to the Taller. He produced the work at times in the company of other Congo artists and often in collaboration with them. This space of shared art-making allowed sustained casual conversations about the tradition that illuminated details for everyone involved. At times Lindsay's academic privilege made him privy to information to which Congo practitioners lacked access. At other times Congo experiential knowledge shed light on areas of Congo history and local Portobelo history about which Lindsay had only scratched the surface. Having participated in the dialogical workshop space of joint art-making through my experiences with the Art Colony, which Lindsay uses as a mode of ethnographic analysis, I have incorporated aspects of this practice into my ethnographic process.

The willingness of Lindsay, Eleta, Yaneca Esquina, and his son, Gustavo Esquina, to share their ties to and familiarity with the Congo community have been invaluable to my research. They made it possible for me to talk with more people in greater detail about the tradition than I, as an outsider with no other ties to the town, would have been able to accomplish on my own. From that introductory experience through its closing in 2013, Taller Portobelo served as the home base of my field research and the primary laboratory for my critical ethnographic praxis. In addition to being a space of artistic production, economic empowerment, and cultural preservation, Taller Portobelo included rental housing for visiting artists and scholars interested in collaborating with local artists and community members. The Spelman program was housed there, and I have resided in Eleta's home or Taller Portobelo rental spaces during subsequent field research trips.

In addition to the field research I completed as part of the Spelman Art Colony in 2001–2002 I was awarded a Fulbright Grant to spend ten months in Portobelo during its centennial celebrations in 2003. I returned for two to three weeks to conduct field research during the summers of 2004 through 2009, 2012, 2013, and 2014, as well as two- to four-week trips to witness Carnival in February–March 2004, 2007, and 2013.

## CREATIVE CURRENTS: ART + CULTURE + COLLABORATION

Oronike Odeleye and I began our intellectual and artistic journey together in Portobelo during the 2000 Art Colony. With a shared interest in the people, politics, and cultural traditions of Portobelo as well as cross-cultural experiences throughout the Black Diaspora, we have collaborated on projects throughout my research process. During the 2000 Spelman Art Colony, we worked together as part of a research team that included the University of Pittsburgh Professor Yolanda Covington-Ward (then Yolanda Covington). Each of us had come to Portobelo to work on independent projects that required intense community engagement. Lindsay wisely suggested that we pool our resources and time to minimize disruption to the town and maximize our ability to achieve our goals. With little Spanish-language training, I relied heavily on Odeleye for translation and transcription. Odeleye and I returned in 2001 as "*ahijada*" ("goddaughter") teaching assistants for the Spelman program. We continue our collaboration through my research projects and through an independent cultural arts organization that she founded in 2001 entitled Creative Currents: Art + Culture + Collaboration (formerly Taller Portobelo Norte). Creative Currents is an Atlanta-based organization focused on creative critical engagement with Africa and the Black Diaspora. Honoring the legacy of Lindsay's model, the organization creates artist/ scholar retreats that embody his workshop design of shared artistic creation and cultural emersion as methods of building bridges between individuals, communities, and perspectives *in* the process of and *as* a process of creating solid, meaningful work.

With the exception of my extended field research year, my experiences in Portobelo have thus been "homeplace" moments of reconnection, reflection, and deepening levels of engagement within a supportive transnational community of artists, scholars, and friends more than the experiences of a solitary ethnographer working alone. Equally important, the scholar-artist Portobelo Diaspora of which I am a part has benefited from engaging with the town as an intimate, stable, and receptive community that finds our relationship generative and mutually beneficial.

## Positionality and Dialectics[9] of Difference

Two cornerstones of Black feminist scholarship, Kimberlé Crenshaw's (1995) theory of intersectionality and Patricia Hill Collins's (2000) standpoint theory, serve this project as valuable analytical resources. They also provide important strategies to help bracket aspects of my ethnoracial, gendered, and cultural identity in order to maintain a space of curious wonder between my subject position and those of Portobeleño community members. As a U.S.-born southern Black woman living and working in a predominantly Black, rural Panamanian town, I find striking similarities between Portobelo and my "homeplace." In fact, most of the people in the community look like my kin. Therefore, throughout my fieldwork, I have used a reflexive praxis of tracking the various axes of the experiential, embodied perspectives I carry with me in order to check for "blind spots" and to resist the trap of reducing similar phenomena to "like mine" or "like me."

My phenotype, dress, and cultural performativity make me invisible to many outsiders and sometimes hypervisible to insiders. I can, for example, join Portobeleños sitting on the steps of the *aduana* (Customs House) surveilling predominantly White, U.S. tourists who, mistaking me as Portobeleña, have said things they may not have had they known I, too, spoke English and was from the United States. Often, I have witnessed local friends use these tourists' preconceived notions against them. At those moments, I was in on the joke; at other times, I was the joke.

Although braids are popular among young girls in Portobelo, no one has (dread)locks as I do, and few Panamanians outside of the country's small Rastafarian community wear them. Because of my locked hair, I was often mistaken for Jamaican when I traveled outside of Portobelo. After hearing me speak Spanish, people just as often mistook me for Haitian. I was told that my slower, melodious way of speaking Spanish reminded people of native French-speakers. In any case, my hair and speech mark me as Black "other" more so than Panamanian Black. "Gringa" is a floating signifier that my Blackness sometimes deflects and my privilege in being able to travel and study in Portobelo sometimes absorbs. Whereas I am more conscious of my racialized identity in the United States, I continue to be more aware of my gender and nationality in Portobelo. In the States, I am a Black American; in Panama, I am an American Black. The differential nature of my "Black" subjectivity and performatives in relation to the people with whom I work is tied to our unique experiences of exclusion and belonging within nation-states enmeshed in neocolonial relationships. Our ideologies as well as our bodies bear the mark of the land on which they are cultivated. As an African-descended researcher attracted to the Congo community of Portobelo, in part, because of Black Diaspora cultural connections, I am cautioned by theories of intersectionality not to make the mistake of the White tourists mentioned above who allowed phenotype to glaze over vectors of difference. Rather, I must be ever mindful that the ethnoracial identity I carry with me and that which I encounter in Portobelo are neither neutral nor "invisible."

I began my field research as an unmarried, English-speaking woman in her late twenties with no children. Each of these personal attributes made me an "odd" woman. Had it not been for Lindsay's introduction of me to the community as his *ahijada* (goddaughter), establishing meaningful relationships would have been much more difficult, especially among women who were understandably suspicious of a foreign woman living and working in close proximity to the male-dominated space of the Taller workshop. To help mitigate my status, I was careful to dress modestly, not to entertain male friends inside my home alone, never to enter the *cantina* (neighborhood bar) except during festival times, and to stay in the park or on the stoop only as long as other women did, even if close male friends stayed longer.

Lindsay and I sometimes compare notes and are intrigued by the impact of our gendered identities on which parts of the tradition we have come to know experientially. These meta-dialogical performances between scholars working in the same area represent another productive opportunity to check for blind spots and to contextualize perceptual particularities. He once told me that he would never know what it is like to put on the Congo pollera skirt, sing in the chorus, and gossip with the women, all experiences in which I have participated. Likewise, I will never know what it is like to paint my face with charcoal, turn my trousers inside out, go in the woods with macheteros/men with machetes, or story-talk over drinks in the exclusive company of Congo men—experiences he has shared. Our gender and sexuality matter in the field and not always in expected ways. They frame what we are invited to witness, what we feel comfortable witnessing, and what we will be excluded from as much as they frame how we may perceive phenomena.

## Overview: Scenes of Performance

### PERFORMANCE OF/AS ETHNORACIAL IDENTITY

Congo traditions in Panama experienced a significant shift in national reception at the beginning of the twenty-first century. By the dawn of that new millennium the country's two African-descended populations were less marginalized, "Black" ceased to signal "foreign," and the December 31, 1999, turnover of the Canal both opened the way for greater tourism in Panama and increased the need for it as an economic urgency. This shifting impetus toward tourism elevated the status of unique cultural markers that might be branded to attract patrons. Congo performance once had been enacted exclusively by Afro-Colonial practitioners as a celebration of their specific Panamanian history and culture. By the first El Día de la Etnia Negra celebrations in 2001, it was "presented" not only by Congo practitioners but also by West Indian communities, paid performers associated with tourist bureaus, school-children, and members of various cultural and civic organizations as a more general Afro-Panamanian folkloric performance.

Focused on its evolving location within twentieth-century discourses of Blackness, chapter 1, "'Una Raza, Dos Etnias': The Politics of Be(com)-ing 'Afropanameño,'" utilizes critical race and decolonization theory as well as theories of race and nationalism to examine the dialectical relationship between two distinct African-descended populations and how they came to fit strategically (although sometimes contentiously) under the category "afropanameño." It historicizes Panamanian "Blackness" within the contexts of twentieth-century Latin American and Caribbean ethnoracial ideologies and the internationalization of U.S. Jim Crow. Further, it focuses on the shifting contexts and meanings of Congo performance in local and global discourses of "Blackness" as articulated in four moments of heightened Pana-manian nationalism. I refer to these moments as Construction (1903–14), Citizen vs. Subject (1926–46), Patriots vs. Empire (1964–79), and Recon-ciliation (1989–2003). I analyze each period through Victor Turner's (1982) theories of social drama and "communitas." The phases of Turner's social drama are breach, crisis, redressive action, and reintegration (9–10). Com-munitas represents a feeling of communion that cuts across social divisions such as ethnicity, race, gender, class, age, and nationality (47). Whether Afro-Colonials and West Indians stood in opposition to or in solidarity with each other at the end of each nationalistic moment depended largely on their experiences of communitas during the redressive action and reintegration phases of each period.

## CULTURAL AND RITUAL PERFORMANCE

Articulated through Turner's (1982) figure-eight Möbius strip that illustrates the relationship between social drama and cultural performance as a dialogi-cal process of reflection, representation, and (re)interpretation, Congo Car-nival traditions are "cultural performances" that use parody to manifest the "social drama" of Cimarron resistance to Spanish enslavement. As such, they afford practitioners the opportunity to celebrate their history, renew their bonds of community, and experience a sense of solidarity. Engaging Congo traditions as cultural performances, *When the Devil Knocks* examines how the tradition has changed in the living memory of contemporary intergen-erational practitioners as well as the relationship between various perceived changes in the tradition and those within the broader community.

Nested within the larger frame of "cultural performance" are a set of "rit-ual performances" that serve as "scenes" for the Congo drama—the culminat-ing episodes of Congo Carnival that begin on Shrove Tuesday and conclude on Ash Wednesday. *When the Devil Knocks* attends to the Congo drama as a repeatable secular ritual performance with unique costuming, movements, symbols, space, and temporality. In doing so, it explores the ways in which contemporary practitioners continue to "improvise" ritual elements in order to keep it organic, tactical, and responsive.

Chapter 2, "Christ, the Devil, and the Terrain of Blackness," analyzes the Congo tradition as cultural and ritual performance within the "mise-en-scène" of Portobelo—an Afro-Latin town whose history and tourism are grounded in the cultural contexts of Spanish colonialism, cimarronaje, and El Cristo Negro (the Black Christ). With attention on the complex matrix of globalization and globalism, "mise-en-scène" signals my analysis of the space, place, characters, costumes, movements, and ritual temporality of the tradition as performed and interpreted by intergenerational practitioners who actively negotiate its meaning and significance.

Further, chapter 2 engages Raymond Williams's (1977) theories of "official consciousness" and "practical consciousness" (130) to contrast Congo ritual performance as it exists as a more rigid script to my field research of it as a dynamic and improvisatory process. How has the Congo tradition changed over the course of the twentieth century in the living memory of its practitioners? Which characters have changed most dramatically and why? How do intergenerational practitioners define the role and function of the tradition? How does the Congo tradition affect the ethnic identity of the town?

## PERFORMANCE AS/IS THE (RE)MAKING OF CULTURE

Congo traditions are sociopolitical cultural performances situated in discrete locations but constituted through processes of departure and return. They evolve not just through intragroup negotiations within "home" locations, but also through intergroup encounters and reckonings. Whereas Paul Gilroy's (1993a) *The Black Atlantic* and Joseph R. Roach's (1996) *Cities of the Dead* name a trafficking of bodies, performatives, ideologies, and cultural commerce back and forth across the Black Diaspora, chapter 3, "Baptizing the Devil," develops a "circum-local" paradigm to analyze the restless micro-migrations of these same contemporary phenomena within discrete diasporic locations.

Placing the cultural performance practices of the character El Diablo Mayor (Major Devil) center stage, chapter 3 focuses on Congo performance as a site of subversion, empowerment, innovation, and cultural preservation. Using a circum-local paradigm, I analyze the cultural contributions of the three men who have played the Major Devil role in the living memory of Congo practitioners. First, I examine the way in which the most renowned Major Devil in Portobelo influenced the local tradition mid-nineteenth century when he migrated to the town from a neighboring community and reinstituted the Major Devil character as well as the practice of "baptizing the Devil." Second, I explore the ways in which the current mayor of Portobelo inherited the role in the early 1980s and the ways in which his political and cultural roles amplify Portobelo's position as a nexus point and conduit for Congo performance. Finally, I engage the ways in which a recent Major Devil co-created a cultural innovation entitled El Festival de los Diablos y Congos, which serves as a means of cultural preservation as well as a cultural show-case. Developed to bring Major Devils and their Congo communities together from throughout Panama in the space of Portobelo, the festival extends prac-titioners' ability to celebrate Congo practices as well as offers national and international tourists a unique opportunity to view a "sample" of Congo per-formances as they exist throughout the Republic.

Chapter 3 concludes with my analysis of a generational shift in the popular interpretation of the Devil character and its significance to both the commu-nity and broader tradition. This shift was triggered, in part, by the traditions' increasing visibility and popularity. How has the Devil character been used as a site of cultural preservation as well as a means of cultural subversion? What is the significance of "baptizing the Devil" to the Congo tradition of Portobelo and to its relationship to Congo traditions throughout the country? By what criteria does the Congo community of Portobelo judge other Con-gos and their Devils? What types of adjustments or negative judgments do they make of or to their own Congo embodiment? What does a circum-local paradigm do for the study of Black Diaspora identity formation and cultural production?

## DUALITY, DOUBLE-CONSCIOUSNESS, AND THE TRICK OF PERFORMING FOR "OTHERS"

Chapter 4, "'¡Los gringos vienen!' / 'The gringos are coming!': Race, Gen-der, and Tourism," examines the dialectical relationship between Congo tourist presentations and more ritualized performances for local audiences. Combining theories of "respectability" with those of "duality" and "dou-ble-consciousness," I explore differences between Congo "local" and "like-local" performances. "Local" refers to Congo performances within Portobelo intended primarily for the community. I use "like-local" to name Congo "packaged" presentations intended primarily for global tourists who enter Portobelo by bus or boat for one- to two-hour midday excursions. Whereas chapter 2 focuses on Congo performance primarily for "local" spectator-ship, and chapter 3 focuses on Congo performances for both "circum-local" and tourist audiences, this chapter focuses on Congo performance exclu-sively within the political economy of global tourism. The broad spectrum of Congo characters are active within the first two realms, while only the cho-rus, drummers, dancers, and representations of King, Queen, and Pajarito are active for tourist presentations. The Devil character, which only appears in Congo ritual performance, is absent from tourist presentations.

Congo practitioners are agents and witnesses, watching just as actively as they are watched and attempting to control how they are consumed by external audiences. "¡Los gringos vienen!" attends to a doubling of the gaze whereby the Congos watch tourists watch them. How is the Congo tradition packaged for midday presentations to primarily White, overwhelmingly U.S. tourists? How do these packaged representations differ from the tradition as it is performed for the community? How has globalization in the form of media, trade, and tourism influenced the tradition and its practitioners?

## STAGING "DIALOGICAL PERFORMANCE"

Chapter 5 was inspired by the conceptual artist Adrian Piper's (1996) theory of "meta-art," which describes an artist's writings about her own work that examine its processes, presuppositions, reception, and sociopolitical contexts from a critical distance. The chapter, "Dancing with the Devil at the Crossroads: Performance Ethnography and Staging Thresholds of Difference," offers a reflexive engagement with staged dialogical performance as it has been used in this study and the knowledge gleaned through moments of perceived success as well as those of perceived failure. In so doing, it provides a nuanced perspective on Congo traditions and of Panamanian Blackness as revealed through my artistic processes, practices, and missteps. As the concluding chapter, "Dancing with the Devil at the Crossroads" also summarizes previous arguments and reflects upon performance as a method, theory, and object of research in this study. What nuanced questions about or interpretations of the tradition resulted from each performance project? How might such performances create new opportunities for dialogues and deeper analysis? How might critical attention to misunderstandings and misinterpretations reveal taken-for-granted assumptions that the ethnographer brings to bear on the communities with which she works?

## DIALOGICAL PERFORMANCE AND THE DIGITAL HUMANITIES

Returning to the ways in which arts- and performance-centered models of creative, cross-cultural collaboration, activism, and scholarship continue to shape this research, the epilogue considers the state of Blackness in Panama and the Congo tradition's ever-evolving relationship to it from the 2003 Centennial to the present. As outlined in previous chapters, the Congo tradition has remained resilient despite the passing of Congo elders; the relocation of community members to larger cities for greater employment and educational opportunities; the impact of a type of cultural tourism that emphasizes the spectacular aspects of the tradition while silencing its more community-centered ritualistic details; a growing disassociation among younger Congo generations, and shifting discourses of Panamanian Blackness. Still, these changes have influenced the ways in which the community frames, enacts, and reflects upon its tradition.

Looking toward the future of this research and in dialogue with the persistent discourses and concerns mentioned above, this chapter introduces Digital Portobelo: Art + Scholarship + Cultural Preservation, a collaborative, interdisciplinary, digital humanities initiative that extends the audience, impact, and scope of my performance-centered critical ethnographic work.

Digital Portobelo responds to a call from the community for greater cultural preservation as well as a desire from researchers on the topic to have a better platform to share and expand upon existing research. Ultimately, it seeks to 1) establish a digital space for researchers to return the stories and interviews we have collected to the population most intimately connected with them; 2) foster a collaborative digital environment in which community members and researchers may share information, correct absences and errors, and create ongoing dialogues related to Congo traditions and culture; 3) create a mechanism for local community members to archive and share their cultural practices and memories; 4) develop skills in the local community for recording and studying oral history through a curriculum on media literacy and production; and 5) offer local, national, and international communities a new digital resource through which to study Afro-Latin history and culture. The epilogue concludes with a consideration of how our "digital present" is reshaping critical/performance ethnography and the ways in which it has the potential to facilitate more reciprocal, collaborative experiences between researchers and the communities within which we work.

**Figure 1.1** Preparing for Congo Carnival (Photo by Elaine Eversley)

# 1

# "Una Raza, Dos Etnias"

## The Politics of Be(com)ing "Afropanameño"[1]

> The narrative of one life is part of an interconnecting set of narratives;
> it is embedded in the story of those groups from which individuals derive
> their identity.
>
> —Paul Connerton, *How Societies Remember*

> In Panamá, Blacks are not discriminated against because they belong
> to a low social class, they belong to a low social class because they are
> discriminated against.
>
> —Justo Arroyo, *African Presence in the Americas*

> *Los blancos no van al cielo,*      Whites do not go to heaven,
> *por una solita maña;*              for a single reason;
> *les gusta comer panela*            they like to eat sweet candy
> *sin haber sembrado caña.*          without sowing sugar cane.
>
> —Chorus to a Congo song[2]

On Friday, May 26, and Saturday, May 27, 2006, I witnessed the inauguration of the first Festival Afropanameño in the Panama City convention center. Supported by the Office of the First Lady, the Panamanian Institute of
Tourism, and the Special Commission on Black Ethnicity, the event included
twenty booths featuring Black-ethnicity exhibitions, artistic presentations,
food, and wares representing the provinces of Panamá, Coclé, Bocas del Toro,
and Colón—the areas with the highest concentrations of afropanameño populations. As the Friday celebration reached its apex, a special commission

appointed by former President Martín Torrijos in 2005 presented him with the fruits of their year-long endeavor: a report and action plan titled "Recognition and Total Inclusion of Black Ethnicity in Panamanian Society."[3] Using public policy advances in other parts of Latin America and the Caribbean to bolster their case (such as Colombia's Law of Black Communities, 1993; Brazil's body of laws against racial discrimination, 1998; Nicaragua's Law of Autonomy of the Atlantic Coast, 1996; and Peru's Anti-Discriminatory Law, 1997), the Special Commission built on the progress made through El Día de la Etnia Negra (The Day of Black Ethnicity) to open a wider space for the recognition of social, economic, and cultural contributions of Black ethnicity to the nation-building process.

This chapter analyzes twentieth-century Black identity in Panama by examining how two distinct points on a spectrum of Panamanian Blackness came to fit strategically (although sometimes contentiously) under the category "afropanameño" at the end of the twentieth century. The dynamism of contemporary Blackness in Panama exists around the politics of Afro-Colonial and Afro-Antillean identities as they have been created, contested, and revised in the Republic's first century.[4] In the micro-diaspora[5] of Panama, Black identity formations and cultural expressions have been shaped largely by the country's colonial experience with enslaved Africans via Spain's participation in the transatlantic slave trade and neocolonial experience with contract workers from the West Indies via the United States' completion and eighty-six-year control of the Panama Canal.[6] Blackness in Panama forks at the place where colonial Blackness meets Canal Blackness.

The complexity of Black identity in Panama is evident in the following glossary of terms, which the Commission (Comisión 2006) included in a document it forwarded to the press after the May 26 festival:

Afrocolonial (Afro-Colonial/Colonial Black)
Afroantillano (Afro-Antillean/Black West Indian)
Afrodescendiente (African descended)
Afrohispano (Afro-Hispanic)[7]
Afrolatino (Afro-Latin)[8]
Afropanameños (Afro-Panamanians)
Diaspora Africana (African Diaspora)[9]
Discriminación (Discrimination)
Equidad (Equality)
Etnia negra (Black ethnicity)
Inclusión social (Social inclusion)
Justicia social (Social justice)

Racismo (Racism)
Tolerancia (Tolerance)
Xenofobia (Xenophobia) (13)

Twentieth-century Panamanian Blackness evolved through a tug-of-war between West Indian and Latino ethnoracial politics, which Norman Whitten and Arlene Torres (1998) would argue translate into *négritude* versus *mestizaje*[10] forms of nationalism.

When I began this project, I had no interest in the Canal. Knowing little of its history apart from its significance as an engineering marvel, I had no idea about its implications for North American race and trade relations. During the early days of my research, it seemed to be my albatross. Every time I attempted searches on varied combinations of "Panama," "Blackness," "race," "Afro-Colonial," and "Congo"—the keywords at the heart of my initial inquiry—scores of references regarding "West Indian," "Afro-Antillean," "Panama Canal," and "The Zone" would appear. I quickly learned that little has been published, especially in English, on Afro-Colonial identity in Panama and less on Panamanian Congos.[11] It was not until I stopped trying to excavate around the scholarship on the Canal in order to "expose" work related to my topic that I realized the impossibility of studying twentieth-century race in Panama without critically engaging U.S. intervention and the Canal.

Through its "internationalization of Jim Crow"[12] and its imperialistic relationship with Panama, the United States significantly influenced the development of race and nationalism in the Republic. As indicated by the terms in the second half of the commission's glossary, twentieth-century Panamanian Blackness was enmeshed in debates around discrimination, equality, the terrain of Black ethnicity, social inclusion, social justice, racism, tolerance, and xenophobia. This struggle for belonging played out in various historical periods in ways that I will explore over the course of this chapter. Combatants struggling over the terrain of belonging ranged from the Panamanian and U.S. governments, to West Indians and the Panamanian government, to Afro-Colonials and West Indians, to both of these Black-ethnicity populations and the Panamanian government.

The political theorist David Theo Goldberg (2002) contends that central to the constitution of the modern state is "the power to exclude and by extension include in racially ordered terms, to dominate through power and to categorize differentially and hierarchically, to set aside by setting apart" (9). Because moments of heightened nationalism provide opportunities for the state to publicize its criteria for belonging and exclusion, this chapter analyzes the major discourses that shaped Blackness in four key moments of heightened nationalism in twentieth-century Panama. I refer to these moments as Construction (1903–14), Citizens vs. Subjects (1932–46), Patriots vs. Empire (1964–79), and Reconciliation (1989–2003). Following Ann Laura Stoler (1997), I use "discourse" to mean the intellectual constructs of Blackness, its material practices, and the human agency that moves and molds them (194–95). These discourses not only affected the country's two major African-descended populations and their relationships to the state but also how the Republic perceived itself.

Common Panamanian attitudes regarding the Canal punctuated each twentieth-century surge in nationalist sentiment and united a politically fragmented populace: anger at being coerced into trading the Canal for (in) dependence,[13] contempt at its control by the United States, resolve to reclaim it, and celebration at having done so—conditionally. The moment I refer to as "Construction" marks the foundation of Panama as an (in)dependent Republic and the construction of the U.S.-owned Panama Canal. "Citizen vs. Subject" is the period during which West Indians associated with the Canal fluctuated between being "undesirable immigrants" and "prohibited immigrants," and shared a space with the United States as targets of the "Panamá for the Panamanians" campaign of the 1930s. "Patriots vs. Empire" signifies the tumultuous era within which the 1977 Panama Canal Treaty guaranteeing full transfer of the Canal to Panama by December 1999 was signed, and West Indian descendants embraced the classification "Afro-Panamanian" as a tactical method of integration. This was also a pivotal moment in Portobelo history because it is the era when the road was built connecting Portobelo and the Costa Arriba with the rest of Panama. Finally, "Reconciliation" indicates the period within which Panama gained complete control over the Canal; the West Indian Museum of Panama was inaugurated; El Día de Etnia Negra was instituted as a national celebration; and Panama expanded its tourism industry in response to the U.S. military's departure.

I have chosen to mobilize the cultural anthropologist Victor Turner's (1982) theories of communitas and social drama as the analytics that drive this chapter. Doing so gives me a performance-centered mechanism to examine how discourses of Blackness were catalyzed in these moments of crisis in ways that either splintered the two main African-descended populations in Panama or united them. His theories of social drama and communitas offer a valuable method for deciphering how Afro-Colonials and West Indians shifted in national, intragroup, and intergroup imaginings of race, ethnicity, class, and nation during the Republic's first century. According to Turner:

A social drama first manifests itself as the breach of a norm, the infraction of a rule of morality, law, custom or etiquette in some public arena. This may be deliberately, even calculatedly, contrived by a person or party disposed to demonstrate or challenge entrenched authority—for example, the Boston Tea Party—or it may emerge from a scene of heated feelings. (70)

The phases of Turner's (1982) social drama are breach, crisis, redressive action, and reintegration (9–10).[14] Just as the Boston Tea Party created a breach in the social contract between Great Britain and its American colonists, which is credited with sparking the American Revolution, each aforementioned period begins with a traumatic breach in the social contract of Panama's national identity. The scope of each period spans roughly from breach to reintegration. Whether Afro-Colonials and West Indians experienced the stages of redress and reintegration together or in opposition depended heavily on their experiences of communitas following these periods of crisis. Turner defines communitas as a feeling of communion that cuts across social divisions such as gender, race, class, age, and so forth. He explains, "When even two people believe that they experience unity, all people are felt by those two, even if only for a flash, to be one. Feeling generalizes more readily than thought, it would seem" (47).

With particular attention on the Congo tradition of Portobelo, Panama,[15] this chapter traces what Paul Gilroy (1993a; 1995b, 19) calls the "routes" of Black identity rather than merely its situated "roots." How did the dialectical relationship of Afro-Colonial and West Indian identities define Blackness and non-Blackness during these four moments? How did Panama's two "Black ethnicity" communities create intra- and intergroup antagonisms and solidarities as methods of resistance and survival? How did two distinct African-descended populations, which began the century as Afro-Colonials and Afro-Antilleans, *become* Afro-Panamanians? What was the relationship between these fluctuating discourses of Blackness and twentieth-century Congo performance?

Feelings of communitas following the first two periods pitted Afro-Colonials and West Indians against one another by using discourses of Blackness to signify (Black) nationals versus (Black) immigrants. The antagonistic presence of the United States and its racist practices facilitated these tensions. By the latter half of the twentieth century, West Indians were more assimilated into Panamanian life and culture. With the agreed withdrawal of the United States and the dismantling of the Canal Zone, Panama's two national Black ethnic populations began to come together. Furthermore, the Day of Black

Ethnicity offered West Indian communities the opportunity to signal Panamanian-ness and Afro-Colonials the opportunity to signal political Blackness.

I begin each section with an installment of a first-person poem entitled "Citizen Congo" that stitches together knowledge gleaned from archives, histories, interviews, and my coperformance in the field. It represents my situated "awareness" and dialogical reflections on the meaning, purpose, and commitments of Congo cultural nationalism during each era. "Citizen Congo" represents an analysis of and reckoning with the Congo tradition's sociohistorical position in each historical frame through the medium of performative writing and sets the stage for more in-depth discussions.

## Construction (1903–14)

> The border alters the way that bodies carry and, indeed, perform themselves not only in the moment of encounter but also for years (and even generations) afterward. Entire cultures have been defined by their proximity to a border or by the border crossing of ancestors.
>
> —Ramón H. Rivera-Servera and Harvey Young. *Performance in the Borderlands*

*Citizen Congo I*

I am
a bold secret—
A steadfast crease
At the center of a
global crossroads—

The melodious exhale
Of a feminine wailing
dancing barefoot
on the edge of agony turned
sweet
Made urgent by
a defiant
mestiza Black
drum beat.

Animal skins
Treated and stretched taut
Over the mouths of
hollowed timber—

a hallowed pact between
generations of warriors
dispersed as wide as
Diaspora
Protected by fierce jungles—
Rebellious vegetation and
African descended bodies
Daring to be free
Together

A port
The tribes of Columbus
Thought beautiful enough
To burden with tons of
fortress rock and canon weight

A port
The tribes of Roosevelt
Blew holes through
To feed the mouth
of a ravenous canal

I AM
The lyrical hopes
Children of a Black Christ sing
in a Spanish litany
for redemption
in a Congo chorus
for revolution

During the Construction period, Panama coalesced as a nation by separating (gaining independence) from Colombia (*La Separación*) and being separated by the United States. The influx of West Indian railroad and Canal workers at the beginning of the century increased the need to differentiate between Panamanian-Black (assimilated) and immigrant-Black (non-assimilated) African-descended populations. "*Afrocolonial*" and "*afroantillano*" became critical markers of both national and ethnoracial identity.

When Panama achieved its (in)dependence in 1903 and continuing well beyond the eleven-year Canal building process, Afro-Colonials and West Indians allied with two different brands of "cultural nationalism." According to Will Kymlicka (2000), "Cultural nationalism defines the nation in terms of a common culture, and the aim of the nationalist movement is to protect the survival of that culture" (243). As Spanish speakers living pre-dominantly in the isolated coastal communities of their grandparents and great-grandparents, Afro-Colonials strongly identified with their local towns and regions. Their expression of cultural nationalism, rooted in their experi-ences as a "national minority," most often manifested itself as Congo cultural nationalism through participation in Congo tradition(s) and an affiliation with a particular Congo community or "kingdom." Comparatively, Barbadi-ans, Trinidadians, Jamaicans, and other citizens from the Greater and Lesser Antilles entered the century largely as an "immigrant minority" (242). These diverse groups experienced "West Indian-ness" in Panama through soli-darities informed by shared cultural values and traditions as well as shared oppression under U.S. and Panamanian systems of ethnoracial control; and they lived in more urbanized multinational spaces associated with the U.S. Canal Zone. Facilitated by a common English language and a lexicon of racial oppression consistent with that expressed in the post–World War II Black press, West Indian cultural nationalisms connected to what Brent Edwards (2003) refers to as a global "Black internationalism." Whereas Afro-Colonials' twentieth-century worldview was shaped largely by Latin American ideolo-gies of mestizaje, West Indians lived in and understood the world primarily through ideologies of Blackness.[16]

## AFRO-COLONIAL (CONGO) CULTURAL NATIONALISM

Over the next two sections, I show the ways in which Afro-Colonial (Congo) cultural nationalisms and West Indian cultural nationalism shaped each com-munity's ethnoracial identity. The "routes" of Panamanian Afro-Colonial cul-tural nationalism are linked to the Spanish colonial period and manifested through the Congo tradition's cultural performance of cimarronaje.

Some form of the term "Cimarron" maintains currency throughout North and South America as a way to name communities that liberated themselves from servitude, escaped into the hills and rain forests, and established inde-pendent settlements. In his book *Maroon Societies: Rebel Slave Communities in the Americas*, Richard Price (1996) defines "Cimarron" as the mother term of the various derivations. According to Price:

> The English word "maroon," like the French "marron," derives from Span-ish "Cimarron." As used in the New World, Cimarron originally referred to domestic cattle that had taken to the hills in Hispaniola (present day Haiti and Dominican Republic) and soon after to Indian slaves who had

escaped from the Spanish as well. By the end of the 1530s, it was already beginning to refer primarily to Afro-American runaways, and had strong connotations of "fierceness" of being "wild" and "unbroken." (1–2)

The Congo tradition is a cultural performance that celebrates this spirit of cimarronaje, of "fierceness" and being "unbroken."

The late ethnomusicologist Ronald Smith (1976) noted that "the most serious battles between the Spaniards and Cimarron bands occurred between 1549 and 1582" (35). Smith discusses two categories of self-liberated African-descended communities. The first are those "who remained fugitives and fought a guerilla-like war in the jungles and suburbs of the major population centers." The second "settled in villages (palenques) and began to establish a new social order" (37). Following Price (1996), I offer a third, hybrid category, of those who used their palenques as their home base while members of their communities continued to do whatever was necessary to protect them, which sometimes included guerrilla-like warfare and other times trade for mutually beneficial material goods. The Cimarron experience celebrated in Portobelo and throughout various Costa Arriba communities is more closely aligned with this hybrid view. Even as they existed in autonomous communities, Price makes it clear that there was always some form of interdependence between Cimarron communities and colonists to satisfy each group's basic needs.

As in most Latin American and Caribbean countries, centuries of inter-marriage between African, indigenous, and, in the case of Panama, Spanish populations yielded a large mestizo (mixed race) classification. Throughout the twentieth century, the Congo tradition has consistently been identified by the community and the State as a Black performance tradition even though the bodies of its practitioners have been categorized by demographic data as "mestizo." Four centuries of evolving interchange and dialectical assimilation in a territory the size of South Carolina has rounded the edges of Panamanian Blackness and Whiteness without removing them as opposing place-holders on a spectrum of privilege. Considering "Whiteness" at the apex of privilege and "Blackness" at the base, Afro-Colonial communities remain on or near the bottom, even within the category of mestizo.[17] As Peter Wade (2003) argues regarding mestizaje in Colombia (and the same could be said of Panama), "Black people (always an ambiguous category) were both included and excluded: included as ordinary citizens, participatory in the overarch-ing process of mestizaje, and simultaneously excluded as inferior citizens, or even as people who only marginally participated in 'national society'" (263).

Origin narratives surrounding the name "Congo" take two potentially interrelated positions: 1) that "Congo" might have functioned as a generic nomenclature, similar to "Negro," that Spanish conquistadors and colonists used to refer to African slaves; and/or 2) that a significant number of enslaved people might have initially been transplanted from the former Kongo kingdom of Central and Western Africa. Contemporary Congo practitioners do not place themselves or their tradition in a genealogy of Central African Kongo traditions or in direct relationship to Kongo-derivative traditions in the Americas. This does not negate the connections they celebrate between their tradition and broader notions of African heritage. One of my collaborators, Gustavo Esquina, summarized it this way when I interviewed him on July 25, 2012:

> *Bueno, en Panamá y en como el resto de todo el mundo, o sea, cuando se escucha el sonido del tambor tiene una relación directa con África. Y entonces los portobeleños somos descendientes africanos, no? Entonces hay una tradición que quedó [. . .] ese pasado que hubo aquí africano y que son los Congos.*

> Well, in Panama as in the rest of the world, that is, when one hears the sound of the drum there is a direct relationship with Africa. And therefore we people from Portobelo are African descendants, no? Therefore there's a tradition that remained [. . .] of that African past that was here and are the Congos.

Rather than link the tradition to a specific country or region on the continent of Africa, the community of Portobelo uses "Congo" as a rhetorical strategy to signal a particular trajectory of Blackness in Panama. After self-liberated communities achieved capitulations with Spanish colonists, for example, they were no longer "Cimarron"/run-away. They were freed Blacks/"Congos." Important work remains to be done in comparing and contrasting Congo ritual and cultural elements in Panama with those in Central Africa as well as other "Congo" communities in the Americas.

Whereas Congo cultural nationalisms celebrate sixteenth-century Cimarron resistance to racial domination in Panama (Price 1996; Rodriguez 1979; Lander and Robinson 2006), West Indian cultural nationalisms are tied to nineteenth- and twentieth-century struggles for national belonging, recognition, and inclusion. As Whitten and Torres (1988) assert, "Like marrons in the interior of Suriname and French Guiana, [Congo] self-conscious historicity is alive with events establishing their own communities, called *palenques,* in their own territory by their own creative volition" (21). Congo cultural nationalism embraces both Panamanian and African cultural routes and roots.[18]

## WEST INDIAN CULTURAL NATIONALISM

The routes of twentieth-century West Indian cultural nationalism and anti–West Indian Panamanian nationalism link directly to the former Panama Canal Zone. Although there had been a documented West Indian presence in Panama since colonial times,[19] the largest population surge came with the construction of the Canal. When construction concluded in 1914, West Indians represented almost half of the total Canal Zone population and ninety-three percent of Canal non-U.S. contract laborers (Brenton 2001, 75; Mitchell 1998, 5; Panama Canal Authority 2002b).[20] In order to understand a particular type of West Indian cultural nationalism born of the Canal Zone, one must examine "The Zone" and its racial discourses.

Logistically, the Canal extended over five hundred square miles from Panama City to Colón and was guarded by a high metal fence. Although both cities remained outside the Zone, the United States was empowered, through a series of treaties, to "keep the peace and provide for [its] sanitation" (Conniff 1992, 69).[21] In 1904 two parallel governments were established: one for the U.S.-controlled space of the Zone and the other for the fenced-off Republic it tore through. The Canal Zone impaled Panama at its core, effectively segregating it from its most valuable resource. The Canal's Theodore Roosevelt mythology would have us believe that the United States gave birth to Panama when, in fact, Panama was an unhappy surrogate whose geopolitical location and natural resources helped deliver the United States as a leading actor on the world stage. Following from the Monroe Doctrine in 1823 to discourses of "manifest destiny" that began circulating in the 1840s, the creation of the Canal made U.S. imperialistic aspirations unquestionably tangible.

Part of the animosity directed toward West Indians was caused by Canal Zone Jim Crow policies, which not only segregated West Indian workers as "Black" and therefore inferior but also constructed "Blackness" as elastic enough for *all* Panamanian workers, regardless of ethnicity, to fit uneasily and resentfully alongside them.[22] Although the system of paying salaried workers in gold and day laborers in silver began under the French-controlled Canal, these practices became codified in racial discourses consistent with U.S. Jim Crow laws, translating "gold roll"/"silver roll" into "whites only"/"blacks only."[23]

Not only did the U.S. system treat Panamanian Canal workers as Black *immigrants* in the belly of their own country, but also it privileged West Indians over them because West Indians spoke English. Living in substandard conditions, in the staunchly segregated society of the Canal, and paid a fraction of "gold roll" salaries, West Indian workers still received wages almost double those paid to Panamanians outside of the Zone. Further, the more fluid Panamanian ethnoracial caste system that had produced darker-skinned Panamanian presidents and allowed for greater upward mobility within the system by acquisition of wealth, education, and/or marriage stiffened as a response to U.S. Jim Crow attitudes and legislation (LaFeber 1979, 49–51). For these reasons, many Panamanians, including Afro-Colonials, resented West Indians even though they often both fell victim to the same oppressive Jim Crow attitudes. To make matters worse, the "collusion" of West Indians with the United States through English had rendered Panamanians foreign within their own home country. This enduring sense of injustice exploded into a mid-century nationalist movement that inverted the paradigm, privileging Spanish and unjustly relinquishing the citizenship rights of non-Spanish speakers, thus pitting Afro-Colonial communities against West Indians.

## RACE/ETHNICITY/CLASS

Whereas West Indians, the clear majority in the Canal Zone, were confronted daily with a racism that forced them to drink from separate fountains, eat at separate establishments, study at separate overcrowded schools, and watch "gold roll" workers enjoy movie theaters, parks, and other recreational facilities prohibited to them, Afro-Colonials lived in similar situations but not by *legal* mandate. Afro-Colonial communities, like the Congos, experienced de facto discrimination in the twentieth century with fewer economic and cultural resources allotted to their communities and a negative stigma associated with their darker skin color. English-speaking West Indian communities, on the other hand, experienced de jure discrimination within the Zone (in the form of pay and housing) as well as in Panama proper through fluctuations in their citizenship. Although the two groups' material realities might have been similar because of their ethnoracial identities, their psychological realities and "racial consciousnesses" were quite different (Hanchard 1991). Afro-Colonials could, at least in theory, achieve the same wealth and prominence as White Panamanians through the acquisition of certain cultural and economic capital. Regardless of status or skill, Canal workers from the West Indies could not. West Indians, therefore, represented a *fixed* low socioeconomic class because of the rigidity of race as constructed by U.S. Jim Crow policies within the Zone. Afro-Colonials represented a more *fluid,* although lower, socioeconomic class. Although their ethnoracial identity did not completely forestall their upward mobility, the economic legacies of their enslavement in Panama and the country's uneven development left them in relative geographic isolation until the latter part of the twentieth century and without the means to pursue that mobility.[24]

Peter Wade (1997) explains race as a socially constructed category with material consequences based strongly on phenotype, and ethnicity as a likewise constructed classification based on "culture" (16–17). The United States engineered West Indian and other "silver roll" subordination based on notions of *race*, while Panama did so based on *culture* (language, religion, customs, place). Because the two categories are nonexclusive and rely on each other for their meaning, their material consequences are similar. Furthermore, the Republic justified its asymmetrical distribution of resources, which crippled Afro-Colonials' opportunities for economic and educational advancement, through ethnic/cultural discourses with veiled racial undercurrents. In Panama, as in other parts of Latin America, "nation" superseded "race" whereas the reverse was true in the United States. As Wade argues, "economics, politics, race and ethnicity . . . mutually influence each other . . . economics and politics and social life in general are lived *through* the medium of culture" (112; italics in the original). "Race" and "culture" produce and circulate within their own unique political economies. Like all currency, their value in local markets is not necessarily the same as their value in global ones. Like the Balboa,[25] Panama's official currency, and the U.S. dollar, which is legal tender in the country, race and culture sometimes stand in for each other and have the same structural *effect* even though they may have radically different *affects*.

As a redressive measure, Panamanians collected themselves under a shared hispanicized cultural identity, separate (and forcibly separated) from the Anglo imperial space of the Canal Zone. Panamanians' euphoric communitas surrounding *La Separación* from Colombia and traumatic communitas at being separated by the Canal Zone helped congeal Afro-Colonials as Panameños. By the same token, the trauma of U.S. Jim Crow policies as well as the negative reception of Blacks associated with the Canal in the broader Republic helped to create a distinct sense of "West Indian-ness" out of a diverse people.

The historian Gail Bederman's (1995) work as well as the subsequent work of the political theorist David Theo Goldberg (2002) make it clear that the United States used the Canal to help construct itself as *White* and *male* partially by strategically constructing Panama and other Latin American and Caribbean nations as *Black* and/or *female*. Analyzing cartoons in the popular U.S. press, for example, John Johnson (1980) argues that between the late nineteenth and early twentieth centuries, cartoonists tended to depict Latin America and the Caribbean either as White or fair-skinned women to be wooed or dark-skinned children, in a Blackface minstrel tradition, to be tamed. The United States, in contrast, was most often portrayed as Uncle Sam or an adult White male politician in a business suit. He writes, "Latin America caricatured as female has been weak, dependent, inadequate, in very crucial ways. Nations and peoples so depicted have been denied characteristics which might have qualified them as equal partners in the hemisphere" (73). Likewise, he states, "The republics were lampooned variously as cheerful, improvident, carefree Blacks, meant to recall the myth of 'the happy and contented bondsman' or the popular minstrel of an earlier age" (158). Panama's symbolic relegation to the status of "Black" and/or "female" is an important factor in understanding the country's nationalistic itinerary. I assert that anger over this symbolic Blackening and/or feminizing helped move the country toward a mid-century racist nationalism that projected its rage against the United States onto West Indian bodies.

## Citizens vs. Subjects (1932–46)

*Citizen Congo II*

I am
Portobelo
The gray haired elder
Soaking his callused feet
in Caribbean salt water
Face painted
with charcoal or indigo
(like a warrior)
Pants turned
inside-out
(like a joke)
Waist
knotted with rope or twine
Tugged by the weight
of a hand-me-down satchel
Heavy with food and rations
Body
Steadied by a thick walking stick—
A tool
for balance and combat
Mouth
Open—
Pouring the ear canals

of moreno y café con leche
Great-grandchildren
So full of experience
that they overflow
the lips with song
and legs with dancing

I am
An old body in newer clothes
When Panamá was
A soldier in Simon Bolivar's
Gran Colombia
and a slave in Columbus'
promiscuous Spain-topia
I was still
Portobelo
I am the same
But
"Blackness" shifted
elsewhere

[Economic] "Depression" is just a word
like "drought"
It means the same
to cracked, callused feet
soaking in bay water
as it does to limp Hibiscus—
time to migrate

"Elsewhere"
is just a season
away from home
I live in bodies
Not in dirt
What is our dance
But movement

During the Depression era leading up to the World War II, mass unemployment fueled Panamanian anger over the anglophone space of the Canal Zone and threatened the citizenship rights of its workers. Among its effects, the Depression decreased the worth of gold, making the U.S. government's annual payment for use of Canal Zone land less valuable. The burgeoning Republic depended on these funds but found them increasingly insignificant and unjust considering the property's benefit to the States. Further, Panama had taken out large loans from the United States to "help underwrite the expense of governing the nation, [which] required monthly service payments of $182,500" (Pearcy 1998, 75). Panama's annual debt to the United States was more than eight times the $250,000 annuity the United States paid to lease the Canal Zone.

By 1933 silver roll workers outnumbered U.S. gold roll workers nearly four to one (Conniff 1985, 85). Because West Indians made up the greater portion of silver roll laborers, so, too, did they constitute the highest percentage of the unemployed. As resources in rural coastal communities also began to wither, Afro-Colonials moved to urban centers in large numbers in search of work only to find themselves among the throngs of unemployed West Indian workers.[26] Exacerbating the problem, the United States had encouraged a new wave of West Indian immigration in 1931 for a Canal construction project (McCain 1965, 244).[27] Many of these new immigrants joined earlier arrivals as unemployed and unwelcome. With West Indian competition for scarce jobs overflowing the Canal Zone, the resentment toward them and a desire that the United States repatriate some of them reached its peak. The political climate of the 1930s was ripe for race-based and economic nationalisms to reach the level of territorial nationalism, which had been raging since the Canal divided the country.

Two brothers from the country's interior, former presidents Harmodio and Arnulfo Arias, rode this wave of economic and racial nationalisms in divergent trajectories, although they started at the same root. Long after the wave's crest, it continued to produce ripples in contemporary Panamanian leadership. Until Harmodio's presidency, the country's highest political posts were occupied by an urban oligarchy. Following in his stead, several of Panama's most charismatic leaders, including General Omar Torrijos (1968–81), who led Panama during the 1977 Carter–Torrijos Treaty guaranteeing the complete transfer of the Canal, rose on a populist platform from the country's interior rural middle class. Running on the party ticket of her deceased husband Arnulfo, Mireya Moscoso, the country's first female president (1999–2004), guided the country for the first four years of my field research in Panama and was replaced in May 2004 by Torrijos's son, Martín.

The common root from which the nationalisms of the Arias brothers sprang was Acción Comunal, a "moderately nationalist middle-class civic organization [that] consisted largely of engineers, lawyers, doctors and various bureaucrats" (Pearcy 1998, 60–61). Founded in 1923, Acción Comunal achieved an unprecedented, albeit temporary, cohesion among the emergent middle class by rallying under a common banner of distrust of the "pro-

American" ruling elite, frustration over the pervasiveness of the English language and the United States' influence in Panamanian life, and commitment
to fostering a love of country, flag, and the Spanish language within Panamanian youth (61). Their slogan was *"Panameñismo"* ("Panamá for Panamanians"). Attracted by these tenets, the Arias brothers joined the organization in
1930 and participated in the country's first armed coup, which "ended thirty
years of elite domination of the nation's government" (66) and left Harmodio Arias in the presidential seat. Unlike his brother, Harmodio had a broad
base of support, which included and embraced West Indians. He had acted
as the lawyer for one West Indian community during an urban renters' pro-
test and understood their issues as reflective of other members of Panama's
poor and working class. Harmodio's was an economic nationalism elastic
enough to include poor and middle-class populations, regardless of race,
negatively affected by the politics of the Canal Zone and ruling elite (68–69).
His policies benefited both African-descended populations, and their coali-
tion benefited him. For these reasons, Acción Comunal billed him as "The
Poor People's Candidate." Moreover, he recognized and tapped into the power
of Panama's vocal student populace by founding the University of Panamá in
1935 to "preserve Panamanian nationality" (75). Once in power, however, he
replicated some of the former ruling class's habits of filling powerful positions
with family members and voting in favor of economic benefits for landown-
ers like him, whereas he once had defended the rights of poorer renters (72).

Harmodio had rallied together all poor and middle-class Panamanian residents against the empire, but Arnulfo blamed West Indians for the economic
state of poor and middle-class "Panamanians" and demonized them alongside the United States. Using his brother's economic nationalism as a point
of departure, he railed against the English-speaking West Indians who were
competing with Spanish-speaking Panamanians for scarce jobs and bloating
the country's unemployment. "For the first time," LaFeber (1979) summarizes,
"demands for radical social change linked up with Panamanian nationalism"
(75). Wielded thus, Arnulfo's brand of panameñismo stripped West Indian
citizenship rights and branded them "undesirable immigrants." Legislated in
Title 2, "Nationality and Immigration," of the 1941 Constitution, this represented the first case of legal discrimination outside of the Canal Zone based
on race.[28] Many conjecture that Arnulfo's racial politics splintered from his
brother's as a result of his stint as Minister to Italy in the mid-1930s during
Mussolini's reign, subsequent audience with Hitler in 1937, and fascination
with both forms of fascist nationalism (73). The effects of his regimes[29] on
African-descended communities, however, are more aligned with South African experiences than those in Italy or Germany. Just as the former South

African system of apartheid, which was solidified during the same era, trounced cohesion between "coloureds" and "Blacks," Arnulfo's panameñismo shattered some of the fragile coalitions between Afro-Colonials and West Indians by embracing the former as *citizens* under the law and bracketing the latter as *subjects* of the law.

Although Arnulfo couched his racism in terms of language, which protected Afro-Colonial communities like the Congos from his legislations, his angst involved more than the immigration of non-Spanish speakers. The 1941 Constitution lists as "prohibited immigrants" those who did not add to the "*mejoramiento étnico*" ("ethnic improvement") of the country. Translated, this included "the Black race whose native language is not Spanish, the Yellow race and the native races of India, Asia Minor and North Africa" (Constitución 1941). LaFeber (1979) writes:

> Arnulfo received strong support in Panama City and Colon, where most of the middle class lived, when he attacked Blacks. The new class was the most anti-Black of all Panamanian groups, due partly to fears of economic competition, partly to a proud nationalism that feared outsiders might mistake their country for a "Black republic." The very success of the Canal Zone, and its thousands of West Indian laborers, had created a middle class whose anti-Yankeeism and dislike of Blacks formed the basis of Arnulfo's burgeoning power. (76)

In LaFeber's analysis, the marker "Black" excludes Afro-Colonial populations, regardless of their history of enslavement and cultural performances. "Black" in LaFeber's commentary, as well as in official records, signals the West Indian population.

Arnulfo's spin on panameñismo ostracized West Indians, labeled them as part of the problem, and created a nationalist agenda aimed against all non-hispanicized people. During this period, "race" and "ethnicity" were teased apart; West Indians represented an inassimilable "race" while Afro-Colonials were an already assimilated "ethnicity." His brand of panameñismo did more to polarize Afro-Colonials and West Indians than any nationalistic movement before or after it. In addition to the violence engendered by making "Blackness" coded as "West Indian-ness" punitive, oral history also suggests that Arnulfo reinforced the divide between the two communities by having Congo groups as well as indigenous groups perform at his political rallies. Although I have not yet found documentation to support this claim, the act would have buffered him from growing criticism about his "racist" nationalism and kept the two African-descended populations divided. Regardless of any critique that Congo songs might have surreptitiously made against Arnulfo, the spectacle would have visually placed them on the side of his politics for the West Indian spectator. Most studies of this period in Panamanian history acknowledge the differences between the two African-descended groups as though they occurred naturally without attending to the hand(s) that helped legislate their difference—what anthropologists John and Jean Comaroff (1997) would refer to as Arnulfo's "agentive mode," which is "the command wielded by human beings in specific historical contexts" (22).

By taking away West Indian citizenship rights during his first brief administration in 1941, Arnulfo legally solidified differences between West Indians and Afro-Colonials and drove a deeper wedge between the two African-descended populations. Afro-Colonials were protected as ethnic citizens while West Indians were rendered vulnerable as racial subjects governed by the law but without the rights of citizenship. This material linguistic accomplishment reinscribed the same type of rigid Blackness that Canal Zone racial discourse had forced onto West Indian bodies. Although the 1946 Constitution restored the citizenship and property rights that Arnulfo's Constitution took away, the damage to the two groups' ability to form broad-based coalitions had been done and could not be easily reversed with new laws on fresh paper. The shared trauma of having their citizenship rights revoked created a second reinforcing moment of communitas for West Indians communities.

## Patriots vs. Empire (1964–79)

*Citizen Congo III*

I am
Ebony and phonics
Blended with salsa and cilantro
Served on a plate with red beans
And coconut rice—
An Afro-engineered Castellano
An African drumbeat
Kongo-Atlantic feet recognize
Beneath the swirl of a recycled
Spanish pollera

I am
the red devils
Catholic priests sermonized
And Christian Colonizers *were . . .*

The trickster
Waiting at the Crossroads
With Legba
Wailing like blues
Improvising like jazz
Dancing Diaspora

I am
"Patria"
A bloody brown-skinned girl
Wrapped in a red, white and blue flag
That doesn't belong to the States—
I have danced in it
Torn my hymen on it
Swaddled my babies with it
Cut it into pieces
Fried and refried it like patacones
And eaten it with ketchup and hot sauce . . .
It is not only *mine*
It is *me*.[30]

Third World revolutionary movements burned a hole in the 1960s that affected global change. Blackness as a social construct with material consequences that subjugates one population to elevate another was at the heart of these struggles. The United States was fighting a hot war in Vietnam, the Cold War with the former Soviet Union, and a volatile race war at home. The Bay of Pigs stood as a David and Goliath parable for Latin American and Caribbean countries struggling against U.S. imperialism. By the time that the January 9, 1964, Flag Riots catapulted Panama to break off diplomatic relations with the U.S. government, the United States was already growing increasingly uneasy about possible coalitions between Cuba and Panama. To make matters worse from the perspective of the United States, seven constitutional governments in Latin America had fallen to military coups since 1961 (LaFeber 1979, 116). Time, space, and circumstance had made it urgent for the States to negotiate a new Canal treaty that would lead to the eradication of the "in perpetuity" clause that had plagued Panama since its inception.

The 1964 Flag Riots marked one of the two critical twentieth-century moments of shared communitas between West Indian and Afro-Colonial communities. Until the 1960s the U.S. flag had flown alone inside the fenced-off Zone, fueling Panamanian anti-imperialist irritation. Shortly before the riots, Panama had gained slight concessions from the U.S. government, including the right to display the two countries' flags side by side at designated locations. In other locations, neither flag was to be flown. Several Zone residents resented Washington's concessions and refused to honor them. In accordance with other historical accounts (Conniff 1985; E. Jackson 1999; LaFeber 1979), Don Rojas (1990) distilled the tragedy thus:

> On January 9, U.S. students and their parents living in the zone hoisted the U.S. flag at Balboa High School, disobeying the orders of the zone governor, and refusing to allow the Panamanian flag to be flown alongside it. When Panamanian students entered the zone and secured permission to raise their flag, they were stopped by the U.S. students, and the Panamanian flag was desecrated. (21)

The resulting three days of revolts, which extended from Panama City to Colón, ended in more than twenty Panamanian deaths and hundreds of serious injuries.[31]

By the time of the Flag Riots, the Panamanian students from Instituto Nacional who had attempted to hang their flag in the Zone and their supporters were West Indian and Afro-Colonial and fairly representative of the national population. General Omar Torrijos's road and school projects had not yet linked Atlantic coastal towns with the broader Republic. Afro-Colonial parents wanting their children to get a better education often sent them to live with relatives in Colón or Panama City during the school year. As a result, a small percentage of Afro-Colonials and a sizable percentage of West Indians were either Instituto Nacional students or living nearby at the time of the riot. On January 9, 1964, Panameños living inside and outside of the Zone rioted against Balboa High School. Most of the murdered Panameño protesters were from El Chorrillo, an impoverished, formerly "silver roll" neighborhood outside of the Zone, which had been built to house Canal Zone day laborers (Jaquith 1990, 7). The murder of Panamanian protesters by Canal Zone police caused trauma across ethnoracial lines; West Indians were among those patriots who shed blood and tears. The incident was the beginning of the end of the Canal Zone, as Panama broke off diplomatic relations with the United States for the first time.

The 1964 Flag Riots and their diplomatic fallout set the stage for the 1977 Carter–Torrijos Treaty guaranteeing complete transfer of the Canal. Just as Harmodio Arias had done three decades prior, Omar Torrijos rose to power from the country's interior, recognizing the unity of the underclass's struggle and creating a nationalism built on a platform of social justice that challenged the power of the oligarchy. From 1968 until his untimely death in 1981, Torrijos "dominated the Panamanian political scene" (Meditz and Hanratty

1987b). Born in 1929, "he came from the country's small but ultra-national-istic, ambitious, and anti-foreign middle class, the class that first challenged the oligarchy effectively, if briefly, in 1931" (LaFeber 1979, 126). Torrijos took control of the country in 1968 by overthrowing Arnulfo Arias on his third presidential stint, purging the administration and University of Panamá of opposition, and disbanding both the National Assembly and all political par-ties. Although he admired socialist trends in Peru and Bolivia and established a "mutually supportive relationship with Cuba's Fidel Castro," the political label he preferred (and which is most often used by Panamanians to describe him) was "populist" (Meditz and Hanratty 1987b). Having secured his power through an alliance with the National Guard, Torrijos focused his attention on his nation-building projects, which were distinctive in that they focused largely on those who had been "objects of social injustice at the hands of the oligarchy, particularly the long-neglected *campesinos*" (Meditz and Hanratty 1987b).[32] Through aggressive road-building and literacy and housing proj-ects, he incorporated the rural poor into politics for the first time. He also formed fragile coalitions between historically antagonistic groups like the National Guard and student activists by capitalizing on their shared hostility toward U.S. domination as well as their shared desire for complete access to and control over the Canal Zone (Meditz and Hanratty 1987b; Conniff 1992, 128; Brecher, Nissen, and Barnathan 1981). Relevant to this study, one of his nation-building projects, known commonly as "the colonization of the Atlan-tic," created an intra-isthmian migration by guaranteeing to specific interior populations land along the Atlantic coast, the cradle of Afro-Colonial com-munities and the Congo tradition. The government land distribution included "7,000 hectares of land among 61,300 families" (LaFeber 1979, 134). Torrijos's road and land distribution projects exposed formerly closed coastal com-munities like Portobelo to their first major population influx since the early days of the Canal.[33] As Portobelo had done with West Indian migration at the beginning of the century,[34] the community slowly absorbed its newest popu-lation into its Afro-Colonial life and traditions through mutual assimilation, intermarriage, and time.

Having ruled Panama for thirteen years through his authority over the National Guard, Torrijos was the longest-standing dictator in Panamanian history and the third longest in Latin American history. "Torrijos's proudest legacy," Brecher, Nissen, and Barnathan (1981) conclude, "is the Panamanian flag that now flies over the Panama Canal" (46). Indeed, "It is very unlikely," attests the Panama historian Conniff (1992), "that the treaties could have been concluded without him" (128). The gradual dismantling of the Canal Zone, which was sparked by the Flag Riots and began taking shape with the signing of the Carter–Torrijos Treaty, initiated a process of national healing across ethnoracial lines.[35]

# Reconciliation (1989–2003)

The defensive walls around each sub-culture gradually crumble and new forms with even more complex genealogies are created in the synthesis and transcendence of previous styles.

—Paul Gilroy, *There Ain't No Black in the Union Jack*

Appropriation is a key dynamic in understanding race and nation in Latin America.

—Peter Wade, Afterword to *Race & Nation in Modern Latin America*

*Citizen Congo IV*

I am
Community—
A network of families
Able to mobilize
For grassroots resistance
Brandishing
Cultural weapons
In fisted hands
Made for clapping—
Arroz con coco pots,
Duce con leche spoons,
Pans for sautéing pulpo
And banderas de Panamá
Pounding the air with song
Stretched taut to shouting.
Standing shoulder to shoulder with the ancestors
Demanding visibility
Estas Panameña?
YO SOY!
Portobeleña?
YO SOY!
Negra?
*YO SOY! YO SOY! YO SOY!*
Banging

I AM
Singing
I AM
Screaming
I AM I AM I AM!

The December 20, 1989, invasion created the second traumatic experience of communitas that affected Panama's two African-descended populations. Twenty-five years after the 1964 Flag Riots, "Chorrillo was the first neighborhood to be destroyed as U.S. bombers pounded the Defense Force's headquarters located in the heart of Chorrillo" (Jaquith 1990, 7). In addition to the predominantly West Indian community of El Chorrillo,[36] areas of San Miguelitto and Colón city were destroyed. Based on a report compiled by the National Lawyers Guild (1990) located in New York, "In El Chorrillo alone, sixteen thousand people were left homeless by the invasion." In a cruel twist of irony, the U.S. invasion not only further devastated the El Chorrillo community, but it also forced residents to seek housing in the very school many had protested adamantly against during the 1964 Flag Riots.

Dubbed "Operation Just Cause" by U.S. Defense Secretary Dick Cheney, and led by General Colin Powell, both working under the first Bush administration, the stated purpose was to oust former CIA informant Manual Antonio Noriega from his dictatorial seat of power. Noriega began his rise to power in the National Guard during Omar Torrijos's administration. As Conniff (1992) reports, "Noriega served as chief of security, enforcer, and troubleshooter for Torrijos, who once introduced Noriega as 'my gangster'" (149–50). Two years after Torrijos's fatal 1981 plane crash, Noriega assumed control of the Guard, renamed it the Panama Defense Forces, and greatly increased its numbers and might. Like Torrijos, he was never legally elected president of Panama, but his power over the country was unquestionable. Moreover, just as Torrijos had done in 1972, Noriega eventually had himself named "Chief of Government." "Believing he was in good graces at the White House," Conniff summarizes, "Noriega built a machine of repression and crime to enrich himself and his cronies" (153). Despite knowledge of his "gunrunning, money laundering, and drug smuggling," the United States made no effort to intervene in his politics until 1985, when he refused to use his Panama Defense Forces to help bolster the U.S.-sponsored Contras against the Sandinistas in Nicaragua (152). Until that time, despite the Reagan–Bush administration's 1980s "War on Drugs," the U.S. government had turned a blind eye to Noriega's activities as long as his contacts in the region helped "keep the Contra campaign alive" (152).

From 1985 until his removal in the waning days of 1989, Noriega's power became more absolute, his brutality more conspicuous, and his local and global opposition more vocal. Protesters in Panama City often took to the streets banging empty pots or waving white handkerchiefs to express their opposition (Conniff 1992, 156). To justify an immediate military intervention in Panama, President George H. W. Bush claimed that Noriega had declared war on the United States and threatened the safety of the Canal. History has shown Bush's claims to be just as flawed as his son's accusation of weapons of mass destruction that rallied support for his war in Iraq. Although the majority of Panamanians rejoiced at Noriega's removal, local and global observers shook their heads and pounded their fists disapprovingly at the United States' clear violation of international laws in dismantling a monster of their own creation. Noriega was gone, but Panama was again, if only shortly, an occupied country. Moreover, the Canal still kept the country wed to a patriarchal force that had the touch of a sledgehammer. Twelve years after the Carter–Torrijos Treaty, guaranteeing the complete transfer of the Canal by the end of the century, the invasion reinforced the U.S. government's sustained right to intervene in Panama under the auspices of maintaining the neutrality of the Canal. In the end, the war caused approximately twenty-four U.S. deaths and Panamanian fatalities ranging from the hundreds to the thousands (depending on the reporting agency). Eight thousand Panamanian demonstrators called for compensation due to losses and damages caused by the invasion (Weeks and Gunson 1991, xviii).

Carnival season started on January 19, 1990, in the aftermath of the 1989 invasion. In the midst of U.S. occupation, the Congos of Portobelo staged a small coup. Their mayor, the former Panama Canal Zone resident Elaina Maison (pseudonym), had closed the open-air produce market in the town months earlier and sold the land to a couple from the States. She had replaced Afro-Colonial Portobeleña housekeepers with indigenous workers who commuted into town daily. And, most egregiously, she had flown the U.S. flag over the local municipal building. Portobeleña women had had enough. With the help and support of prominent local residents, the Congo women mutinied against the mayor. Wearing their polleras, armed with pots, pans, and loud, angry voices, the women surrounded the municipal building and demanded that Maison step down. Several of the women entered the building, ascended to the Mayor's office, and blended their screaming voices with those on the street. After Maison's daughter and one of the Congas tumbled down the stairs punching and pulling each other, Maison left the building and her position. This was the Congos' indirect response to "Operation Just Cause," the largest U.S. military invasion since Vietnam, and their direct response to an injustice in their town. As an organized community, the Congos were able to mobilize quickly and affect local change. In 2004, fifteen years after the Congo coup, Carlos Chavarría, the current Diablo Mayor in the Congo tradition, was elected mayor of Portobelo.

After the national trauma of the U.S. invasion, there were at least four redressive moments of communitas shared between the Afro-Colonial and West Indian African-descended populations: the complete turnover of the Canal to Panama on December 31, 1999, including a dismantling of the Zone; the 2000 inauguration of the Day of Black Ethnicity; the 2003 Centennial celebrations; and the 2006 Primer Festival Afropanameño. The relations between the two populations are not seamless; however, by the end of the twentieth century, the cultural traditions that both groups claim were framed by a shared national homeplace. Invoking Peter Wade's (1997) definition of "ethnicity" through the "language of place" (18), both groups now represented Panameño "Black ethnicity" communities, and both recognized their shared global space within a hegemonic system of oppression based in part on discourses of race.

The West Indian community remains at the vanguard of overt Black political action in Panama. Afro-Colonial communities, like the Congos, enact parodic cultural performances that portray their history of sociopolitical struggle for inclusion and self-determination within Panama. These performances maintain a space to subvert contemporary matrices of power, but they do so more to carve out livable spaces within existing systems than with an agenda for political change. Organizations with divergent agenda are positioning Congo cultural representations to highlight the cultural diversity of the nation, as a vehicle to increase national tourism, and (in the case of the West Indian organizations) to move forward a platform of social justice and cultural enrichment based on the racial oppression of "Black" people in Panama. The Congo community benefits from West Indian calls for social justice; however, without an equally clear agenda and voice, Congo communities risk being flattened into mere representation.

As a part of the 2006 Comisión "Etnia Negra Panameña" report, the organization included information from the 2001 Durban (South Africa) Conference against Racism, Racial Discrimination, Xenophobia and Related Intolerance. As J. Michael Turner (2002) notes, it was in the preparatory meetings leading up to the Durban meeting that "Afro-Latin" was "accepted officially into the written documentation concerning the UN Conference." He continues, "To break away from the commonly accepted racial terms, to reject the mixed-race category and declare oneself Afro-Latino was a courageous political act, as it represented a defiance of the historic ethnic status quo that defined hemispheric race relations" (31).

Afro-Colonial orientation to Blackness shifted over the arc of the century as a result of U.S. imperialism, the influx of West Indian immigrants, internationalization of Jim Crow, international attention on "afrolatinidad," and nationalization of ethnic folklore. At the beginning of the century, Afro-Colonial communities were coded as "Black" on the census, demarcated as such by the broader Republic, and likely referred to themselves as such. They *became* "mestizo" when "Black" was made to mean West Indian, English-speaking, and foreign. Even then, Afro-Colonials remained "Black" in the national imagination.

As Third World revolutions exploded in the 1960s, linking anti-colonialism and anti-racism, Afro-Colonial and West Indian desires began to merge; West Indian hostility regarding their second-class treatment by the United States resonated with Afro-Colonial angst on the same subject. Just as the United States' intervention largely splintered Panameño Blackness, its withdrawal has helped heal it. Even with the success of revolutionary movements, including Negritude and Black Power, and greater West Indian integration into Panameño culture, a national coming-together of the two African-descended populations would perhaps not have been possible or successful without the dismantling of the Canal Zone.

Figure 2.1 Photo of Portobelo taken from El Mirador (Photo by Elaine Eversley)

# 2

# Christ, the Devil, and the Terrain of Blackness

A fixed and unified culture exists only as a convenient but dangerous fiction.

> —Joseph Roach, *Cities of the Dead*

History everywhere is actively made in a dialectic of order and disorder, consensus and contest.

> —John and Jean Comaroff, *Of Revelation and Revolution, Volume 1: Christianity, Colonialism, and Consciousness in South Africa,*

Far from being grounded in a mere "recovery" of the past, which is waiting to be found, and which, when found, will secure our sense of ourselves into eternity, identities are the names we give to the different ways we are positioned by, and position ourselves within, the narratives of the past.

> —Stuart Hall, "Culture Identity and Diaspora"

## Setting/Locale

There is an everyday magical quality about experiencing contemporary Portobelo for the first time. It is a thriving contemporary town growing between the carcasses of two colonial forts, a community of colorful cinderblock houses planted in the middle of a bayside rain forest. It is a colonial church with a five-hundred-year-old Jesus as brown as or browner than most of the townspeople and a Customs House that protected Spanish gold against pirates and privateers in its youth and that now tells its story to visitors like an elder

Figure 2.2  Portobelo, Panama 2012 (Photo by Andrew Synowiez)

statesman. This, of course, is a cursory view—like climbing to the top of El Mirador, the lookout high above the city, and looking down. The view from below is that of a townscape soaked in saltwater, rained on, and slightly faded by the sun. Clothes, like dishes, are generally washed by hand and put out to dry without the luxury of hot water. Mildew marks humid concrete walls and rust flourishes on pie-pan roofs. Homelessness is nonexistent but hunger is not, despite a fertile rain forest and generous turquoise sea. During the four months of summer, faucets dry up as dead frogs contaminate the aqueducts and amoebas pollute the belly. Alcohol is cheap, abundant, and free of unexpected pollutants. It anesthetizes against both boredom and despair. This is the view from the bottom. Both the "storied" historical and "lived" contemporary views lie somewhere in between the mountain and the ground.

## HISTORICAL "STORIED" VIEW

Portobelo was founded on March 20, 1597, after Nombre de Dios, the site of Panama's first Atlantic-coast Spanish settlement, was looted and sacked by the privateer Sir Francis Drake. Two accounts of the relationship between arriving Spaniards and Cimarrones persist in local oral history.[1] In one version, more than six hundred Cimarrones lived in the rainforest of Portobelo when the Spanish settlers arrived. Outnumbered and fearful, the Spanish made a treaty with Cimarrones offering to recognize their freedom with the mandate that they inhabit an area northwest of Portobelo. Accepting the capitulation, the Cimarrones relocated, renamed the area Palenque, and abandoned the name "Cimarron" because they were no longer runaways; they were free Blacks/free Congos. In the other version, the Spanish and Cimarrones reached an accord before relocating to Portobelo. After a sizable number of Cimarrones helped Drake seize and plunder Nombre de Dios, the Spanish entered an agreement with them, recognizing their sovereignty in return for a guarantee that they would no longer collaborate with the pirates or take up arms against their former enslavers (Rodriguez 1979, 144). In this version, both groups relocated to Portobelo around the same time, the Spanish living closer to the shore and the Congos—freed Cimarrones— living higher in the rain forest. In both stories, the Spanish and at least one Cimarron band negotiated a peaceful coexistence in late-sixteenth-century Portobelo. Not included in these accounts are the enslaved Africans that the Spanish brought with them from Nombre de Dios to Portobelo or those who continued to be imported into the area during the seventeenth, eighteenth, and early nineteenth centuries to build the forts, *aduana* (Customs House), and church as well as to serve as domestics in Spanish households. As early as 1640, when the life-sized wooden El Nazareno/The Black Christ statue arrived in the area, the vast majority of the population were free and enslaved Blacks.[2]

Throughout the seventeenth century and well into the eighteenth, Portobelo was the nexus of trade in the Spanish colonial world. For one to two months each year, the great Ferias de Portobelo (Portobelo Fairs) attracted traders from throughout the empire. After repeated attacks by English privateers and pirates, the Fairs ceased in 1738 and the already small permanent Spanish population shriveled.

With the decline of the Spanish empire in the early 1800s and the mid-century California Gold Rush, which restructured Panamanian trade routes through Colón rather than Portobelo, the town became a ghost of its former self. Emptied of opportunists who exploited its geographic location to benefit the economies of distant homelands, Portobelo retained at least some portion of those residents who had benefited from the protection of its rain forest, learned the contours of its sea, discovered how to farm yucca in the mountains, and read the leaves for prescriptions.

Figure 2.3 View of Portobelo Bay from local fort (Photo by Andrew Synowiez)

## CONTEMPORARY "LIVED" VIEW

By the twentieth century, Portobelo represented a colonial Black town in the middle of the Black province of Colón. As of the 2010 census, 4,559 people resided in the town.[3] Many had lived there for generations. The 2010 census was historic for the town as well as for the nation because it gave people of African descent the opportunity not only to self-identify as "Black" but also to specify the terms of the "Blackness" they chose to claim. A co-founder and the executive director of the Silver People Heritage Foundation, Lydia M. Reid (2010), summarized it thus:

> In Section IV (Page 4) of the Census Questionnaire for 2010, at the top of the page are situated questions 5 and 6 which read, "Does an Indigenous person live here?" and "Does someone in this house regard him/herself as Negro (Black) or of African descent?" Further down the questionnaire you will see the qualifying questions as to which tribal or ethnic group the person belongs. In "Section V—General Characteristics for All Persons"

question 8 asks to which particular tribal group does the person belong, and question 9 asks "Do you consider yourself?:

1. Negro(a) Colonial
2. Negro(a) Antillano(a)
3. Negro(a)
4. Other (Specify)
5. None

This historic piece of Census information is probably the first time that Black and indigenous people will be asked their opinion and how they view themselves, particularly Black persons.[4]

In light of the information gleaned by the recent census, it is possible to state that of the 4,559 residents who were present in Portobelo during the one-day period within which the census was conducted, 993 or 21.8 percent claim African ancestry: 323 identified as Negro/a Colonial, 108 as Negro/a Antillano/a, 521 as Negro/a, 38 as Otro (Other), and 3 did not declare. In addition to the self-identified African-descended populations, other populations include an indigenous community, a mestizo community from the country's interior that relocated in the 1970s in response to a government initiative,[5] and Asian descendants,[6] some of whom run the town's local stores.

As in most rural Panamanian towns, Portobelo's transit system consists of a small fleet of privately owned, recycled U.S. school buses, commonly called "Diablo Rojos," that are painted in Caribbean primary colors and adorned with graffiti-style airbrush art depicting international to local popular icons.[7] In 2003 one of my favorite buses, "Lola," had El Naza/The Black Christ on the hood, Dwayne "The Rock" Johnson on a side panel, and Britney Spears on the rear door. It has since been repainted; Portobelo is a town of active recycling. As Renato Rosaldo (1993) argues, "All of us inhabit an interdependent late-twentieth-century [early twenty-first-century] world marked by borrowing and lending across porous national and cultural boundaries." However, as Rosaldo goes on to say, this process is not without friction. These boundaries "are saturated with inequality, power, and domination" (217). El Real Aduana de Portobelo (The Royal Customs House), which once stored South American gold bound for Spain, has been remodeled into both a museum and the offices of the Instituto Nacional de Cultura (National Institute of Culture). Likewise, the old slave auction block has been surrounded by a cemetery and dwarfed by the neighboring soccer field. Like many rural communities in the Global South, newer technologies have taken root in Portobelo before

Figure 2.4  Congo couple dancing at local event (Photo by Oronike Odeleye)

older ones acquired the infrastructure to do so. For example, with the introduction of local public-access Internet at the library (converted from a jail
in 2002 by the Peace Corps) and the rise of smartphones, electronic mail
has reached Portobelo before "snail" mail.[8] The historical and lived views of
Portobelo are part of the mise-en-scène within which local practitioners participate in Congo traditions. Drawn from theatre, film, and cinema studies,
*mise en scène* is a French term that literally means "putting into scene." This
chapter makes use of it to examine the space, place, characters, costumes,
movements, behaviors, and temporal frame that animate the tradition's more
rigid "official consciousness" and that form a basis to measure the distance
between the Congo tradition as it exists in the memories of ritual specialists
and as it exists in contemporary practice. Following Patrice Pavis (2013), I
approach mise-en-scène as "a system of meaning controlled by a director or a
collective. [. . .] It is the turning of theatre for the needs of stage and audience.
Mise en scène puts theatre into practice, but does so according to an implicit
system of organization of meaning" (4). The meaning of Congo cultural per-

formances in Portobelo is amplified by its location. Congo traditions stage the tension between Portobelo's storied past and evolving present with the same elastic dynamism as the town's landscape.

With attention to the ways in which ritual specialists render, negotiate, and revise the tradition for an audience made up primarily of local coper-formers, this chapter uses Raymond Williams's (1977) distinction between "official consciousness" and "practical consciousness" to contrast the Congo tradition as it exists in third-person, "storied" historical narratives with the ways it exists in the situated first-person, "lived" personal narratives and per-formance practices of local stakeholders. "Practical consciousness," accord-ing to Williams, "is almost always different from official consciousness [. . .] for practical consciousness is what is actually being lived, and not only what it is thought is being lived" (130–31).

Guided by this productive friction, this chapter is divided into two parts. The first part continues the work begun in the initial section by analyzing the mise-en-scène elements that structure the "official consciousness" of Congo cultural performance. By focusing on cultural performance in this section, I concentrate on the ways in which Congo traditions parody the social drama enacted between Spanish colonists and African descendants who escaped enslavement by fleeing into the hills to create self-determined communities. As Victor Turner (1986) argues:

> Through cultural performances many people both construct and partici-pate in "public" life. Particularly for poor and marginalized people denied access to middle-class "public" forums, cultural performance becomes the venue of "public discussion" of vital issues central to their communities, as well as an arena for gaining visibility and staging their identity. (24)

Embedded within the larger schema of cultural performance are a set of ritual performances that serve as scenes for the Congo drama—the culmi-nating episodes of Congo Carnival, which begin on Carnival Tuesday and conclude on Ash Wednesday. These ritual "scenes" stage the social drama of Cimarron struggles to maintain and protect their self-liberated communities from Spanish encroachment, their reappropriation of the devil trope to suit their liberatory narrative, and their use of inversion, buffoonery, and misdi-rection as tactics for survival.

Part 2 of this chapter analyzes the distance between "ought" and "is"—between the tradition as it exists in the official consciousness of ritual spe-cialists and their lived reality of shifts in its twentieth-century meaning and practice. In addition to examining the elasticity of the tradition made evident through their oral narratives, I compare and contrast two Congo Carnival experiences—one in 2003, which was filmed for an external audience, and another in 2004, which was enacted primarily for an internal audience made up of Congo practitioners and local community members. The 2003 filmed performance aligned more with performances for tourists that are often more polished and precise than those done primarily for the community, which means that they adhere more to the official "script" and feel more directed and controlled. The 2004 performance aligned with other performances I have witnessed that were primarily for community spectatorship and participation, and which are more improvisatory, passionate, and spontaneous. Within each, I attend to the real-time contentious meaning-making that informs the tradition's practical consciousness.

## Part One: Congo "Official Consciousness"

When two of my Spelman College Summer Art Colony colleagues and I first interviewed Congo Queen Melba Esquina about the tradition on May 27, 2000, she slipped a three-page document from a manila folder, waited patiently until we positioned our tape recorders, and read aloud from the document, which she later granted us permission to photocopy. The document's header was "El Congo: Folklore Costeño de Colón." As I would later observe during Carnival season in Portobelo and learn through more in-depth interviews with Melba and other local ritual specialists, several of the elements listed in the document as part of the Congo drama are not part of the contemporary Portobelo tradition; however, as I would later come to understand, they were once practiced in the town and inform part of the community's official consciousness. Much of the written information Melba shared with me was similar to Ronald Smith's 1976 ethnomusicological research with a Congo community in Colón. Many of Portobelo's Congos had met Smith, who, if not for his death on June 18, 1997, had planned to continue his research by studying the Congo traditions there. As the primary Congo representative in Portobelo, Melba received questions from reporters and scholars alike about the meaning and significance of the Congo tradition. Years later, after Melba and I had established a greater sense of trust and comfort with one another, I asked her informally about her choice to read from the document. She told me that she wanted to share the "right" version. The written document represented a well-crafted, repeatable, "official" representation that strongly aligned with community elders' memories of the tradition as practiced in their youth.

Each Congo community improvises the tradition to reflect their situated histories, resources, and purposes. Further, as with most rituals that span multiple eras, successive generations adapt elements to meet their interests and contemporary realities. My early questions and orientation toward the tradition presumed a neater and more transparent narrative than complex cultural practices generally reflect. So during my early interviews, I asked for and received the "official" narrative.

Queen Melba's written narrative interspersed with narrative accounts from Congo ritual specialists and community elders form my primary reference for Congo "official consciousness." Part 2 of this chapter places these memories of what was and what "should be" in productive tension with the tradition's contemporary practice.

## CAST OF CHARACTERS, COSTUMES, AND PROPS

The Congo drama is a mythic battle between good and evil. Architects of the tradition cast the Congos/Blacks on the side of the good and the Devil/brutal enslavers on the side of evil. As Michel de Certeau (1984) argues regarding the agency of people living in subjugated conditions, "without leaving the place where he has no choice but to live and which lays down its law on him, [the subjugated person] establishes within it a degree of plurality and creativity. By an art of being between, he draws unexpected results from his situation" (30). On July 10, 2013, I interviewed Carlos Chavarría,[9] who "plays Congo" as the Major Devil. He epitomized the drama this way: "For us, the Congo tradition is a culture. It was born during the Colonial times with the arrival of Black slaves from Africa to Panama, to the American continent. And, mainly, they were first unloaded in Portobelo as slaves."

## RITUAL TIME, SPACE, AND NARRATIVE MEANING

Congo season/Carnival season in Panama officially begins on January 20, the feast day of San Sebastian,[10] with the raising of the Congo flag high above el palacio/el palenque/el rancho—the thatched roof, open-air structure that represents former Cimarron fortresses. When I interviewed the lifelong Portobelo resident and Congo Cantalante (lead singer) Simona Esquina, on May 7, 2003, she concurred with the version of the tradition that Melba and others shared. "Here," she said, "when it is the twentieth of January, it is the day of St. Sebastian. [. . .] That's the day they raise the flag and they start to [dance]

Figure 2.5 Congo palenque/palacio (Photo by Renée A. Craft)

Congos every Saturday and Sunday. [. . .] The Congo flag is black and white. [. . .] From that day, Carnival starts." In Portobelo, the black and white Congo flag symbolizes the peace reached between the Cimarrones and the Spanish.

All of the action of the Congo game, from the beginning of Carnival season through its climax on Ash Wednesday, takes place in and around el palacio. According to Melba Esquina's written narrative:

> The palace or palenque, for the Congos, was their liberty and where they ruled, and whoever entered it should be able to endure the game [. . .] The Congos play/pretend like when they were in Africa and the tribes attacked each other, but in Portobelo it is a gallant enemy. They would notify the enemy, sending a note wrapped up in leaves [. . .] The other Congo [kingdom] prepared themselves, guarded the palace day and night in order not to be surprised and, if the palace [was] taken, they [the invading Congo kingdom] would take the flag and [the kingdom whose flag was taken would] have to recover it from the other palace as punishment, after they form a musical challenge between both groups.

**Figure 2.6** Pajarito performing during local Congo event (Photo by Oronike Odeleye)

Congo elders within the community remember these performances of ritual warrior play as opportunities for neighboring Congo communities to socialize during the days and weeks leading up to Ash Wednesday. A Portobelo community member, retired schoolteacher, and long-time Priest in the Congo tradition, Andres Jiménez, contextualized the encounter this way during our interview on February 26, 2003:

> When [the Congo character Pajarito] would see another tribe coming, he would blow his whistle and everyone would know that they were coming [to] rob the rancho of its flag and that the Congos would have to go look for it. [. . .] And that created an exchange amongst the villages. One Saturday they would go to one village, another Saturday they'd go to another. It was an exchange, like one Saturday [the villagers from] Cacique or Garrote would come and it would be an exchange.

Congo "official" consciousness narrates these exchanges leading up to Ash Wednesday as rich moments of intercommunity bonding, celebration, and interaction.

Figure 2.7  Congo Queen and King (Photo by Renée A. Craft)

## CONGO ROYAL COURT

El Pajarito, the son of the King and Queen and whose name means "little
bird," is part of the three-member royal court that leads the Congo community. "It was like a joke that the Africans were making on the Spanish," said
Simona Esquina. As Melba explained:

> The criticism (mean way of making fun) of the church consists of adopt-
> ing the name of Juan de Dios [for the King] and Mercedes [for the Queen],
> since the Spanish insisted on instilling in [the enslaved population] that
> they [the Spanish monarchs] were their protectors. [. . .] The primary
> personalities are the King, called in Congo language Juan de Dios; the
> Queen, Merced or Mercer [. . .] their crowns imitated the kings, or roy-
> alty, of Spain; the Little Bird; the Princess; the Devil or Memonia; and the
> Angel."

Both the Queen—"Maria Merced" or "Mercedes"—and King—"Juan de
Dioso" or "Juan de Dios"—are distinguished by their crowns, which are made

Figure 2.8  Congo King and Queen (Photo by Oronike Odeleye)

of cardboard, decorated in gold fabric, and adorned with convenient materials like large colorful rhinestones, mirrors, and/or bows. The Queen's crown is further embellished with multicolored ribbons, which flow from its back rim like streamers. In addition to her crown, the Queen is distinguished by a large cross, which she uses to protect herself and her community from the Devil.

The Queen's costume, consistent with other Congo women's costumes, includes a pollera, a white sleeveless or short-sleeve blouse, a petticoat, layers of beads called *lágrimas de la Virgen* (tears of the Virgin Mary), and one or two flowers pinned in the hair. The polleras are generally made of eight yards of inexpensive cotton material with a pattern of small flowers. The blouses feature a frilly collar matching the pattern of the skirt. Often in the style of their mothers and grandmothers, Congo women wear patchwork polleras made of recycled older ones and other discarded fabric.

Unlike the women, the King and Congo men paint their faces with charcoal or indigo and wear both trousers and a long-sleeved shirt or jacket

Figure 2.9 Yaneca Esquina dressed in male Congo costume (Photo by Renée A. Craft)

turned inside out. Recounting a memory of watching her father get dressed as the Congo King, Simona Esquina shared:

All of my life, from the time I peeled opened my eyes, [my father] was Juan de Dios of the Congos. He was the King of the Congos. His Congo name was Juan de Dios but his birth name was Vicente Esquina. I would see him dress as a Congo with his clothes and rope [belt], lots of banana leaves tied on. [. . .] His crown and face painted blue-black. [. . .] then you put on black circles and your red lips. [. . .] He would use charcoal. [. . .] But first he would put on the blue [indigo]. He would get a little bit of water. He would paint his whole face with that, then he would put on black circles with charcoal, and I would watch him as a child. When I would see him painting his face I would ask him, daddy, where are you going? He would say, daughter, I'm going to Congo. [. . .] I'm going to Congo because I'm Juan de Dios and I have to be there together with my women. So then as a child I would go. I would see them dancing Congo and that's how I began. [. . .] I enjoyed it.

Male Congo practitioners' costumes also include a cone-shaped hat. Whereas the contemporary Congo hat is formed by layers of papier-mâché and adorned with mirrors, beads, and feathers, Simona explained that the traditional Congo hat was made from foliage: "Normally, here, the Congo hat has been the *kafucula*. The kafucula is the leaf of a coconut tree. That's the original Congo hat. The Congo adorns the kafucula—he puts on his decorations, feathers, and colorful objects. So the kafucula is the hat, but Congos from other places use whatever [kind of hat, and that is outside the norm]." Expanding upon the Congo costume, she said:

The outfit of the Congos of Portobelo is very different from the outfit of the Congos of Colón, Costa Abajo, and Panama [city]. The Congo here dresses very distinctly. [. . .] There, the Congos dress using lots of bits of torn pieces of fabrics. [. . .] Yes, they all dress like that. In Colón and Panama City, the Congos dress like that. Everybody with little bits of torn fabric. But not here. Here, the Congos don't dress like that. When you see a Congo here dressed with those pieces of torn fabric, you know that he's not from Portobelo. He's not from Costa Arriba.

Each Congo man carries a satchel over his shoulder to collect provisions and wears a belt of artifacts (plastic flashlights, coconut shells, plastic dolls) tied around his waist with a rope. Like the women, men wear layers of long beaded necklaces and stylize their costumes according to taste. During the 2003 Centennial, for example, a Congo elder made part of her pollera from a large Panamanian flag while Congo artists like Yaneca Esquina (pictured in Figure 2.9) and his son Gustavo speckled their jackets and pants with paint in the pointillist style of their Congo paintings.

According to Melba Esquina, "As the Black was treated like an animal, they gave themselves animal names [for the Congo drama]: Rabbit, Sparrow-Hawk, Small Tiger, etc." When I spoke with him, Carlos Chavarría elaborated:

> The Congos would use purely animal names for themselves, for example, Ocelot, Fox, Pig, Rabbit. [. . .] Some would use names like Doctor, others [would use] Lawyer, but that was really unusual because most people used strictly animal names, and only occasionally used names of professions, right? But when they did you would see them with a book. If they were a lawyer, they used a book [as a prop]. If an Engineer, you would see them with their tape measure. If they were a doctor, they'd have a stethoscope. They may be presenting as that, but they were always imitating. [. . .] But if you were going to be seen as that, it was something you lived.

Throughout Carnival season Congo male practitioners alternate between drumming, dancing, and engaging in buffoonery as a tactic of subversion, misdirection, and evasion.

Melba Esquina explained that "Pajarito, with the bicolored flag (black and white) explores the terrain, shakes himself, makes gestures with his hand like a visor observing the area, [to ensure] that there is no danger, [and] calls to the group and they follow him." Simona offers details of Pajarito's role in the game:

> The Little Bird [. . .] He's the one that keeps abreast of everything that's going on in the Congo. [. . .] When we're going out on a trip, The Little Bird is the one that goes out with his whistle to advise everyone and to take a tour of the other palaces. [. . .] Then later to advise us as to the grouping of the [other] Congos—"That palace is unoccupied, let's go there and rob it." So we would go there and we would rob their palace. [. . .] We would go there and rob them. When they finally realized [what had happened], we would already have been in their palace. That is The Little Bird's job. [. . .] To go out touring and advise the King and the Queen about everything that is happening.

**Figure 2.10** Pajarito's costume (Photo by Oronike Odeleye)

In Congo "official consciousness" and in the living memory of Congo practitioners, el Pajarito's primary leadership role was to help guard the community and help guide them in the part of the Congo game that allows competing communities to capture and rob one another's fortresses in the spirit of Carnival fun.

Figure 2.11  "Devil's Den" with Raul and Carlos (Photo by Renée A. Craft)

In Portobelo, Pajarito's costume is generally a long golden tunic made of taffeta and tied with rope at the waist. As the son of the King and Queen, Pajarito also wears a decorative cardboard crown. However, his crown is topped with feathers linked to the meaning of his name, "Little Bird." Unlike the male Congo performers who use indigo or charcoal to camouflage their faces, Pajarito paints his face in a color that coordinates with this yellow and green costume. In the official narrative, Pajarito is the only Congo member intended to carry a whistle, which he blows to alert the Congos that either the Devil or another Congo community/"kingdom" is in close proximity.

## THE MAJOR DEVIL

Carlos Chavarría, the current Diablo Mayor of Portobelo, summarizes the role of the Devil this way:

> The Devil in our tradition represents nothing more than the Spanish who was always abusing the slave with his whip so that he would work. They were always subjecting the Blacks to the whip, and that's the part [of the

Figure 2.12  Celedonio's Diablo Mayor costume (Photo by Renée A. Craft)

Congo tradition] that they've directly maintained as it was; that is, he [the Devil] is the Congo's enemy as it relates to the culture of the race. But when we look at [the role] strictly within the context of the Congo tradition, it's the evil of man, that we search out amongst ourselves. It is celebrated on Ash Wednesday. That is when you can see clearly the fight between good and evil.

Celedonio Molinar Ávila is the primary architect of the Major Devil tradition in twentieth-century Portobelo. When I interviewed him on June 3, 2000, he had this to say:

> The game is between the Congo and the Devil. [. . .] The Major Devil is the oldest man who dressed [as Devil] first. He's the one who has been dressing as Devil longest. That's why they call him the Major Devil. [. . .] [The Devil represents] a controller of the Congos. If someone acts badly with their father or mother, if they act badly, then the Devil comes to punish them.

Whereas all of the other Congo characters appear throughout Carnival season, the Devil character does not appear until Ash Wednesday. As Carlos Chavarría explained, "[Celedonio] only dressed [as Devil] on Ash Wednesday and likewise I only get dressed [as Devil] on Ash Wednesday. Some people have told me that is not right. Some people get dressed at midnight on Fat Tuesday. But not Celedonio. He did not do it because he was trying to remain as hidden as possible."

The Devil's costume includes a cotton jumpsuit, a mask, ankle bells, and a whip. El Diablo Mayor's costume also includes cardboard wings painted black. Although Diablo Segundo (the Secondary Devil) and each of the minor Devils may elect to wear either red costumes or mixed red-and-black costumes, the Major Devil is the only Devil that dresses primarily in black.

## THE ARCHANGEL AND SIX SOULS

Of the Archangel, Melba Esquina explained, "The Angel protect[s] the souls [ánimas] so that they don't fall under the power of the Devil." Celedonio elaborated:[12]

> When the Devil plays with the Congos, a group of people comes, called Angels, to get the Devil for baptism. After they tie up the Devil, they go over to the table where the Priest is going to baptize the Devil. Then they baptize him and the Devil is let free. That's where the association between the Devil and the Congos ends. This happens every year on Ash Wednesday.

The Archangel and each of the six Souls wear calf-length white tunics and white bandanas that are tied around their heads. Las Ánimas move as a

Figure 2.13 Archangel and Ánimas (Photo by Elaine Eversley)

unit, tethered together by a rope and led by the Archangel, who carries a large wooden cross like the Queen. Unlike Congo men and local observers who play with the Devil while dressed in layers of long pants to protect their legs from the force of his whip, the Archangel and Souls play bare-legged, their eventual bloody welts a part of their costume. And while the male Congo performers, including the King, perform in blackface, the Angels, Souls, and Priest do not. The Priest's only distinguishing feature is a basil leaf and container of water, which he uses to bless the Devils.

## THE "HEART" OF THE TRADITION: CONGO DANCE AND DRUMMING

In addition to the Congo royal court and supernatural characters, the heart of the tradition is Congo dance, which is animated by the percussive pulse of three male drummers led by a female chorus and a primary singer. In her book entitled *Paloma, reina de los Congos: El orgullo de una raza,* the Congo specialist Maricel Martín Zuñigan (2002) states:

Figure 2.14 Congo drummers, primary singer, and chorus (Photo by Renée A. Craft)

The "*cantalantes*" are the key to the Congo because in order to have a good Congo dance it is very important to have a good *cantadora*. [. . .] These women also are given their Congo name that differs and sometimes in groups are often called "Re[v]ellín"[13] and "Cicada" because they have a privileged voice for this [type of] song. There are also other women who are responsible for composing songs. (6)

Melba Esquina explained that the Congo percussion section "is composed of three drums: El hondo, el bajo, and el requinto; the lead singer and the chorus that with hand clapping raises the rhythm of the drums." Simona also described the music: "The Blacks, the Black Africans, they created their own drums. They created their own music themselves, and from there the Congo woman created the waist movement, because the Congo [dance] is a waist movement. Yes, and they created their dance themselves. Yes, they created their dance."

From January 20 through the season's culmination, this constellation of dancers, singers, and drummers form the tradition's foundation. During Carnival season, they gather to fellowship, play, and celebrate with one another each Friday and/or Saturday night as well as from dusk on Carnival Tuesday through the end of Carnival on Ash Wednesday.

Outside of its Carnival context, Congo social dance may be performed informally in a cantina, backyard, or wherever an improvised drumbeat or bass line inspires it. According to Melba Esquina, "A Congo woman lead[s] the dance with her hip movements to invite the Congo men to dance. In the dance, he makes all types of faces and advances toward her trying to kiss her and she, with her skirt, tries to cover herself and is always shaking her skirt. It is a tease. Another female dancer replaces her and the dance continues and so on and so on for both sexes." When this social dance element includes the Congo drummers, chorus and revellín, it is referred to as a *congada,* meaning "mini Congo performance." Each Friday and Saturday evening from January 20 until Lent, Congo communities throughout Panama hold congadas. This interplay between the drummers, singers, and dancers forms the foundation of all Congo performance, including Congo ritual performance, parts of which date back to Panama's Spanish colonial period.

## "SCRIPTED" PERFORMANCE:
## CONGO DRAMA AND RITUAL PERFORMANCE

According to the official narrative, before midnight on Carnival Tuesday, el Diablo Mayor visits the palacio without his costume to check that Congos have assembled to play. Then, he returns home, dresses, and reapproaches the space in order to enter it backward. Pajarito, who has been standing guard of the palacio, blows a whistle to let the Congos know that the Devil is approaching. The first dance of the Congo drama is the "Diablo Tun Tun":

| | |
|---|---|
| *Cantalante:* | *Primary Singer:* |
| Ayer soñé con un hombre | Last night I dreamed of a man |
| De dientes de oro | With teeth of gold |
| Y me quiso llevar | who wanted to carry me away |
| | |
| *Cantalante:* | *Primary Singer:* |
| Ay, ¿sabes quien es? ¡ayayay! | Oh, do you know who it was? Oh, oh, oh! |
| | |
| *Coro:* | *Chorus:* |
| El Diablo Tun Tun | The Devil knock knocks |

| Cantalante: | Primary Singer: |
|---|---|
| Ay, que se va | Oh, he goes |

| Coro: | Chorus: |
|---|---|
| El Diablo Tun Tun[14] | The Devil knock knocks |

The Devil dances to the song with his feet perpendicular to one another in the shape of a cross. Carlos Chavarría explained:

[Celedonio] told me, when you go out to play Devil, salute the four cardinal directions—North, South, East and West—because remember that you're imitating the man of darkness. [. . .] Always try to play with your feet crossed. I did not understand what he wanted to say to me and [so] he said, no, look, that way, you always play under the cross. [. . .] I always try to make a cross with my body.

When the Diablo Mayor enters the palacio, he does so to steal the Queen, the seat of the Congo's power. The colonial Spanish Queen's interest was in colonization through expansion, Christianization, and the exploitation of labor through slavery. Enslavers appropriated "the devil" and "the church" as a means to dissuade rebellion and protect the institution of slavery. *El juego Congo,* the Congo game, repositions power such that the Congo Queen uses her cross/the church to combat the Devil/enslaver for the protection of *her* nation.

As the Major Devil dances backward into the palacio, the Queen comes from her place in the chorus with her large wooden cross in hand. She then dances in front of the drums as Congo members play, dance, and mock the Devil in order to keep him distracted. Finally, she grabs the Devil from behind and they dance in a tense battle as the chorus sings "Diablo Tun Tun." Having tricked him by grabbing him from behind, the Queen prevents the Devil from taking her. They dance this way until the Devil jumps up and throws them both back on the drums, thus ending the official Carnival Tuesday portion of the Congo drama.

As the church bells announce the dawn Ash Wednesday service, interested Congos go to mass to have ashes placed on their foreheads. Although this is the beginning of Lenten season for the church, the Congos are not done playing yet. By early evening, the Major Devil and all of the minor Devils take to the streets. The Archangel and the six Ánimas who follow him chase and bind each Devil, starting with the minor Devils and working their way up the hierarchy. Once captured, each Devil chooses a *madrina* (godmother) from among the women in the crowd and proceeds with her to be blessed by the Congo Priest. The Priest tries to get the Devil to call the name of God (Dios), but he refuses and keeps saying "arroz," which means "rice." Eventually the Priest accepts "arroz" as "Dios," and de-whips (takes away his whip) and de-masks the Devil. The game does not end until each Devil is baptized and unmasked. The last to be baptized is the Major Devil. The Congos then symbolically sell the Devil/enslaver house to house just as enslaved people were once captured, baptized, and sold. Carlos Chavarría summed it up thus:

> And that's the moment that everything ends. Good beats out evil, which is when I [the Major Devil] have been baptized. And that's celebrated. It's accomplished, that good imposes itself on evil, and we reach a moment of joy, which is what the tradition recreates. But looking at it from the perspective of Blacks and the Spanish, it's nothing more than [showing] that the Spanish always had his whip enslaving the Blacks.

# Part Two: Practical Consciousness
## THE "CHANGING SAME" OF CONGO CHARACTERS

Congo ritual specialists cite significant changes in each primary character with the exception of the Congo Queen. Her role, costuming, and embodiment have remained fairly consistent in the twentieth century. Meanwhile, the role of the King and Pajarito have diminished, and the embodiment of the Devil character has started to become more violent. I will focus on the King and Pajarito here. Due to the scope, complexity, and relationship of the Devil's changes to what I refer to as a "circum-local" paradigm, I analyze the Devil character in chapter 3.

### JUAN DE DIOS, THE KING OF THE CONGOS

The contemporary Congo Queen maintains an everyday leadership role as the person in charge of community business matters, communication, and organization. Her scripted role in the Congo drama is that of the seat of Congo cultural memory and power that the Devil seeks to take away. The role of the contemporary Congo King, however, has diminished. The space remains open for his leadership in the everyday affairs of the community, but his official role in the Congo performance is not all that distinct from that of other Congo male practitioners. Like them, he dances with and seeks to protect the Queen from the Devil, but his role has shifted measurably from the early twentieth century when Simona Esquina's father was King. She shared commentary and insight on the significance of the change:

> Back when my father [Vicente], who was the oldest Congo, would play, and [. . .] Zacarias Esquina [. . .] my father's brother—they played a different way. [. . .] They had a big responsibility to the Congo women. They went from house to house picking up the women for the Congo. And the same way, when the Congo ended, they took each woman back to the house where they had picked her up. The King had a responsibility to the Congo women. Wherever he went, he would take them and he would drop them off. But not today. Today, the King doesn't have, he doesn't take responsibility for the Congo women. There isn't that [sense of] responsibility that the Congos had before. Today, no [. . .] The King is where he is, the Queen is where she is, and the Congos are where they are. [. . .] There's no formal organization. Because before, the King and the Queen, named Merced, would go out together. They organized themselves and they worked together taking care of the Congos, taking care of the Congo women and the palace.

## THE PRINCESS AND MAMA GUARDIA

The official consciousness of Congo performance consistently includes La Menina/The Princess; yet, I have only witnessed the character at presentations primarily for tourists, special festivals, or outside spectators. Ritual specialists tell of a time when the character was active as a helper and apprentice to the Queen. In discussing the previous role of the Princess, Simona Esquina also spoke of Mama Guardia, a character who was once charged with protecting Congo financial resources:

> There used to be [. . .] the Princess. The Princess is the girl who accompanies the Queen. She's younger than the Queen. She's always at the foot of the Queen. In case the Queen cannot, the Princess takes her place. Now they don't use a Princess, just a Queen and a King. They don't choose or name a Princess, just the Queen and King. [. . .] Maybe 10 years ago or so the tradition of the Princess was lost. [. . .] Just like the Congos always had someone who would guard the money. They called that person Mama Guardian. She would guard the money that the Congos made in what we call "going to take a collection"—the people give money. [. . .] That's over

**Figure 2.15** Photo of symbolic princess (Photo by Renée A. Craft)

now. Now we have someone like a Mama Guardia in whom we have a lot of faith because she's a serious person. Her name is Mrs. Mata, Juana de Mata. We give her the money and she guards it and then turns it in to us. [. . .] The Congo [tradition] has always had a King, a Queen, a Princess, and a Mama Guardia.

## PAJARITO'S WHISTLE AND "CONGO TAX"

After the road was built that linked the towns of the Costa Arriba and created a throughway of what was once a closed community, the Congo game lost the intercommunity war play in which Pajarito had figured prominently. His current role is more circumscribed to warning the Congos of the Devil's approach and indicating the presence of "outsiders" to the community. Tourists and visitors must pay a symbolic tax when entering Congo territory, which might mean driving into a Congo community or entering the palacio during Carnival season. Carlos Chavarría contrasted the tax as it was once exercised to the ways in which some community members choose to practice it now:

> Some friends from back in the day who dressed Congo, called Congo Fox and Congo Ocelot, they came to my grandmother and said, "Hey, Florentina, you want us to help you round up the hens?" And my grandmother said, "No, no, no, I do not need help." And my grandmother gathered up the hens. And when she counted them, one or two were missing. They [my friends] had taken them as a tax for helping her round up the hens, even though she did not want their help. Afterwards when she said, "Hey, they robbed me!" they said, "No, we needed [the hens to feed people at] the fort. We helped you round up the hens, so we had to collect a tax." That ended up being her donation to the fort.

Whereas the tax or "donation" was once a material good that could be confiscated or that offered benefit to the collective, it has now become more cash-based and individualistic. Now, Congo practitioners and those dressed up like them form "tax" checkpoints during Carnival season all along the road running throughout the Costa Arriba. At each checkpoint, passersby are asked to pay a Congo tax or give a donation in the spirit of the season. Whereas Andres Jiménez found this action "annoying and bothersome," Carlos posed the problem as less that the tax has been reduced to a cash contribution and more that some young people engage in it without knowing its history and without providing something in exchange for the "tax":

> When I see the guys in the street with their ropes and everything else and collecting [money], I have told them, look, it is not prohibited to collect money but it is not just doing it to do it. If you are going to charge me for passing by with a car, there has to be a reason. It is not just charging to charge; it is that I am coming onto your land and I have to pay a

**Figure 2.16** Collecting "Congo tax" near the road (Photo by Elaine Eversley)

tax for that. But to charge me for that you have to entertain me so that I feel placated with something. [. . .] I tell them, it is just not charging for no reason. You see a lot of young people putting on their rope and I see them with their little cans and they start to dance and it is for that reason. Because they know they have to entertain so the people get excited. And you will see a lot of them afterwards settling accounts: hey, I earned 15 or 20 dollars.

El Pajarito is often less active in these Congo (street) tax encounters and more active in orchestrating contact between local practitioners and outsiders within the space of the palacio. The Little Bird sees an outsider and ushers him or her into the palenque to dance. Once the visitor has completed a few steps, the Little Bird or another Congo character will signal to the drummers to drop the drums and charge the visitor a fee for trespassing. Whereas the fee was once satisfied with any token offering, now either drinks or a monetary donation is expected. The Congo "tax" as it was previously implemented was about collecting toward a shared communal pot. As implemented today through the checkpoint model, it is sometimes more about the individual than the collective.

The tourist boom, which was facilitated in no small part by the road, has helped the local economy, and improved infrastructures have provided improvements in communications, education, transportation, and media in the town. Still, many elders lament the capitalist bend of globalization and worry that the Congo tradition will suffer because younger practitioners participate more actively in global economies that promote more urban, cosmopolitan culture, style, and values.

## Ritual, Improvisation, and the (Re)invention of Culture

Since I began my study in 2000, whenever I ask "When does Congo season begin?" the official response has been that Carnival season begins January 20, the feast day of San Sebastian. In 2002, however, I learned that the flag that signals the start of Carnival had been raised on January 19. Simona Esquina explained: "The day of St. Sebastian, the twentieth, is the day they raise [the flag], but they raise it at midnight on the day before, that is, on the eve of the morning of the twentieth."

During my extended field research in 2003, when I attended my first Portobelo Carnival, a Congo visual artist and good friend, Manuel "Tatu" Golden, alerted me that the Congo flag would be raised around dusk on January 18. I assumed that perhaps the community had chosen the eighteenth because it was a Saturday. I had arranged an interview on Saturday at a location two hours north of Portobelo. Wanting to return in plenty of time to witness the official start of Congo season, I arrived back in the late afternoon to the sound of drumbeats and a Carnival atmosphere. Local vendors had set up small tables to sell fried fish, *patacones* (fried plantains), sticky coconut candy, beer, fried chicken, hamburgers, and barbequed hotdogs on a stick. The streets were full. As I dropped my things at home, I wondered if the music I was hearing was a kind of warm-up/pre-Carnival/opening-act performance. Sarabi is the youngest daughter of Ariel Jiménez, a Congo practitioner and visual artist who has played the role of Pajarito. As she often did, my little friend screamed up to my window as her older sister, Yaroka, ran around to try my back door. I looked out the window to see their mother also yelling my name and waving for me. "Corre!" ("Run!") she said. I raced down to join the community members who were flowing toward the palacio. The flag had already been raised. When I encountered Tatu, I asked, "But I thought the flag wasn't going to be raised until dusk this evening?" "That's right," he answered, "but it started early." "Why?" I pressed. "I don't know," Tatu[15] concluded with a shrug, "it just did."

During various interviews throughout the years, I have asked about the variation in start times that I have witnessed. Without fail, each community member restates that Congo season begins on January 20. When I ask about a specific year's variation, respondents generally say something akin to, "Oh, that's right. It did." Practitioners living and working within the daily rhythms of the community share a collective "common sense" about the tradition that fills the gaps between official and practical consciousness. Gustavo Esquina, my long-time Congo research collaborator, is the great-grandson of the renowned Congo King Vicente Esquina and the great nephew of the cantalante Simona. Raised in Portobelo in a family whose participation in the Congo tradition spans more than four generations, Gustavo explained the reason for the variation during a telephone conversation we had on November 25, 2013: "I learned that the flag of the Congos, of Carnival, rises [on the] twentieth at 12:00 a.m., but in truth many times [the community] improvises and they have done it a few days before or after as well. That has to do with how well the Queen and King, who are in charge of running it along with the Carnival board, are organized."

These processes of shared knowledge within the community often exist as hegemony rather than ideology, as "taken for granted" rather than "articulated" (Comaroff and Comaroff 1997, 23–24). Zuñigan (2002), the former Portobelo Congo Queen, writes: "One day I asked my mother: How did I learn so much about the Congos? She, in her time, asked me: You want to know why you like it so much? I told her: Yes! She responded to me: Because you have it in your blood" (2).[16]

Taken-for-granted, "in the blood" methodologies of *el juego Congo* (the Congo game) point to embodied "sensuous knowledge" (Gordon 1997, 389–90). One enters into an intimate understanding of Congo culture, performance, and ritual through immersion, repetition, commitment, community, and time. Born in Portobelo in 1931 to Vicente Esquina, Gustavo's great-aunt Simona remembers being introduced to the tradition by going to the palacio with her father and singing and dancing with the Congos. Afterward, she and her friends would try to recreate what they had witnessed: "When I was a little girl, I got a bunch of kids together with cans and we made a Congo dance. And the drums were the cans. The cans were the drums. [We were] little kids, and we began to make up Congo dances."

"In the blood" signals "in the body," steeped into the consciousness from the mundane to the spectacular. Children of Congo practitioners grow up watching their parents prepare for Carnival, participating with them, and mimicking Congo play.

In Congo "practical consciousness," Congo season/Carnival season begins *close to* January 20, but it fluctuates with Lent, Easter, and Congo leadership. An early Easter means an early Lent, the end of all Congo/Carnival celebrations. In years where Lent begins in February, Congo season may begin earlier. Just as the Lenten season shifts to offer believers forty days of sacrifice regardless of when Easter falls, so, too, does Congo season adjust to allow practitioners ample time for pre-Lenten celebration. January 20 functions as a benchmark rather than a precise location. Such improvisation is part of the tradition's "felt" or sensuous meaning, which fits within Raymond Williams's (1977) discussion of history and "structure of feeling." Williams writes:

> It is not only that we must go beyond formally held and systematic beliefs, though of course we have always to include them. It is that we are concerned with meanings and values as they are actively lived and felt, and the relations between these and formal or systematic beliefs are in practice variable (including historically variable), over a range from formal assent with private dissent to the more nuanced interaction between selected and interpreted beliefs and justified experiences. (132)

As Margaret Drewal (1994) asserts in *Yoruba Ritual*, "Performers exercise their options frequently enough to undermine the dominant notion in scholarly discourse that ritual repetition is rigid, stereotypic, conventional, conservative, invariant, uniform, redundant, predictable, and structurally static" (xiv). Regardless of calendar or clock, Congo season/Carnival season begins when Pajarito hoists the black and white flag over the palacio.

## "The Road" and a Tale of Two Palacios

Although the official Congo narrative cites only one palacio/palenque per Congo community, Portobelo had two in 2003. Everyone with whom I engaged in formal and informal interviews agreed that this was an anomaly. When I interviewed Simona Esquina in 2003, she explained: "A long time ago there was another palace around there. Up there, in the Campaña neighborhood. That was years ago, and there wasn't another one until now, this year, that there are two. [. . .] But before there had ever only been one palace in the village."

All active Congos danced at the primary palacio each Saturday, but some of the younger members danced to the rhythm of newer songs and faster drumbeats in the smaller, secondary palacio each Friday as well. Although there had been tension between the groups for years, this was the first time in practitioners' living memory that there had been two palacios in the town. "What we are defining," Williams (1977) argues, "is a particular quality of social experience and relationships, historically distinct from other qualities, which gives the sense of a generation or of a period" (131).

Congo ritual specialists like Simona, Carlos Chavarría, and Andres Jimé-nez talk about a clear distinction between how the tradition was performed when the community was only accessibly by boat and the changes they have witnessed after the main road was built in the mid-1970s, connecting towns along the Costa Arriba, including Portobelo, with the larger Republic. Simona gave this example:

> Look, the Congos have always had a group of women. These women com-mitted themselves to party with the King and Queen until Carnival was over. Those who were lead singers sang, and the others answered them [call-and-response], but they were always willing to be inside the palace. But not nowadays. [. . .] Today, whoever wants to go to the Congo goes [. . .] It's not like before when the Congo women committed themselves to it. [. . .] If they want to go, they go. If they don't, they don't. They come for a while, sing if they feel like it, and from there go off somewhere. When they're tired of doing whatever they were doing, they come back. And that's how it goes. But in reality, Congo shouldn't be like that. Congo is a commit-ment. [. . .] In the old days Congo was a commitment.

Echoing Simona's sentiments about the absence of the sense of communal sharing of time, energy, and resources that preceded the road, Andres added:

> The women would go out on a Saturday at 4:00 in the evening going from house to house. Those who wanted would receive them and they would sing a Congo song. If the owner of the house liked to dance, he would dance, and, if not, he would give some kind of a donation. [. . .] And when the women finished going around the village, they would arrive at the ran-cho and there they would start to play so that the people would come. [. . .] When the road came, they didn't keep doing that. But before there was a road, they would go out from house to house and dance and enjoy them-selves—enjoy themselves a lot! And during the four nights of Carnival, the Congos wouldn't stop.

Offering thicker detail to round out our understanding of the types of communal sharing in which the pre-road, closed community participated, Carlos shared a memory that I have chosen to quote at length:

> It would begin on January twentieth, which was the day of Saint Sebastian, when they would raise the Carnival flag here, and from there on the people of the village—in those days there was no highway—so everyone always came out [to participate]. They worked hard in agriculture, [but] at night when the Congo groups would begin, everyone in the community participated. When Carnival week would arrive—that's Saturday, Sunday, Monday, Tuesday, and Ash Wednesday—then it was a completely closed party, that is to say, strictly for the people of the village. No one would go up into the mountain [to work]. No one would do anything. Everyone quit working and did everything in their own houses [. . .] No one went to clean [their farms]; no one did anything. And they had their vegetables, their food. There was a lot of hunting. [. . .] [lots of smoked, salted meats that they would cut and put out to dry]. A lot of people went up in the mountains. Others went out to fish. And we would eat a lot of salted, smoked meats [and fish]. And when Carnival time arrived, they went out strong to *confiar.* "Confiar" is nothing more than getting everyone together who was dressed as Congos and going out to take up a collection in the village. That is what was used to get the food for the fort. They would seek contributions of vegetables, fish, hens, [. . .] they even got iguana eggs that they would see drying. They would take them to the fort and cook them for everyone, and they would stay there until Ash Wednesday, until the game of the Devil would end. Then everyone would go back to their houses like normal. Those were the moments of the tradition that I experienced a lot [. . .] me and the older people.

Contemporary congadas leading up to Carnival Tuesday generally start around nine in the evening and continue until shortly before sunrise. During the course of these performances, there are also locally sponsored parties at the cantinas as well as those hosted by Panamanian radio stations in found and installed spaces throughout Portobelo.

Those Portobeleños born after the road was built experience greater access to national and international culture through advances in communications and media infrastructures as well as through a wider array of educational and job opportunities that the road helped make possible. However, the presence of the road and the rapid globalization that followed the 1999 turnover of the Panama Canal from U.S. to Panamanian control ushered in an end to the part of the Congo tradition that centered on intercommunity flag capturing, robbing, and warrior play. Greater access and exposure to a broader array of professional opportunities and entertainment also wound down the clock on the types of intimate, prolonged, communal sharing that inform Congo ritual specialists' and elders' official consciousness of the tradition.

Over the course of Carnival 2003, Congo practitioners, especially young adults, as well as local and visiting coperformative witnesses flowed back and forth between the two palacios and discos hosting salsa, merengue, hip-hop, and reggaeton parties. For them, the Friday palacio did not threaten the traditional one. They maneuvered between them as "both/and" rather than as "and/or" spaces, similar in outlook to feminist theory, Eastern philosophy, and what I would call a Latin American mestiza theory. The Friday palacio offered an extra day of festivities and another way to participate in them. Although many, many Congos danced in both palacios in the days leading up to the Carnival's climax, all activities coalesced at the traditional palacio with the different subgroups melding into one for the ritual performances of Carnival Tuesday and Ash Wednesday.

The expanding exposure that the road helped make possible shapes the "present" of younger generations' Congo experiences, just as lived experiences in the once isolated community shape the recollections of Congo elders. As the cultural theorist Connerton (1989) argues, "We will experience our present differently in accordance with the different pasts to which we are able to connect that present" (2).

## Congo Drama: For the Camera versus for the Community

When I witnessed my first Congo ritual drama in 2003, it followed the "official" script I had been given almost perfectly. The Jason Foundation for Education, a Massachusetts-based nonprofit organization dedicated to developing a lifelong passion for learning in middle school students, filmed Carnival that year. They had come with several Panama collaborators and Arturo Lindsay, founder of the Spelman College Summer Art Colony, to film the Portobelo celebrations as well as some of the area's ecological and historical sites. The result was "JASON XV: Rainforests at the Crossroads," a video and printed teaching companion that middle school educators could use as a supplement to their standard texts. At the appointed hour, the Carnival's female chorus sang in two thick rows, each of its members beautifully dressed according to tradition. Congo men, also dressed in full costume, ran through the crowd in groups of three and four making music with whistles, like the one carried by Pajarito. With the exception of the bright camera lights, which threatened to set the palacio's dry thatch roof on fire, and the bulky video equipment, which congested the walkways, Carnival Tuesday 2003 unfolded exactly as I had imagined it would, exactly as I had been told. The following year, I would learn how much of that exactitude related to the bright spectatorial eyes of the professional cameras.

When I returned for Carnival in 2004, I expected the same polished performance I had seen the previous year. In the absence of lights, cameras, or an external impetus for formality, the 2004 Carnival was more improvisational and also more modest. The drama started much later in the evening than it had the previous year, and many female Congo practitioners dressed as informally as they had in the weeks leading up to Carnival. The chorus was smaller, consisting mainly of elders. Whereas in the previous year, young women expecting to dance in multiple venues had worn jeans or cotton pants underneath their polleras, in 2004 most donned their polleras like aprons over their fashionable pants to facilitate even easier transitions between club and Congo spaces. Although most Congo men dressed in full costume on Ash Wednesday to play with the Devil, only a handful consistently dressed in Congo costumes and painted their faces prior to Carnival Tuesday. Most, especially teenagers and young adults, dressed for the parties but danced in each of the spaces.

For some Congo elders, projects like the Jason Foundation's create a catalyst for intergenerational community members to perform Congo in ways that more closely relate to its "official"/"storied" past. In that way, Simona Esquina sees some value in it:

> The Congo tradition changed years ago. Now is when it is [. . .] forming again and being revived because the Congo tradition was being lost. Now, with the arrival of tourism, the Congo tradition is being revived. [. . .] Because at least when tourism comes, they ask for Congo. We present Congo to them and they see it, and they also dance Congo, in their way. But they dance and they enjoy themselves.

As we have seen throughout the world, globalization has accelerated and altered processes of change that are a part of our collective evolution. Congo elders, therefore, are witnessing larger changes in the tradition than their parents did. The younger generation's greater exposure to the world at large vis-à-vis music, television, and tourism filters into the tradition on their bodies and in their consciousnesses. However, the youth are also experiencing an ever-increasing sense of pride, which global exposure has affected. As more international tourists enter the area, as Congo art gains international recognition, and as its young artists gain exposure and capital, the Congo tradition is becoming "cool" for savvy young practitioners to associate with and brag about. As Lindsay often puts it, "It's easy to think the grass is much greener on the other side until your neighbors start coming over to your lawn, admiring how green yours is." Watching tourists marvel over taken-for-granted elements of their home tradition has sparked a new level of interest among many Congo youth. In this way, greater exposure to global tourism and media is stimulating greater appreciation for local culture.

## WHEN THE QUEEN TRUMPS THE DEVIL AND THE DANCERS DIRECT THE DRUM

The official Congo drama narrative positions the Queen as the seat of Congo cultural power, a commodity that the Major Devil seeks to steal. According to the story, the Devil enters the palacio to capture the Queen but is distracted by the tactics of male Congo buffoonery and female Congo dancing. Eventually, the Queen grabs the Devil from behind and maintains her hold until he throws them both against the drums, wherein the Carnival Tuesday portion of the drama ends. This rendering limits the Queen's assertive power to her ability to capture the Devil before he captures her, and concentrates Congo women's agency to their ability to control space and attention through their singing and dancing. Congo women's lived reality of the tradition and their active role in the Congo drama are more subtly powerful and complicated than the official narrative documents.

As in most African/Black Diaspora call-and-response traditions centered on the drum, there is a relationship between the drummers and dancers as much as there is between the primary singer and the chorus. Although Congo dance is a couple's dance, a female practitioner always enters the space alone to begin a new dance before being approached by a male Congo "suitor." At the start of a new Congo song, one female dancer stands in front of the drummers and chorus as the lead singer begins to sing and mark time by clapping. The chorus and drummers match the lead singer's tempo, and the dancer marks time by stepping side-to-side with rhythm. Both the dancer and the lead singer have the ability to goad the drums faster or slower depending on how they choose to interpret and conduct the rhythm through their voices and bodies. Holding up the edges of her skirt, for example, the dancer may attempt to increase the pace of the song by waving her skirts to the tempo she desires. Likewise, lead singers often start a new song using a single-clap-per-beat tempo and increase to a faster double-clap-per-beat tempo to urge the drummers to pick up the pace.

Likewise, Congo Queens use their physical strength to prolong the game, and the female chorus may choose not to sing if the game and drama do not proceed according to their expectations. In 2004, for example, the person scheduled to play the role of Major Devil was running late. The female chorus was furious. As time ticked on, they complained about the lackadaisical way the young people were doing Carnival and reminisced about how special it had been in their youth and how much fun they had had the previous year.

As the evening hours of Carnival Tuesday melted into Ash Wednesday, the palacio crowd dissipated into the local cantinas and clubs. Everyone was becoming frustrated by the long wait. Finally, the Major Devil's jingling bells sounded in the distance and the palenque once again soaked up the interest of the dispersed crowd. Pajarito's whistle provided final confirmation of the Devil's proximity. When the Major Devil entered the palacio, however, the Queen was angry with him for making everyone wait so long and refused to dance the "Diablo Tun Tun." The elders, slightly inebriated from the Seco liquor that had helped fill their long wait, chided him and told him to go get someone else to play Major Devil. When the elders refused to relent, that Devil retreated and a new Major Devil appeared. As soon as he arrived, the women took to their feet and began clapping in time with the swelling drumbeats. The Queen lifted her cross and began dancing toward the Major Devil, and the crowds swelled thicker than before.

Although the official narrative gives most of the Congo game's agency to the Major Devil and male primary characters, the Queen, chorus, and other Congo members also have space to assert their desires and will. Both Delia Barrera Clifundo, the 2004 Congo Queen, and Melba Esquina, her predecessor, for example, had the physical strength and will to alter the course of the game. In the official narrative, the Carnival Tuesday drama ends when the Major Devil throws himself and the Queen back on the drums. In practice, however, each of the two Queens active in the tradition during my research has been able to sink her weight and position her body such that the Major Devil could not throw her into the drums until she so desired, thus prolonging the game. In 2004, just as the Congos and chorus had supported the Queen in her refusal to dance with the scheduled Devil, they also intervened in the ritual to extend the evening's festivities. Once the Queen was satisfied with how long the Congos had been dancing and playing, she acquiesced to allow the Major Devil to jump backward with her into the drums. However, the Congos were not yet ready to stop playing, so they rushed behind her to buttress her as she started the fall. They intervened this way through several more refrains until they were ready to conclude the evening's drama. In this way, Congo practitioners negotiate power and agency in the midst of Congo drama.

## ASH WEDNESDAY AND PLAYING WITH THE DEVIL

Just before dawn on Ash Wednesday 2004, the Congos began to assemble outside of the town's church. By the time the 5:00 a.m. bell rang signaling the 5:30 mass, many tired but jovial Congos were waiting outside the church door. Only a few went inside. Although some of the Congos active in the Catholic Church participate in the Ash Wednesday service, many do not. Most Congo members are spiritual, but not all participate in organized religion. The Congos waiting outside the church that day were generally quiet during most of the service. As mass ended, however, their whistles and chants began to compete with the Priest's recitation. I exited the church to find the King, Queen, Pajarito, drummers, and most of the chorus resting against the building at the side of the entrance. Other Congos were engaged in mini street performances in front of the church. There was, for example, a Congo boatman who sat on the ground with an oar but no boat. Every few beats, he would use the leverage of the oar to lift his body and propel himself forward. Once the remaining Congos exited the church, the chorus started up again; the Major Devil appeared and the Queen took turns dancing with him as well as with Congos in the chorus; and each character danced in his or her own style. After the early morning activities, community members retreated either to the palenque or to their homes in order to rest and prepare for the Ash Wednesday game between the Congos and the Devil.

## WATCHING CELEDONIO TRANSFORM

When I arrived at Celedonio Molinar Ávila's home in late afternoon of Ash Wednesday 2003 to witness him transform into the Major Devil character, his adult daughters and granddaughters were readying his costume, and his great-grandson was running through the house with excitement and expectation. Celedonio's granddaughter guided me into one of the bedrooms of the home where he was beginning the *pujido* (grunt), but his legs ached and he did not know if he would be able to play. Celedonio had explained the *pujido* to me in our interview in 2000:

Figure 2.17 Congos waiting outside church on Ash Wednesday (Photo by Renée A. Craft)

The grunt is something that comes out of a person when that person puts on the costume before going out. It comes out of you. It comes out of you. It's an arrogance that you didn't have before, but the moment you put on the costume a different emotion comes out of you—an emotion of how you're going to walk, which is [the persona] that you are going to [be seen as]. When you make it look like you're the Devil, you're going to put fear into the people with the grunt that comes out of you. [. . .] a grunt that, if it doesn't end up being what you wanted it to be, doesn't work.

The transformation that I witnessed in 2003 was not at all what I had imagined. Celedonio's leg pain and deep desire to play his role in the Congo game merged into something that looked and felt like a deeply embodied prayer. Wearing a loose-fitting black cotton jumpsuit, Celedonio sat on the edge of one of two twin beds, tapping his heels in unison while rocking slightly back and forth. Although I was proficient in Spanish by that time, I could not understand much of what he muttered and quickly stopped trying. His words and gestures felt private, like a supplication; they weren't meant for me. So I let myself be still and humbly witness him. He touched his bad leg every so

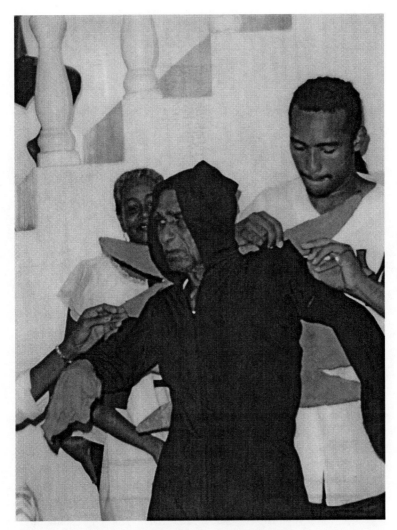

Figure 2.18 Celedonio getting dressed (Photo by Renée A. Craft)

often and looked up as if begging. The words that registered with me without my straining to understand were, "Please, [. . .] please let me do it. [. . .] I don't know if I can do it [. . .] Please [. . .] please let me do it." Something in me was moved close to tears. There was a tension in the house, a deep communal yearning. I could feel the "please" emanating from his family members. I could feel it from the other Devils starting to gather in his living room. I shared in this palpable longing.

Figure 2.19  Devils gathered in Celedonio's den/living room (Photo by Renée A. Craft)

Like Celedonio, the Devils gathered in his den started to tap their heels and stomp their feet to build up energy and to let him know that they were there. Each Devil wore layers of ankle bells, which entranced the house. Drawing from personal experience, I likened the ambience to the way an impassioned song builds in a small, rural, Southern Baptist church whose seated members stomp on hardwood floors in time with their own choral singing, or to the mounting feeling of being wrapped in sound that builds toward the end of a well-spun house music set. Celedonio let out a "Pu-u-ha" sound and the other Devils echoed him. As he explained it: "The grunt comes casually from you. You grunt and you go outside in accordance with what [the grunt helps you to] 'see.' You are going to go out and you 'see' an atmosphere, you know, that can make a person change."

After one of his daughters helped to tie on his ankle bells, Celedonio's legs started to jiggle in unison with the other Devils. "Pu-u-ha," he let out again, and an echo of staggered, strong "pu-u-ha" refrains followed. He was on his feet now, but the strength that I had seen mounting in him seemed struck by pain and waned. "I can't do this," he said, looking up again. "*Sí, puedes, papá* [Yes, you can, daddy]," one of his daughters reassured as she slipped

Figure 2.20  Photo of Celedonio (Photo by Renée A. Craft)

his hands into thin red cotton mittens. He let out another "pu-u-ha," and the living room shook with bells and echoes. He started to move now from the bedroom to the kitchen. One daughter readied his mask and another readied his cardboard wings. As I moved to see him better, I caught a glimpse of the den and the screen front door just beyond it. The whole den was full of men dressed in red-and-black Devil costumes, some leaning on canes with whips coming out of the ends, others sitting in chairs jiggling their feet, and still

Figure 2.21  Carnival Devil in the Street (Photo by Ashley Minner)

other, younger ones sitting on the floor. Outside the door, rows and rows of
children and teens sat in a neighbor's yard waiting to see the Devils. The ones
sitting on a nearby wall propped themselves up on their hands so they would
be ready to leap and run as soon as all the Devils spread out of the house.
Inside, Celedonio was somewhere between his prayer and *pujido*. He let his
daughters guide him without seeming to notice them. He stretched his arms
above his head the way I had seen people "catch the spirit" in church, and

Figure 2.22 Photo of Raul (Photo by Renée A. Craft)

then one of his daughters gave him his cane-whip and he started crossing his feet and jiggling them toward the living room. In explaining the process of transformation, he had said that "You want to jump, so you grunt. It comes out and you jump, jump up high. Then you're changed. [. . .] You can throw yourself from a house and land softly. It's a mystery. [. . .] because it's something that comes from inside of a person. [. . .] It's like a genie, a genie that comes out of you."

Figure 2.23 Peaceful devil (Photo by Elaine Eversley)

I had expected to be a little afraid. Instead, I was as excited as the children sitting on the wall. Celedonio came out to the Devils in the living room, and the sounds they made reminded me of the ways I imagine a lion's pride answering the alpha male. With Celedonio's call as their license, all the Devils exploded from the door, crossing their feet in jiggling steps and running hops up the street as the children fled and screamed with glee. Carlos and Raul, two Major Devils whom Celedonio had trained, stayed behind with their mentor. Ilusca, Celedonio's adult granddaughter, scooped up her young son and exited the house behind her grandfather. Her son was a diablito, a little Devil, dressed in a red-and-black costume that looked like his great-grandfather's. He had been talking about being a Devil all week, but now he clung teary-eyed to his mother. Celedonio moved slowly down the street flanked on both sides by his mentee Devils, both of whom also played the Major Devil role in various capacities that year. When Celedonio looked a little unsteady, Carlos would reach for him as though whipping him, but he hit him only lightly and used the contact as an opportunity to grab onto his mentor until he was more stable. Carlos likewise whipped Diablito in his mother's arms as she smiled, but his hand lingered gently. The farther Celedonio walked, the stronger he appeared. I had prepared myself for many things, but I had not prepared myself for something so intimate and tender.

They were three Major Devils moving toward the park to join the Congo game and to be "blessed" one by one until the game ended. In the official Congo narrative, there is always only one Major Devil in the tradition, but the lived reality is more complicated, contested, and contextual.

## THE GAME BETWEEN THE CONGOS AND DEVIL

What once included a competition among Congo kingdoms along Costa Arriba to capture and rob one another's palenques/palacios in the spirit of Carnival fun has evolved into a game principally between the Congos and the Devil. Intergenerational Congo practitioners dispute the role and ideal embodiment of the Devil character more than any other character in the Congo tradition. Celedonio, Carlos, Raul, and other Congo ritual specialists explain the Devil character as representing colonial enslavers who personified evil in their abusive treatment of enslaved people. Colonialists appropriated the Christian trope of devil to dissuade rebellion, and are rumored to have put on devil costumes to frighten runaway slaves into surrender.

Practitioners in their mid-twenties and younger, however, define the Devil character in flatter, more literal terms. They view it as a *metaphor* of the Christian devil rather than a *parody* of Spanish enslavers. According to Simona Esquina:

> The game between the Devils and the Congos has changed a lot. Because look, before, the Devil played on Ash Wednesday only. [. . .] Before, you didn't see the Devil all throughout Carnival. You didn't see the Devil. Now what happens is that from the moment the Congo game begins, the Devils are out playing with the Congos, and it shouldn't be that way. The Devil should just be for Ash Wednesday, no more [. . .]. But now the Devils is out every day. Every day they're playing Devil. [Before,] when [. . .] the last Angel tied up [the Devil], that's where it ended, at 6:00 [p.m.] After that, they didn't keep going because the next day was Lent.

When colonial enslavers watched the Devil characters whip seemingly mischievous Blacks/Congos, what they saw was their anti-rebellion Christian teachings made flesh, and so they looked upon the tradition with approval. All the while, though, the Congos were openly dramatizing their contempt. Devil as parody takes a weapon from the hand of the enslaver without his knowledge and uses it against him; Devil as metaphor gives it back. This type of flattening by the younger generation of today distances the Devil character from its context and allows it to "easily become an act of complicity" rather than continuing to "serve as critical intervention, as a rite of resistance" (hooks 1995, 211). Not only does this nullify part of the power of *el juego Congo,* but it also changes the terms of play. Simona described such a change:

> The Devil used to dance and play with the Congos, [. . .] but not now. Now, they're at it [i.e., whipping] from the moment they come out. No, no, it's not like that. I get so mad on Ash Wednesday when I see those young guys working themselves into a rage with all that hitting. No, the Devil should play with the Congo men and women. It's about playing. It's a game. They should not work themselves up with hitting, hitting, and hitting. [. . .] If a Congo woman threw herself to the ground, a Congo, the Devil would do his feet like this and he did like that and he played. It was a game the Devil played with the Congos. But not now. The moment the Devil arrives it's whip, whip, whip, whip. That's not how you play Devil. Please, it's a game. But now the Devil doesn't play. No, sir, the Devil doesn't play. Now, from the moment they arrive it's whipping. They're so enraged as if they carry some hate inside for that person, they give it to them so. No, it's not like that. They don't know how to play Devil. The truth is that they don't know. Ask Celedonio. [. . .] That man knows how to play Devil. He doesn't go beating people.

Ritual specialists believe that the Devils in the Congo tradition establish power and presence through the dance. Devils, like Raul and Carlos, who apprenticed under Celedonio were well trained in the proper means of Congo/Devil play. Speaking about the advice he received from his mentor, Carlos said:

> [Celedonio] told me not to run after anyone because the people come out to play with you. You do not have to go out looking for them. They come to play with you. If you run after someone it is because you want to mistreat them. Do not run after them. And I have seen it myself since I have taken his advice. Certain people come out to play with me. I do not have to go looking for them. They come to me and they respect me. It is something I have noticed.

Younger members, however, sometimes attempt to assert the power and presence of the Devil through flashy costumes, speed, and the force of their whips.

"You know what the Devils do now?" Simona asked at the conclusion of our 2003 interview. "They even put razor blades on the end of their whips!" This is part of the escalating material danger she feels in younger people's metaphoric interpretation of the Devil character that contradicts the *burla* ("joke") it originally was making about Spanish enslavers. She added:

> Over there in [the town of] Nombre de Dios, they've had to take the whips away from the Devils because they put razorblades on the tips and cut people. And [the game] isn't like that. That's not the tradition. That's not the game. [. . .] It's been like this for a while but it's over now because the Queen took it upon herself to check all the Devils' whips. So now you have to check all the whips of the Devils. That's why I'm saying that everything has changed. It takes an evil heart to put razor blades on the ends of whips to cut people. [. . .] The tradition is being lost. It's being lost because of that and that's bad.

The power of the tradition throughout Costa Arriba is experiencing a shift from the symbolic to the literal as the tradition circulates in the broader world context and dances from the margins toward the center. Yet, the shift is neither unidirectional nor irrevocable. Community-led festive celebrations that focus on cultural preservation, networking, and intracommunity knowledge sharing, like El Festival de los Diablos y Congo (The Festival of the Devils and Congos), which I discuss in chapter 3, as well as newer innovations like El Festival de las Polleras Congas are working to create intergenerational and intercommunity dialogues, performances, and play among Congo communities throughout the country.

The road along the Costa Arriba marks the epochal shift in the tradition for many elders. Before the road, the Portobelo Congo tradition saturated the political economy of everyday life such that complex exchanges among layered identities operated in a closed system. Congos lived, worked, and made meaning primarily in Portobelo among *vecinos* (neighbors). Although newer members are inducted into the tradition by participation and time, they come with less context than did older members whose families have firm roots in the tradition. For older members, being Congo was part of their primary identity. For newer members, it is one of many points of identification and not necessarily the most important one.

Speaking about the ways in which the Congo ritual specialists, elders, and community members are working to help young people maintain a sociocultural grounding within the tradition, Carlos Chavarría said:

Today we're trying to teach the young people to uphold the value of their tradition. [. . .] Remember where you come from. You can become the President, but remember where you are from. [. . .] because when you go out into the world you'll realize the richness that there is out there. In the little that I've traveled, I've realized that we are also rich in culture, and that makes you want to maintain your tradition, your culture, as it was something that was given to us by our ancestors. We have to continue with it as much as we can.

For Carlos and other ritual specialists, it is most important that young people understand "*de donde nace la tradición Congo y porque se celebra* [where the Congo tradition was born and why it is celebrated]." He continued: "It's what I think they should know so they can understand it. Because if they do not know where it is from, they'll be celebrating something they do not know, but if they know where it is from, they'll understand why it is celebrated."

Regardless of changes that twentieth-century practitioners have witnessed to certain ritual elements of the tradition or the embodiment of specific Congo characters, one thing remains true: the centrality of Congo dance and music to the community and its persistence as the heart of the tradition. Speaking about this centrality, Carlos concluded:

There are a lot of young people who do not like to dress Congo, but they still dance, right? Others do not want to have their faces painted, but they still dance. [. . .] When Carnival is happening, little kids with their little drums playing and singing, everybody dances. That is what happens. [. . .] That is the way it is. It is in the blood, and I would like to see it continue. [. . .] Perhaps it's because they sacrificed so many people and so many Black slaves died here that there's something here. If that's it then I think the tradition will always continue and won't get lost. Regardless of all the modern dances that come out, Congo is Congo.

Figure 3.1  Blessing the Devil 2013 (Photo by Elaine Eversley)

# 3

# Baptizing the Devil
## Circum-Local Transmission and Translation of Culture

> In all cultures, most of the choreography of authority is expressed through the body.
>
> —Paul Connerton, *How Societies Remember*

> If ethnography once imagined it could describe discrete cultures, it now contends with boundaries that crisscross over a field at once fluid and saturated with power.
>
> —Renato Rosaldo, *Culture & Truth*

> *El Diablo nace en Portobelo. [. . .] El Diablo se crea en Portobelo.*
>
> The Devil was born in Portobelo. [. . .] The Devil was created in Portobelo.
>
> —Raul Jiménez, former Diablo Mayor de Portobelo

As discussed in chapter 2, the contemporary Congo "game" is a parodic bout between the characters of Congos/self-liberated Blacks and Devils/Spanish enslavers. In general discourse, the Congo "game," "tradition," and "drama" implicate or directly involve the Devil character. In practice, Congos and Devils have specific costuming, performatives, and rituals that form a distinct ethos for each character. Whereas the previous chapter used Raymond Williams's dichotomy between official and practical consciousness to analyze the elasticity of twentieth-century Portobelo Congo traditions, this chapter uses what I have coined a "circum-local" paradigm to analyze the ways in which movement, migration, and assimilation have distilled twentieth-century Devil traditions in Portobelo. Congo and Devil traditions in Panama are cultural performances situated in discrete locations but constituted through processes of departure and return. They evolve not just through intragroup negotiations within "home" locations but also through intergroup encounters and reckonings. Following this circum-local process of cultural reproduction, this chapter tracks the cultural contributions and performative innovations of the three primary people who have played the Major Devil role in the living memory of current Portobelo practitioners.

First, I examine the ways in which Celedonio Molinar Ávila, the longest-playing Major Devil in Portobelo, influenced the local tradition mid-century when he migrated to the town from a neighboring community and instituted the Major Devil character as well as the practice of "baptizing the Devil." Second, I explore the ways in which Carlos Chavarría, the current mayor of Portobelo, earned the right to play the character in the early 1980s and the ways in which his ascent to the role solidified the community's adoption of Celedonio's innovation, albeit on its own terms. Finally, I engage the ways in which Raul Jiménez, a Major Devil tapped to play the character from 1982 to 1986 when Carlos traveled abroad to study and who has performed the role at various points since, co-created El Festival de los Diablos y Congos, an innovation that serves as a means of cultural preservation as well as a cultural showcase. Developed to bring Major Devils and their Congo communities together from throughout Panama to Portobelo, the festival extends the time frame for practitioners to celebrate their Congo tradition and offers national and international tourists a unique opportunity to "sample" Congo performances as they exist throughout the Republic.

This chapter concludes with my analysis of a generational shift in the popular interpretation of the Devil character and its significance to the way the tradition is practiced in the broader Republic. This shift was triggered, in part, by the increased visibility and popularity that the tradition has received since the dawn of the twenty-first century. With the following questions in mind, this chapter examines Congo performances as sites of subversion, empowerment, innovation, and cultural preservation. How has the Devil character served as a site of cultural preservation, innovation, and subversion? What is the significance of "blessing" or baptizing the Devil to the Congo tradition of Portobelo and to Congo traditions throughout the country? By what criteria does the Congo community assess the quality of

Major Devil performance, and who has the authority to pass judgment? What nuanced perspectives might a circum-local paradigm offer the study of Black Diaspora cultural production and transmission?

## Toward a Circum-Local Paradigm

Whereas Paul Gilroy's (1993a) "Black Atlantic" and Joseph Roach's (1996) "Circum-Atlantic" name a trafficking of bodies, performatives, ideologies, and cultural commerce back and forth across the Black Diaspora, I use "circum-local" to name the restless micro-migrations of these same contemporary phenomena within geographically discrete diasporic locations. Black Diaspora citizens travel across the Atlantic when able and/or interested, but they more frequently micro-travel within their home countries or regions, returning to their places of origin with nuanced Black performatives on their bodies, in their mouths, and in their consciousnesses. Inspired by the aforementioned theorists' focus on the mixing and mingling whereby the New World was "invented" (Gilroy 1993a, 4) in the Caribbean through "flow, exchanges and in-between elements" (190) that constitute identities, I offer "circum-local" as a means to examine the ways Black Diaspora communities, which "are always unfinished, always being remade" (xi), experience other such communities within their own national boundaries through processes of departure and return—city to city, village to village, town to town, neighborhood to neighborhood, and/or between any mixture thereof. While Gilroy uses the chronotope of "ship," which he defines as "a living, micro-cultural, micro-political system in motion" (4) as a guiding trope in his study,[1] I suggest "bus" as an appropriate spacio-temporal model for a Caribbean/Latin American "circum-local" paradigm. Urban and rural commuters as well as lower- and middle-income travelers throughout the Diaspora rely on this form of transit more frequently than any other.

Like Roach's (1996) circum-Atlantic model, for circum-local "intercultures," "performances so often carry within them the memory of otherwise forgotten substitutions—those that were rejected and, even more invisibly those that have succeeded" (5). Roach continues, "The key to understanding how performances worked *within* a culture, recognizing that a fixed and unified culture exists only as a convenient but dangerous fiction, is to illuminate the process of surrogation as it operated *between* the participating cultures" (5; italics in the original).[2] Not only have flows and exchanges between cirum-local communities augmented or otherwise altered small elements of the Congo tradition's contemporary practice, but also some of the elements regarded today as foundational have been drastically altered by microdiasporic processes of departure and return.

## Celedonio Molinar Ávila—The (Re)invention of Culture

> Stanislavsky said of the theater, when a person, the public, enters a theater space and sits down and the play begins and they know already how it's going to end—that is not theater. That is not art. Art should surprise. The art should appear to be a miracle to the public. Like with kids, the public should be on the edge of their seat. Like this. Like this. They follow you. They want to eat you up, right, with all of their senses. So, well, that's what Celedonio did the first time I saw him.
>
> —Ileana Solís Palma, Professor of Theater, University of Panama, and the first woman to dance Devil in the Congo tradition of Portobelo, Panama

From our first encounter, Celedonio Molinar Ávila drew my attention. It was not his embodiment of the Major Devil character; I did not witness his performance until three years after I first met him. Rather, it was his captivating presence. During my July 2013 interview in Panama City with Ileana Solís Palma, the first woman to train with Celedonio and perform the Devil role in Portobelo, she described his magnetism: "In the West, we think of energy as movement [. . .] we see that a person has a lot of energy because we see them moving around. No, it's the energy that comes from inside out and from outside goes in, like a yin and yang. Knowing how to control that is a gift [. . .] He had that gift. He had the gift to capture your gaze."

More than the strength of his presence, Celedonio knew how to "story" himself. Like most of the Congo practitioners I interviewed, he spoke about the tradition with great pride, but he also spoke about it with a strong sense of authority. Credited with a major intervention in the tradition, Celedonio revised the Congo game and reinvented the twentieth-century Portobelo Devil tradition.

Born on March 3, 1916, in Nombre de Dios, a town northeast of Portobelo, Celedonio began playing the Devil role in 1939 while still living in his place of birth. He learned the Devil tradition from a Portobelo native named Viudo Ceballos [sic],[3] who had relocated to Nombre de Dios for marriage. According to Celedonio when I interviewed him in 2003,[4] "They [Congos in Nombre de Dios] would play, but they didn't dress as Devils. When [Ceballos] arrived there, he organized the Congos and the Devil. He himself dressed as Devil." Ceballos had been a Devil in Portobelo, so he named himself Major Devil in Nombre de Dios since he was the only local practitioner with knowledge of the Devil tradition. With that knowledge from his experiences in Portobelo, he augmented the tradition in Nombre de Dios. Celedonio continued, "The Major Devil is the one who has the most years of service [. . .] He's the one who's been dressing as Devil longest. That's why they call him the Major Devil."

Completing the circum-local path begun by his mentor, Celedonio migrated to his bride's hometown of Portobelo at the age of 29. "I arrived here in 1945 and started to dress as Devil," he said, "that was when the Major Devil [tradition] was established here. I became the Major Devil here [. . .] I got the title here [. . .] I brought that tradition from there to here." Portobelo had had a Devil tradition before, but it had not included the Major Devil character. Celedonio returned to Portobelo as the only local Devil who had studied under the first Major Devil. He thus claimed the title of Major Devil and taught local practitioners how to play the Congo game in the way that he had been trained. He explained that "They [had] dressed [as Devils] and put on their Congo costumes, but they didn't know about the Major Devil. [. . .] They kept dancing, but they didn't baptize [the Devils]. The Congos and the Devils kept playing with each other. [. . .] So I realized that they weren't doing it like it should be done."

Ceballos had taught Celedonio the practice of "blessing" or "baptizing" the Devil as a way to conclude the game. Rather than a practice that he brought with him from Portobelo, "baptizing the Devil" appears to be a unique intervention that Ceballos initiated in Nombre de Dios. Celedonio learned it as a part of his training there and incorporated it into the Portobelo tradition. In doing so, he also migrated the Devil's dramatic foils, the Angel characters and the Priest. "Before Celedonio, there were no Priests," Raul Jiménez confirmed in our 2003 interview. "He implemented that. That is to say, that when he got dressed [as Devil], he said, 'Baptize me, baptize me.' No one knew [what that was], so he explained about the baptism and from there it began. [. . .] He taught my father [Andres Jiménez] how to baptize."

No contemporary Portobelo Congo practitioner recalls a tradition of blessing or baptizing the Devil character before Celedonio arrived. Prior to his arrival, Devil characters were merely captured and released to play again until the community grew tired of doing so. Adding the element of baptism gave the Congo game a dramatic arc that signaled when the game might end. It also added another complete "scene" to the Congo drama. In the first scene, the Devil comes to the Palacio on Carnival Tuesday to capture the Queen but is thwarted. In the second, the Devil seeks to punish the Congos for their defiance and independence by whipping them, but the Angels and Priest help the Congos to successfully defeat him and take away his power. Speaking about how this second scene concludes, Celedonio said, "When they baptize the Devil, everyone donates based on their generosity, like they do in Nombre de Dios. They buy drinks, no money, to have a party that night, and they make a big pot of soup so that all the Congos can eat, and that way everyone feels satisfied because everyone has participated."

Throughout Panama's Atlantic coast, Congo communities have incorporated some form of the Devil character into their Congo traditions. "Official consciousness" narrates the character's existence as though it has always been. However, "practical consciousness" reveals its existence, at least in Portobelo and Nombre de Dios, as acts of migration, imagination, organization, and will. After the road linking the Costa Arriba to the rest of the country was built, the freedom that Congo communities had had in relative isolation to capture one another's flags, raid one another's palacios, and play "war" diminished, and the circum-local interventions of Ceballos and Celedonio of having Congos play with and baptize Devils *became* the contemporary game.

## Carlos Chavarría—Mayor and Major Devil of Portobelo

> [Regardless of] me being the Mayor, I dance Congo all the same. I take off my shoes and I dance Congo. That's who I am; it doesn't make me any difference. I stay the same. I'm still the same Carlos Chavarria. I'm still the Mayor Devil. I'm still the Mayor. You must enjoy the moment.
>
> —Carlos Chavarría

Portobelo native Carlos Chavarría has played the role of Major Devil in the town's Congo tradition since Celedonio Molinar retired the first time in 1980. During our 2013 interview, Carlos stated, "In 1979, [Celedonio] had played Devil for 49 years, so, in 1980, he decided not to play anymore as he had served seven seven-year cycles." Those who commit to playing the role of Devil pledge to do so for a seven-year period. After seven years, they may continue as Devil or they may choose to play in the role of a Congo, which has no time restrictions on play. Except for the years he spent studying abroad in Russia (1982–86), Chavarría has continued in the role for over forty years, including playing alongside his mentor for over two decades until Celedonio officially retired in 2003. In 2004 Chavarría was elected mayor of the district of Portobelo. As a long-standing Major Devil and the civic leader of the town, he has an important perspective on the meaning, purpose, and transformations of the role.

Although Carlos grew up watching Celedonio perform the Devil role, he was not immediately attracted to playing it. Over time, however, it appealed to him. When we spoke in 2013, Carlos described how he came to the role:

> When I was a kid in school I dressed as a Congo. But one day, I decided to play as Devil, and my mom told me no. She wasn't on board with that [but] I told her that I wanted to play. And I wanted it so much that [to earn money for my costume] I had to go out to the mangrove to make coal with a guy called Ricardo Robles. We cut wood and we made an oven [. . .] and from that I bought my first bells and everything else. A sack of coal cost 50 cents. A woman named Melida Jiménez, may she rest in peace, was the one that bought the coal, and from there I bought [what I needed].
> I made my first attempt to dress as the Devil. Later, an aunt named Antonia Solio sewed my costume for the first time. She made my costume because my mother wasn't in agreement. The second year, I had to work shoveling as a mason's assistant to earn enough to make my costume, and in the following years my mother began to help me [. . .] I began dressing in my costume, and, well, I enjoyed it [. . .] I think my interest was more because some of my friends dressed as Devil and I wanted to play too, so that's where I stayed, playing Devil.

Whereas young men who choose to play Congo are able to create their Congo costumes by turning existing clothing inside out and fashioning their hats and props out of materials found in nature or around the house, the Devil's costume requires a jumpsuit, mask, whip, and layers of bells. Like other youths desirous of playing the role of Devil, Carlos had to work odd jobs to be able to afford the materials for his costume, but he did not do so alone. Just as the community would later choose him as their Major Devil, so, too, did various family and other community members choose to help him acquire the resources he needed in order to play. From the creation of one's costume through the execution of the game, Congo/Devil culture is communal.

In addition to the attraction of dressing up and performing the Devil role alongside friends, Carlos's attention and curiosity were captured by the Devil's mask and the insider/outsider perspective it provided. Speaking about the experience, he explained:

> When I played Devil the first time, what most caught my attention were the masks. When I wore the mask, I saw people run and be afraid, and inside

of the mask, I laughed. From the outside one cannot see the face inside. [The Devil wearing the mask] can enjoy what is happening. Also, when you [see] the Congo playing with the Devil, it is graceful and you see how the community celebrates it. That fills me with satisfaction and emotion. That is the great thing that this tradition has given me. So, that is what most attracted me to it and what most makes me play Devil.

Wearing the Devil's mask allowed Carlos to experience what Du Bois (1994) described as a sense of double-consciousness, of witnessing the world through his unique first-person perspective as well as through the third-person perspective of Congo co-witnesses. However, unlike Dubois's concept of "the veil," which he posits created a psychosis in Blacks by simultaneously allowing them the perspectives of the bodies they animated, which were as capable and deserving as those of Whites, and to witness themselves through the stifling perspective of their oppressors, playing Devil afforded Carlos the opposite view. He could move within a veil of power, a parodic veil of Whiteness, watching those around him responding as if the construct were real, all the while knowing his own limits and the necessary illusions that were designed to perpetuate and amplify the community's perception of his power. Having previously played the role of Congos/Blacks, Carlos was even more aware of how to project the type of Devil embodiment that would meet the community's expectations of how the role should be played.

Respect is an important principle regarding how one embodies the Devil. To be respected as Devil, especially as Major Devil, one must maintain the performative integrity of the role, play the Congo game with commitment and finesse, and honor the rules sanctioned by the Congo King and Queen that govern how the Devil character interacts with Congo characters. In discussing his ability to maintain the community's respect, Carlos talked about the ways in which he stays in character until the Congo game and drama are complete:

I walk backwards into my house and I take off the mask, and because of that I have always maintained the respect [of the people] because I only take my mask off in public after I have been baptized. I mean, the local people all know who I am, but the tourists ask, "Who is that? Who is that? Why does he not take it off?" Not until the moment I am done do they see me. During the game, I try to remain incognito with people because it is important to retain that respect. And I have noted that since I took my position as Major Devil, I have maintained my respect.

Carlos's refusal to break character enhances the game's enjoyment for all practitioners. Staying within the movement vocabulary of Devil, and retaining his mask until baptized allows Congo practitioners to immerse themselves in the world of the game, including the anticipation and fear of being confronted by a whip-wielding Devil. Speaking about the difference between community members' everyday interactions with him compared with their responses to him as Devil, Carlos said:

The people sincerely respect me as Devil [. . .] I have seen that sometimes I am here in my house not dressed [as Devil]. People will be playing up there [at the fort]. I will go up there to watch for a while, and the kids will come by while I am there. [But] the moment I dress as Devil and go out, I see that everyone moves aside, and I wonder why that is. It is because the people are scared of me? I don't know why because I don't mistreat them; I just go out to play with them [. . .] and when the game begins, they come out to play with me. But they fear me, from the smallest ones to the biggest. Why? I do not know. I have acquired the respect of the group, and I have maintained it, thank God. In terms of the tradition, I have maintained it.

The emotional range that Carlos arouses between fear and respect is not born of impending bodily harm or mistreatment. Rather, it reflects his ability to create suspenseful anticipation and tension through the way he dances and carries himself as Devil. Carlos learned this sense of performative integrity and finesse by watching his mentor, Celedonio, perform the role. During our interview, Carlos reminisced about one of the ways his mentor captured the community's imagination and interest:

When I was young, I would see that the older people were scared of Celedonio. They were scared of him when he played Devil. Even the youngest among us, we would go running away from him. Later, I noticed that all of the houses here in Portobelo were right next to each other. So here, facing the church, there were various houses that people would play in front of, and I do not know how he came to jump on top of the roof, but he went running from roof to roof. I was surprised. Everyone in the village said he could fly! And I did not see that, but I did see him running from roof to roof. Well, of course, between the houses there were alleys, so he would jump from one roof and land on the other side. Yes, I witnessed that personally.

Growing up with the model of Celedonio's embodiment of the Major Devil helped to emphasize for Carlos the importance of performance over force in garnering the community's respect and in sustaining their excitement about the game.

Carlos's virtuosity with the Devil's dance movements as well as his overall manner of playing the game led the Congo community to select him to succeed Celedonio as their Major Devil. This manner of passing the baton was not aligned with the selection process that Celedonio had brought with him from Nombre de Dios. During our 2000 interview, Celedonio asserted, "The people can't choose the Major Devil. [. . .] The Major Devil isn't named that way. It's earned. It's a school. [. . .] I appoint the Major Devil. It's earned."

Carlos had apprenticed under Celedonio with other Devils, but he was not next in line to become Major Devil when Celedonio retired. So, the community intervened. After adopting the practice of baptizing the Devil, which Celedonio had introduced, as well as absorbing into their local tradition the additional characters required to perform the baptism, Portobelo's Congo community also expressed its agency in determining who would play the pivotal role of Major Devil. Carlos described the initial, improvisatory selection process, which occurred at the conclusion of the 1980 Carnival:

> When we were playing Devil, there was a man called Francisco Amoreti, and it was thought that he was the one to be the next Major Devil. When we were getting baptized, there was no one left but him and me, so I went out to play with the Angels and the Congos. And they said to me, "Not him, you." And the Angels said to me, "Not him, you." And I am asking them, "What is going on?" And they tell me there is going to be a duel [i.e., a performance competition] between [me] and Pancho [Francisco Amoreti] [. . .] So they created a duel between him and me. The advantage that I had over him was that he was deaf, but I knew that he still played Devil very well and I recognized that. So, I told the Congos to render unto Caesar that which is Caesar's if he is the Major Devil. And they said no. There [was] a duel, and when we started playing he did not hear the music and could not follow the rhythm, and that was to my advantage. And I have been able to play from 1980 until now as the Major Devil.

Carlos's ascent to Major Devil at once marks the success of Celedonio's circum-local cultural intervention and the friction that often comes when a cultural innovation shifts from the exclusive control of its creator to that of its host community. Beyond that initial intervention, the Congo community continued to tweak the "official" rules of the game in order to honor their desires about how it should be played. During our interview, Carlos discussed his choice to study abroad and his assumption that choosing to do so would mean forfeiting the role of Major Devil:

In 1982, I went to Russia to study. So I did not play in 1983, 1984, and 1985, until I came back in 1986 and was motivated again to play Devil. I knew that there was another person [Raul Jiménez] playing Major Devil for me, and I gave it to him, but the Congos told me, "No, you were on vacation. You have come back to your culture, and these years [when you were away] count." I told them, "No, Raul is here." They said, "No, you are the Major Devil." It was like they gave me a license to study and they kept counting the years.

The community considered Carlos's time away to be a sabbatical, allowing that time to count toward his total years of service as Devil. As previously noted, practitioners who commit to playing the Devil role do so for seven-year periods. These periods may be served consecutively, as Celedonio did, with the goal of retiring at the end of a seven-year multiple. Talking about his own future, Carlos continued:

Unfortunately, [in 2013] we had to suspend the games because of a few security problems that happened in the district [but] I will play next year and, God willing, I'll reach 42 years of playing Devil [. . .] I do not know if I will achieve 49 years of playing Devil like my ancestor Celedonio, may God keep him in His glory. He played seven seven-year cycles in a row [. . .] I do not know if I will achieve [that], seeing as how he had more strength and everything, but you know that the minute you dress as Devil and you have the gift and responsibility to be the Major Devil, you have to try to do it as best as possible [. . .] [to] maintain the tradition so that the people respect you and you respect them.

## Raul Jimenez and El Festival de los Diablos y Congos

Like Carlos, the Portobelo native Raul Jimenez was raised in the Congo tradition remade by Celedonio with the existence of the Major Devil and the practice of baptism. Raul's father, Andres, was one of the first practitioners to learn the role of Priest, which Celedonio also introduced. Raul's older brother, Fernando, once played Pajarito, and his younger brother continues to play as a Devil. Even though members of his family played various characters, that Raul would perform as a Devil was far from predetermined. As he explained during our 2000 interview, he came to the Devil character by way of a prank:

It was practically like a joke. What happened was, back in those days, the Congos had their own rules, no? They were strict about their rules. So, I stole a cane from one of them [and after that] each year [during Carnival] they would chase me. I could not be relaxed anywhere [. . .] In order for me to have some safety, I started dressing as Devil, and here I am. I was really interested in the game [. . .] I went to the home of Mr. Celedonio Molinar, who was the Major Devil [. . .] and he taught me how to play Devil. When Carlos went to Russia, [. . .] I was left in charge.

Although he initially chose to perform the role as the solution to a problem, Raul has continued to participate in the tradition as Devil because of the sense of presence that playing the game from the vantage point of the Devil affords him. He explained:

I like it because it gets me directly involved with the Congo—I mean, I arrive at the center of what is Congo [. . .] When I go out, there is a tension [. . .] At the time that I go out, which is midnight, the whole world has that tension: Here comes the Devil. Who is the Devil? When is the Devil coming? And when they hear the Devil—that is, [when] the Devil grunts in the street—the people stay there; they live in that moment. [. . .] Congo and Devil, I mean, they are tied together.

Having served as Major Devil in Portobelo during Carlos's absence from 1982 to 1985, Raul not only continues to act in the role when called upon, but also he has made a lasting contribution to the tradition by conceiving of and helping to implement one of the town's largest festivities. In 2000, he partnered with the photographer Sandra Eleta, the visual artist Noel González de Carrera, and a committee of Congo practitioners to found El Festival de los Diablos y Congo. Planned as a biennial celebration of culture and history, the Portobelo-based festival attracts Devils and their Congo communities from throughout Panama for a day-long showcase of each community's talent and skill.

Raul and others in the community feared the deterioration of the Congo tradition, especially the significance and meaning of the Devil character, and so planners organized the festival as an intervention into cultural erosion. During each festival, Congo "kingdoms" have an opportunity to share, borrow, and critique various ways of embodying the Devil characters and enacting the Congo/Devil game that exist within hours (in some cases minutes) of their home communities. This cultural intervention harks back to the days before the construction of the Costa Arriba road when Congo communities

Figure 3.2 Devil mask from El Festival de los Diablos y Congos (Photo by Elaine Eversley)

visited one another as part of the game and restores an important aspect of the Congo tradition's circum-local praxis.

Unlike presentations for tourists, which are intended primarily for an outsider's gaze and do not include Devils, the Festival of the Devils and Congos not only features the Devil character but also depends on Congo community spectatorship, approval, respect, and engagement in order to succeed. Each kingdom's royal court, primary singer, chorus, and drummers take turns performing on an elevated stage while their Devils and male Congos exhibit a portion of their Ash Wednesday performances in front of the stage. Because practitioners generally are in their home communities during Ash Wednesday ritual celebrations, they do not get to observe the full array of Congo characters active in neighboring communities. The festival allows them that unique opportunity. Congo ritual specialists from Colón, María Chiquita, Palenque, Nombre de Dios, Puerto Pilón, Viento Frío, Portobelo, and other regions along the Atlantic coast as well as Congo communities from throughout the country showcase their talents, skills, and particular styles of Congo performance for an immediate audience of other practitioners and an extended audience of national and international spectators.

Just as respect is an important element in maintaining the integrity of the game between Devils and Congos within their home communities, each community's adherence to an overarching set of ethical principles maintains a spirit of play, celebration, and good-natured rivalry during intergroup play. Communities entering Portobelo for the Festival de los Diablos y Congos do so understanding that they must submit to the local community's rules. Accordingly, visiting Major Devils subordinate themselves to the Major Devil in their host community. Carlos discussed this aspect of the tradition during our 2013 interview:

> When all the young people come to play Devil for the Festival of the Devils, they all know who the Major Devil of Portobelo is and we all talk and play together. But if I were to go to another community, I cannot be the Major Devil because that community has one already so I have to be under the rules of the Major Devil of that community. In that moment I would be a junior to him [. . .] I would have to ask him how they play Devil there, what are the rules, and I have to stick to them. It is the same as every community having a fort, and you have to follow the rules of the King and Queen [of that fort] [. . .] When others come here, they ask me what the rules are. They submit to the style that the Congo reign [King and Queen] has given me directly because the [rules of] Devil play are what the Congo reign has outlined. We submit to whatever the Queen and King say in order to maintain the tradition. It's because of that that I tell them, "Sirs, you know how this game is. We do it with respect. Do not abuse it." And that is truly why you have seen here, that no one gets hit [with the Devil's whips] here during the Festival of the Devils. You've seen the quantity of people that come here to play, and [the Devils] don't hit anyone. [Play during the festival] is really a game with a different style. It is not like our Ash Wednesday [during Carnival]. Ash Wednesday is the game where the whip comes into it.

The rules of play established by the Portobelo King, Queen, and festival organizers allow Devils to display their whips, but disallow their use. This helps to safeguard against unintended consequences.

More than a "showcase," planners designed the Festival of the Devils and Congos as an opportunity for discussion, education, and mentorship. Each festival includes 1) opportunities for local youth to apprentice under established artists working within the Congo aesthetic in set design, mask-making, and general costume preparation prior to the festival; 2) a free public exhibition held on the second floor of Portobelo's colonial Customs House of art and history related to some aspect of the Devil tradition; and 3) set-aside moments during the festival for younger and more established Devils to talk among themselves. These experiences combat the cultural forgetting

Figure 3.3  Devils participating in El Festival de los Diablos y Congos (Photo by Elaine Eversley)

that elders within the tradition fear and extend young people's network of Congo friendships throughout the Coast. In this way, El Festival de los Diablos y Congos serves as both a larger cultural performance honoring Cimarron history in Panama and a meta-performance about Panamanian Congo performance.

Some members of the religious community in Portobelo see the festival as an act of defiance that attempts to extend Carnival season further into Lent; given the history of the Carnival tradition, their assumption is likely valid. Although all Carnival activities in other parts of the country conclude on Ash Wednesday, the Portobelo festival gives celebrants one final opportunity to play Congo a week or two after Ash Wednesday. In 2003, the year of the country's Centennial, the festival had one of the largest audiences of any public event in Panama, attracting over five hundred Devils (nearly twice the population of Portobelo) from throughout the Atlantic coast, along with their Congo communities and more than *six thousand* spectators (Meneses 2003, 58).

The event's success can be credited to the inclusion of Devils from throughout the Atlantic coast in its planning as well as to support from a wide range of local and national sponsors, including Panama's National Cen-

Figure 3.4 Partial view of El Festival de los Diablos y Congos spectators (Photo by Saleem Reshamwala)

tennial Committee, the Spanish Embassy, the National Institute of Culture, the National Institute of Tourism, and the University of Panamá, as well as corporate sponsorship from one of the largest communications companies in the country, a major grocery store, and a major beer brand.

More than simply measuring other communities' performances against their own, Congo members also look for material markers of distinctions in their fellow Congos' histories and, conversely, use physical markers to raise questions regarding their neighbors' histories. The distinction that generated the most speculation among those who witnessed the 2003 festival was one Congo kingdom's performance by two Pajaritos, one male, the other female. The pair performed synchronized mirror movements, jump-dancing with their arms extended as in flight and their legs bent low while blowing their whistles to accent each step. Portobelo Congos wondered if the female Pajarito was a contemporary addition, or if she signaled a Black female interlocutor in their history who had served as a lookout or a messenger alongside a brother, father, mate, or compatriot.

As the event concluded, several teenaged Devils began strategizing their masks for the next year. Although younger Devils are often drawn to the ability of larger masks to capture the attention and admiration of the spectators, Carlos discussed the virtues of traditional masks at length during our 2013 interview without disparaging younger members' choices:

> In respect to the masks, I have seen that they have made a lot of changes. You will see big, extravagant masks that the young people are creating. I do not criticize them because the creativity of the old days is not the same as now, and that is good. That is what I tell the older people. [. . .] Before, we used to make the masks, [and] I still stay with a traditional mask, a mask resembling an animal or any other kind of design, but small. It lets in good ventilation so you can breathe well [. . .] We would make a mud mold. We would cover it with newspaper and a paste that we made from wheat—we would boil it and make a paste [. . .] We would use that to stick on the newspaper. Afterward, we would put the mask in the sun for one or two days. We would take out the mold and leave the paper mask drying until it hardened. From there we would cut it and start to decorate it, paint it, and put whatever we wanted on it. That is the way our masks were [. . .] [As the years passed,] I decided not to make the ones from mud molds as they take a lot of time. I would get cardboard. It [covers] half my face and from there I would design it and add decoration to it. I would go out with my mask—it was more lightweight—and that is how I would go out to play [. . .] [Younger Devils] ask me, "Why don't you play with a bigger mask?" (*Laughs.*) I tell them that I see when you all [who play with large masks] all lower your head and raise it [. . .] two or three times [and] have problems with [your] neck. Not me! With my mask, I can raise and lower it and I do not feel a thing. [Large masks] weigh a lot. It is for that reason that I do not want a big mask. Leave me with my traditional small mask, and I play all I want. I have kept it this way, and they respect my decision. And what is more, sometimes after I am finished playing Devil, some of them come to borrow my mask to go do a [Congo] presentation. Even my son has borrowed my mask. He takes mine and he takes his. When he is tired, he takes his off and puts mine on. But yes, the ones of today are exaggerated. You have seen them in the Festival of the Devils, those big extravagant masks that the young guys make. And we have told them: six hundred and something guys will come here dressed as Devil and, truthfully, one mask looks like the other. But they are not the same; you can see the difference in creativity that the guys have, you understand? There are people that take up to two or three months making their masks because a lot of them sew the decorations with a sewing machine. They do have their creativity.

The festival has had two unintentional consequences. One has been that it perpetuates the fascination that many young people have with the grandeur of some of the Devil costumes. They mistake them as markers of successful Devil embodiment rather than the performers' attention to rituals of preparation and dance movements. The other unintended consequence has been in greatly increasing the number of practitioners who play the Devil character in any given community while reducing the number who desire to play the role of Congo dancers or other characters. Nonetheless, people continue to participate in the tradition and, like their predecessors, make adjustments to it that favor their aesthetics, interests, and methods of play. As long as these adjustments do not violate the rules of the game as set forth by the King and Queen, practitioners are free to add their own unique innovations without fear of dishonoring the game.

Among the three "scenes" of Congo performance, the "local" and "circum-local" esoteric performances are most active in cultural preservation and community building, while "like-local" performances package the tradition for consumption for a more conservative global exoteric public. Throughout each of these arenas of spectatorship, Congo practitioners are agents and witnesses watching just as actively as they are watched and attempting to control how they are engaged. Further, Congo "circum-local" performance traditions like El Festival de los Diablos y Congos bolster a more public sense of "Congo nationalism."

## The End of an Era: Celedonio Officially Retires as Major Devil

In the midst of Panama's Centennial, Celedonio Molinar Ávila, the man who introduced the Major Devil character to the Congo tradition of Portobelo and served in the role for 49 years, officially retired. Such a momentous occasion demanded the audience, spectacle, and flair that the Festival of the Devils and Congos provided. Carlos recounted his memory of that moment during our 2013 interview:

> The last time that [Celedonio] played with us was for a Festival of the Devils [here] in Fort San Jerónimo. They did an homage to him. [. . .] He was so emotional in that moment to see all of his colleagues who had come from all around to play with him, and when the group from Portobelo entered to play with him, it was so emotional for him that he began to cry. [. . .] It was really strong, the emotion that he felt.

Figure 3.5 Celedonio retires (Photo by Renée A. Craft)

The highlight of the 2003 festival was Celedonio's march from the fort's entrance to the middle of the space in front of the stage. Amid an onslaught of camera lights and cheers from the estimated six-thousand-member crowd (more than twenty times the number of people living in Portobelo), Celedonio danced, posed, and was saluted by fellow Devils. That was the front-stage finale. As Carlos detailed, the backstage finale did not occur until 2004:

The next year we played again, and he was a judge. He judged the dance and cross of the Devil [. . .] The young people who were playing did not know what he was judging them on, so he explained: it is not about the mask; it is the dance and the cross. The kids did not know. So we suggested [that the judges] not give out prizes because that was going to damage the essence of the game. It is better not to give out first, second, or third prize; it is better that it just be about participation. So [Celedonio] was playing, [. . .] and he was very excited. I was outside. I was not dressed [as Devil] [. . .] and they sent me in to look for him. He was totally possessed by the game—in plain clothes, totally possessed, transformed. You saw the transformation in his face. And they called to me, "Hey, you, careful." They said, "Since you are replacing Celedonio, you go and play with him." When I arrived and saw him, I asked, "What has happened to Celedonio?" He did not answer me. "Cele!" I saw that he heard me, but he did not answer. Yes, the man was totally possessed in that moment, and we played together [. . .] me in plain clothes and him in plain clothes, but we kept up the grunts and behaving as Devils. And there came the moment when the encounter was so strong (he had taught me some things, some steps) that I had to use them with him directly, and I do remember what he said to me—"Hot water." I said to him, "Hot water, hot water, hot water." "Hot water" in the Congo culture—excuse me, Devil culture—means "I am angry; I am mad." [Celedonio] ended by telling me that he was mad, "I am hot!" So it was a challenge between us. We looked at each other intensely, and when the pressure lessened he said to me, "You are ready to replace me." I did not think that was what was going to happen, but it is what he wanted, to shed himself of his power and transmit it to me. But I do not play with secrets [. . .] A lot of people cried that day [. . .] After that he did not play anymore. Occasionally he would do a short presentation on Ash Wednesday with his sons [. . .] but he did not keep up the tradition of playing every year because he had retired.

## THE DEVIL, MAKING A CROSS WITH THE BODY, AND BEING BAPTIZED

Of all the Devils I have witnessed in Panama, Celedonio's costume and mask were the most modest. He used the same type of mask throughout his career. It was made of cardboard in the mold of half of a hollowed-out calabash, painted, adorned, and tied around his head with two strings. Yet, in his time, he was the most respected and feared of all Devils. During our 2013 inter-

Figure 3.6  Celedonio's mask and shoes (Photo by Renée A. Craft)

view, Ileana Solís Palma summarized it thus: "His costume wasn't anything spectacular. It was just a cardboard mask and cardboard wings. But I couldn't stop looking at him. I said, who is that Devil? I mean, how he jumped, the energy that he has. It's something that you can't stop looking at him." Celedonio believed that the Devil character's physical embodiment, not his whip, was his most powerful tool. As Devil he moved slowly, then exercised sharp, precise dance movements with strategic bursts of energy. He bounced, one foot crossed in front of the other, ankles layered in cuffs of bells; one arm stretched forward, the whip-arm stretched back; bells jingling ominously. As he moved forward, he intermittently jumped, crisscrossing his feet mid-air. One of the most important elements of the Devil's movement practice involves creating and maintaining the form of the cross with one's body. Carlos discussed this during our 2013 interview:

> I am always trying to make a cross with my body, and that is what [Celedonio] was trying to say. [. . .] You always have to create a cross and walk, [but] do not walk straight. [. . .] That is to say, always find a way to make

[your body or movements] the cross since you are imitating the man of darkness. As you are imitating him, you should do everything [like invoking the sign of the cross to protect yourself]. Walk bent over, because then you are in a better position to create a cross with the body and that gives the game greater acceptance because when you walk straight up like that your Devil performance loses respect.

Part of the suspense generated through the Congo game is the community's sense of playing at a crossroads between good and evil that might open a space for the *real* Devil to enter. As such, community members take various precautions. Male Congo practitioners keep a "cross" on their bodies through part of the game's parody. They wear their trousers and jackets "crossed," meaning inside out, as part of their costuming. Female Congo practitioners are encouraged to wear some intimate clothing inside out, and the Devil character dances with his "cross" in/as his body.

## "THE END OF THE MAGICIANS": THE BEGINNING OF A NEW ERA

Unlike those who have succeeded him as Major Devil, Celedonio observed the prior tradition of going off alone to engage in ritual preparation, including mixing special herbs and reciting special prayers. These practices generated an air of ritual sacredness and mystery around his embodiment of the character. As Sandra Eleta, co-founder of Festival de los Diablos y Congos, shared during our January 3, 2003 interview, "There was some magic about [Celedonio as] El Gran Diablo. When he would get dressed, he would go to the other side of the bay, and everything was, like, sacred. He would never show up in town before he got dressed, and people even said that when he was at his house, the roof would shake." Remarkable stories abound about the heightened abilities that Celedonio appeared to possess when he transformed into the Devil character. As discussed in the previous chapter, Celedonio credited part of his ability and energy to his practice of enacting the Devil character's "pujido" or grunt, which taps into an internal power that one may not realize that he or she possesses. However, Celedonio and those closest to his Devil praxis talk about the possibility that he tapped into something deeper as well. When we met for an interview on February 10, 2004, Sandra spoke of Celedonio's embodiment of Major Devil as an "existential compromise":

He was more existential. He was totally compromised [. . .] not with his role but with his being as a big Devil [. . .] He recited all the prayers—all the "Perro Negro" [prayers]. Everyone would be totally afraid of even saying the name "The Perro Negro," and he would dare to pronounce the big prayer of the Black Dog [. . .] you are not supposed to say that prayer if you don't want to deal with the ["real"] Devil [. . .] Celedonio would use that prayer [but] no one else wants to know anything about it.

Those who have come after Celedonio fear the implications of such mysticism. They resist this type of "compromise," and avoid some of the old rituals.

Both Raul and Carlos reflected on the Major Devil character as Celedonio chose to embody it with this sense of existential compromise. During our 2000 interview, Raul began his reflection by stating that "the Devil has a mystery." He continued:

That is, we see that when I grunt, I am challenging the other Devil, the Devil of . . . the ["real"] Devil Lucifer. When I grunt, I am imitating him with that grunt, right? So then when I leave my house, I grunt three times before leaving. [. . .] It's like calling to the Devil forcefully, right? So then when you go out, [. . .] he, on the third [grunt], sometimes he answers you. So that sometimes I'm left with [Lucifer's] grunt, right? And we go playing from there. That's the mystery that sometimes a lot of people won't tell you. Well, I don't play that game, but various ones that have, like Celedonio and before Celedonio, those people would go up into the mountains to dress as Devil. When they would come down and walk, one could feel the earth shake. It's like a force, yes, from the other side, to represent the real Devil [. . .] People aren't going to tell you that because it's something that they have hidden. One can feel a force inside of you. The moment that you get dressed as Devil, you feel like you're another person, a total other person.

When we spoke in 2013, Carlos shared an experience that echoed Raul's characterization of the pujido and Sandra's discussion of the prayer:

One year I went dressed as Devil to [Celedonio's] house to play with him. He would always get dressed up in the mountain, but this year he said he was getting dressed at home. He said, "When you come to get me, when I give the second grunt, move away from the door." He grunted the first time, grunted the second time, and it was normal, but when he grunted the third time, it was like a force shot out of him, like a spring that he had pushed outward. And it left me wondering, what was that? [. . .] I also remember that Celedonio, may he rest in peace, told me one time, "You play very good, but something is missing." And I asked him, "What is it?" And he said, "I'm going to tell you a secret." And I told him, "No, no, no, no. I play from emotion." And he said, "Yes, but I am going to tell you a secret." And I said, "But a secret about what?" He said, "A secret prayer." And I told him, "No, no, no, no. Excuse me, I do not know what kind of prayer you want to give. No, no. I play from emotion. I do not use any prayer. I play from emotion and, when I do not want to play anymore, I will quit. I do not want to make a pact with anyone." He said, "No, but—" I told him, "Excuse me. I respect you and everything, but I play for emotion. When I do not want to play anymore, I will simply retire and not have any commitment with anyone." And that is how I have kept playing. Yes, that is exactly how I have stayed, thank God.

Ever curious, I can't help but wonder what might have followed Celedonio's "No, but—." Ever cautious, I never asked Celedonio about the prayer or this sense of compromise directly. The ethnographic challenge of serving as a co-witness is the same as any act of witnessing. Some things, once known, cannot be unknown. Toward the end of the interview I had with Celedonio in 2000, I wanted to clarify whether he perceived the energy he felt from the pujido as a "possession," something foreign to him, or as an amplification of an internal energy. He responded with a lyrical caution:

He that doesn't really know what the Devil costume on a person is, shouldn't put it on. It's not anything miraculous because it has something that you can't see, but when you do the movements [. . .] You fly without wings [. . .] You start jumping, like in the sea, like when the waves from the sea are coming in, like that. It comes from inside you. You don't know what you're doing. The people see, the people see you. You don't know what you're doing. You are like, what's the word, like a bird. You do the steps as if you were a bird that was flying like that.

Like the ritual specialists and elders within the Congo tradition, Sandra Eleta has seen more of a split with traditional ways and in the enactment of the Devil role since the coming of the road and greater global connectivity. Having witnessed the end of the era of practicing the Congo tradition within a closed community and the passing away of those practitioners whose everyday life identities were more intimately tied to their Congo personas, she made the following observation toward the conclusion of our 2004 interview: "There was no 'role,' no performance of a 'role' before. It was only one thing— a person was involved existentially in what he was doing. Now, there is a separation. There is a character. It's performance. But before, there was something together. So, it's like, you know, the end of the magicians." Interpreted within the language of performance, Ileana Solís articulated it this way:

> Well, when you construct a character, at least in theater, one of the basic things is the breath of the character. Breath is the life of the character. [. . .] I believe it's the most important thing as a creator of characters. [. . .] that energy that comes from inside out and returns back inside, that cycle. Not just anybody can do that, right? And, well, [Celedonio] had that. He had the breath of, the breath of the Devil. [. . .] You don't need a great big mask to be a demon, a Devil, right? With just some cardboard you can transform, transform the vision of the spectator to something deeper.

At the time of his death in 2005 at the age of 87, Celedonio Molinar Ávila was undeniably the most respected and influential Diablo Mayor on the Atlantic Coast of Panama. His method of Devil embodiment was sociocultural critique as much as it was ritual performance and play. His popularity, longevity, and legendary Major Devil embodiment are key factors in the cultural currency of the Congo and Devil traditions of Portobelo, Panama, and their status as "traditional" and "authentic." "The whole world respected him," Carlos said in our 2013 interview. "His legacy was to keep up the Devil tradition," Carlos continued, but it was also more than that:

> As a citizen of the village, he was a marvelous person. What is more, he was a deacon in the Catholic Church and worked with the Boy Scouts. He was always trying to instill it in the kids. On Sundays you could always find him at the church as a deacon, and outside of that he was a person always on the move. You never saw him sitting around. He was always active. He was a very admired person in the village. He was respectful and was always respected by the people. They took care of him. They respected him. We, the Devils during that time, all knew who he was. So we would all give him respect whenever we would see him coming. He always said to me, "Carlos, when you play Devil, as I've told you, do not waiver. Enjoy it. Play with it. Look and see what you are doing." That is what I do. I enjoy it. I live it. I play with it. That is what I always try to do [so] that [we] maintain [our] traditions.

Cultural innovations must be adopted by community stakeholders in order to survive the passing of their catalysts. Viudo Ceballos succeeded in introducing the Devil character into the Congo tradition of Nombre de Dios and organizing it into a unique cultural tradition that not only persisted there but also migrated back to his place of birth on Celedonio's body and in his consciousness. Likewise, Celedonio not only introduced the Major Devil character as well as the tradition of blessing the Devil to Portobelo, but also saw it so accepted within the local culture that its practice successfully passed to other practitioners and its influence became amplified through the Festival of the Devils and Congos, which has the cultural preservation of the Congo/Devil game at its core. Every two years, Devils within the Congo tradition and their communities pack their local performance practices on their bodies and travel with them to Portobelo, which has become a gathering space for the Panamanian Congo Carnival diaspora. The festival provides discrete Congo communities an opportunity to check, critique, and share their cultural orientation to Congo/Devil culture within a broader community before completing their circum-local journeys back home with performatives potentially influenced by their encounters. Celedonio, therefore, got to witness his innovations take root and bear fruit before his passing. "That's what I've always wished for," Celedonio said toward the end of our 2000 interview, "that they [the Devils] do the steps well. The people come to enjoy themselves with what the Devil's doing, how the Devil plays with the Congos. It's lovely. And it came to me, it came to me [. . .] the resolution that this doesn't end, that the tradition doesn't end."

Figure 4.1 Congo women awaiting a tourist presentation (Photo by Oronike Odeleye)

# 4

# "¡Los gringos vienen!" / "The gringos are coming!"

## Race, Gender, and Tourism[1]

It is the Saturday night before Ash Wednesday, and we are leaning, body to body, on the walls of the palenque, a seven-hundred-fifty-square-foot temporary space with a thatch roof supported by wooden beams. A three-foot-high railing connects the beams with two catercorner entryways. More thatch has been used to fill in the "walls" below the railing. Pressing against the wooden frame and rocking the walls is a crowd of multi-brown bodies three rows thick. Even the sparse "white" bodies register faintly brown as a result of the dry season's relentless sun. Uncles, aunts, grandmothers, daughters, godsons, neighbors, visitors, friends clapping, rocking, pointing, laughing, cheering, make the small space more intimate. Inside, Simona starts a new song, clapping the rhythm she wants the three male drummers to follow: "*Micaela, Micaela, yo no bailo contigo morena.*" The rhythm of her hands is slow, marking every third beat. After one verse, the chorus—older women dressed in polleras with flowers in their hair and younger ones in blue jeans or shorts, hair pulled tight in ponytails—echo her clapping in time: "*Micaela, Micaela, yo no bailo contigo la plena.*" The rap-tap-tap of the center drum smacks the others awake and matches the women's rhythm. Simona raises her voice high and, without altering the rhythm of her singing, speeds up her hands to two claps per beat. The drummers follow in time, as does the chorus. A very skilled Congo woman in her early twenties, wearing fitted jeans and a halter top, slips out of her sandals and transfers her weight from side to side, matching the rhythm of the music. The drumbeats rise to meet the pitch of the singing and the young woman enters the space with a twirl. Standing in front of the drums, she stretches out her arms like a fan, as if holding the corners of a pollera, and goads the drummers faster. She swirls and dips, gliding willfully on a current of black sand. When even the air is dancing, a male Congo practitioner enters the space. With his brown face made black with charcoal and his pants turned inside out in the Congo way, he shifts his weight in dialogue with the music. The Congo woman uptilts her chin, confident and defiant; it is a command more than an invitation. With hips and shoulders a flurry of syncopation, the Congo male approaches, front leg bent, back leg straight, front thigh bouncing to the push of the back leg. The dance between the two is a negotiation of power and will. He wants a kiss. She teases, he pursues, and she thwarts his effort by shielding her face with her (invisible) pollera and/ or by twirling away. Another Congo male pushes his way through the crowd and replaces the first as the dance continues: "*Micaela, cielo, lindo, yo bailo contigo la plena.*"

Seizing his opportunity, an inebriated foreign White male spectator trades places with the male member of the Congo couple and attempts the dance. The woman stops for a second, looks at the chorus, smirks, and points displeasingly at her new partner as he continues to dance sluggishly around her. The female chorus laughs and fans her on, encouraging her to dance with him. She acquiesces, but with much less enthusiasm than before and with a noticeable grimace. Just like the women, the Congo men tease her. She repays them with looks of playful scorn, nonverbally urging any of them to replace the visitor or any Congo woman to replace her. The visitor, egged on by his male companions, dances in closer, grabs her waist, and pulls her toward him. She pushes him away harshly. Drunk and easily knocked off balance, he stumbles backward to the amusement of his companions and to the indignation of his dance partner. The Congo men come closer but do not intervene. The female chorus also does not intervene, but rather continues singing without hesitation, except for a few chosen chides from the elders castigating the visitor and daring the Congo woman to teach him a lesson. After a few shakes of her finger and a twist of her neck, the Congo dancer smirks again, opens her arms wide, and dances with even more charisma than she had with her Congo partner. She recaptures control of the space, forcing the man to dance-walk backward in any direction she chooses. She smiles as his face reddens, and when she has danced him directly in front of the Congo drums, she presses her body next to his, quickly squeezes his crotch and dances away to the celebra-

**Figure 4.2** Local Congo performers relaxing after Carnival season performance (Photo by Oronike Odeleye)

tory roars and laughter of the audience. Only then does a Congo man come to rescue *the visitor* who seems relieved to have been replaced. This chapter focuses on the ways in which the Congo community of Portobelo negotiates encounters with global tourists. More specifically, I attend to how practitioners perform gender and sexuality differently in the ritual space of the Congo tradition, the palenque or palacio, where tourists represent a convenient outgroup, compared with how practitioners do so for "packaged" presentations where tourists represent the primary audience. How is the Congo tradition packaged for midday presentations to primarily White, overwhelmingly U.S. tourists? How do these packaged representations differ from the tradition as it is performed for the community? How do space, place, spectatorship, and desire determine when "respectable" signifies "performative mastery," as in the opening anecdote, and when it signifies a performative measure of female "decency"? (I define these terms more fully below.) What might respectability as performative mastery offer Black Diaspora performance like the Congo tradition?

As a method of analysis, I use the term "local" to focus on the tradition as it is produced and consumed during Carnival season primarily for the community. I have coined "like-local" to signal Congo "presentations" of the tradition for the consumption of global tourists. Whereas local performances are more active in cultural preservation and community building, like-local performances are more active in the commoditization of the tradition. I contend that distinctions between Congo local and like-local performances may best be accounted for through a nuanced understanding of "respectability" as an aspect of the dualism and doubling endemic to Panamanian Congo traditions.

By using the term "respectability," I mean to invoke the anthropological and historical debates regarding the term and its cognate, "reputation" (Wilson 1969, 1973; Besson 1993; Burton 1997; Sutton 1974). In his foundational work on systems of social and moral valuation in the Anglophone Caribbean, Wilson (1973, 1969) theorizes a binary system of respectability/reputation within which women and men vie for power and status (respectively). Within his bifurcated structure, Wilson formulates *respectability* as a female domestic domain governed by outside/foreign norms of Eurocentric middle-class values, and *reputation* as a male public domain governed by inside/indigenous valuations of talent and achievement.[2] Over the course of my fourteen-year engagement with the Congo community of Portobelo, Panama, however, I have witnessed female Congo practitioners embody a different kind of "respectability" in their performances for local spectators—one that is rooted in notions of mastery, confidence, and dominance. While in like-local Congo performances, "respectability" among female performers might take on some of its more traditional (within this genre of literature) meanings, such as female "decency," my analysis shows that local Congo performances instead derive "respectability" from successfully actualizing one's talent, skill, attitude, and flair such that the practitioner earns honor and praise for herself as well as for her community. In other words, female Congo practitioners make a performative choice to forefront qualities that Wilson associates with reputation for local spectators and those he associates with respectability for outside spectators. In keeping with the messy dynamism of cultural performance, I want to empty these qualities out onto the table to examine how racialized, gendered, classed, cultural agents who code-switch for local and tourist audiences take them up to use as needed. Including qualities often ascribed to "reputation" in an analysis of female respectability reclaims the breadth of the term as it relates to women's *ability* to earn *respect*.

For the purpose of this analysis, I extend "inside/home" to signify local spectators and "outside/foreign" to signal tourist spectators. When expanded thus, many of the qualities associated with the "street" in the schema that Bur-

Figure 4.3 Congo female practitioners preparing to give a tourist presentation (Photo by Renée A. Craft)

ton (1997) extends from Wilson (play, chaos, freedom, mobility, noise) exist in female Congo performance for the local community. Many of those he posits as "home" (order, discipline, decorum, work, self-restraint) exist in female Congo like-local performances for tourist audiences (162).

## Congo "Local": Dualism, Parody, and Double-Consciousness

Congo performance is a marriage of interdependent dualisms: good and evil, insider and outsider, sacred and secular. These dualisms manifest themselves in Congo consciousness and material practice. Connected to a quality of Du Boisian double-consciousness, Congo collective consciousness is a dialectical engagement with how community members perceive themselves as Congo versus how national and global outsiders perceive them; this is what Frantz Fanon (1967) refers to as "third person consciousness" (110). Speaking about the Congo tradition and this sense of double-ness during our 2003 interview, Elsa Molinar de la Fuentes,[3] a Congo ritual specialist, recounted the dilemma of Congo practitioners in the early- to mid-twentieth century: "*Sentíamos la vergüenza con la puerta abierta y el orgullo con la puerta cerrada* [We felt shame (about our tradition) with the door open and pride with the door closed]." When I spoke with the Congo ritual specialist Andres Jiménez that same year, he echoed this sense of self-consciousness that was tied to perceptions of class as well as race. He said, "There was this mistaken concept that the ones who dressed as Congo were the poorest people, the people without culture and all that. [. . .] That was the idea, but now that people have studied it more, they see that Congo is a tradition and that it is beautiful." As Afro-Colonials whose history and cultural performance link them to an enslaved past, Congo practitioners represent an exoticized Black presence in the equally exoticized Black space of Portobelo. Congo consciousness represents a kind of thinking about oneself and one's culture from the perspective of insiders keenly aware of the fissure between insider and outsider perceptions of their tradition.

At the same time, Congo consciousness and material practice also reflect double-consciousness as a "strategy" to use the outsider's preconceived notions against her (Morrison 1997, 12). Double-consciousness as a strategy aligns with Michel de Certeau's (1984) concept of subversive consumption and Marta E. Savigliano's (1995) analysis of the ways subjugated groups use cultural products to "trick back" on those in power.[4] Just as Savigliano argues of Argentinean tango, Elizabeth McAlister (2002) of Haitian rara, and Carolyn Cooper (2004) of Jamaican dancehall, I assert that Panamanian Congo performance may likewise be used as a "strategic language, a way of talking about, understanding, and exercising decolonization" (Savigliano 1995, 16). This conception of double-consciousness as strategy aligns with Deborah Thomas's (2004) articulation of cultural duality as "maintaining and enacting one or another repertoire of behavior that is considered appropriate for a situation, given a common comprehension of locally specific relations of both material and symbolic power" (232).

In Colonial times, Congo Carnival performances were done under the watchful gaze of enslavers who saw the reversals of clothing, heard the Congo dialect, and participated in the joke not knowing that they were its objects. Congo traditions depend on an in-group that gets the joke and an out-group that is the joke. As Thomas (2004) notes, "Descendants of Africans throughout the Atlantic world have been forced to develop a worldview that enables them to negotiate Western tenets of civilization while at the same time creatively critiquing them. This inherently double-sided structural formation has meant that for black people, *at least* dual visions, lifestyles, and consciousness are not only possible, but necessary" (258; italics in the original).

Moving from colonial to contemporary times, local and global tourists easily form a convenient out-group.[5] Many non-Congo Portobeleño spectators and visitors from neighboring towns have witnessed the tradition throughout their lives without understanding the significance of the reversals or the Congo dialect. This local out-group as well as national and international visitors who happen to witness Carnival in Portobelo become the object of the joke for local performances.

Congo performances continue to preserve the subversive space of spectatorship that allows Congos to watch the watcher watch. The space of Congo performance puts both Congos and their audiences "on stage" in full view of one another. Whether done in the palacio during Carnival season or in an alternative public space, like the Customs House, for tourist presentations, Congo practitioners create the space of their performances through a dialectical relationship with their audiences as well as through the natural limits of the physical places they inhabit. Practitioners create Congo space through the sonic connection they produce by drumming, singing, and clapping. They also do so through the embodied invitation they make to audience members to join in as visual witnesses and through their ability to extend and amplify sound by clapping in time with the beat. Those who gather to witness Congo performances do so most frequently by creating a semicircle that begins where the semicircle of the chorus ends. This round configuration creates sight lines that put everyone in full view of one another. Although the central "stage" of Congo performance is where male and female Congos dance in pairs in front of the drummers and chorus, this central space is made more malleable and porous through the act of Congo men moving among the spectators as well as across the "stage" to engage with both the performers and the audience.

Compared with local performances in which Congo practitioners and knowledgeable community members form the largest part, like-local *presentations* feature a larger out-group to make fun of and a smaller in-group privy to the joke. This larger out-group creates a heightened sense of ethnoracial and class inflected self-consciousness, which shifts female "respectable" Congo performance from the arena of "mastery" to that of "decency." By decency, I am evoking what Evelyn Brooks Higginbotham (1993) refers to as the "politics of respectability" that African American women's movements used as a part of what she calls "uplift politics." These class-based discourses attempted to combat negative stereotypes of African-descended people by having them outperform the dominant society's norms of moral propriety. Although well intentioned, this strategy often reinscribed the dominant culture's stereotypes on "lower class" cultural practices and agents who failed or

Figure 4.4 Speaking in Congo (Photo by Elaine Eversley)

refused to conform (1–4).[6] This understanding of respectability aligns with Besson's (1993) analysis of Afro-Caribbean respectability as "cultural resistance rather than Eurocentric respectability" (26). Language was one of the primary means through which enslaved people subverted Spanish colonial rule and Cimarrones enacted community and culture. It remains one of the most political and dynamic elements of Congo culture. The "Congo dialect"[7] is a coded intra-group lexicon that successive generations of Congo practitioners have used to exercise resistance while appearing complicit. It emerged as a part of the culture of enslaved people in Panama just as "Negro" spirituals served as a coded message system among enslaved people in the United States. Unlike spirituals, however, which have maintained their racial and historical specificity but are no longer used as code, the Congo language maintains its multiplicity. Speaking "Congo" is not only a way of organizing knowledge about the world but also a way of thinking about the self and the world. Further, it offers a means to "trick back" on systems of power over which Congo practitioners may have little control.

Frantz Fanon (1967) theorized that language was one of the key areas that created psychosis among Blacks (17). "To speak," he said, "is to exist absolutely for the other." We think and exist in the structures of the languages we speak. "A man who has a language," Fanon suggests, "consequently possesses the world expressed and implied by that language" (18). He goes on to say that "every dialect is a way of thinking" (25). African slaves combated this "psychosis" by creating a creolized, secret language strategically couched in the dominant discourse. Contemporary Congo communities continue to follow this model.

In order to give an example of the contemporary political currency of Congo speech, the Taller Portobelo co-founder, visual artist, and Congo ritual specialist Yaneca Esquina shared an anecdote with me during our May 2000 interview about the time he and other Congo members were asked to perform before Panama's former military dictator, Manuel Noriega. Understandably, they could not refuse. According to Yaneca, everyone called Noriega "pineapple face" behind his back, so the Congos called him "pineapple face" in coded language as they sang and danced in front of him. Speaking in Congo allowed the practitioners to simultaneously comply with a request they could not refuse and subvert the request by saying the unsayable. In the language of James Scott's (1990) well-noted schema, the Congo dialect allowed the community to express a "public transcript" that aligned with their host's expectations while enacting a "hidden transcript" that expressed their contempt. Noriega formed part of the extended group of "outsiders" who were unwittingly part of the joke, while the small group of Congo performers and those community members assembled to support them served as "insiders" who understood the layered performance and got the joke.

Many Congo community members have reconciled themselves to the fact that much of the nuanced complexity of the Congo dialect is fading as a result of globalization and the deaths of knowledge community elders. Still, ritual specialists like Major Devil and Mayor Carlos Chavarría encourage younger members to preserve as much of the dialect as they can in ways that are easy for them to reproduce. During our 2013 interview, he said:

What I try to tell the young people now is to try and save the Congo dialect, which is very difficult. I am, and I still keep a few Congo words, but if they can't rescue it—because the majority of it has been lost—they can try to speak backwards. At least say, "Good morning" if it is night. [. . .] or say it is raining if it is sunny. If the moon is out, say the sun is out. That is, look for a way [. . .] to keep it up so that something is maintained. But do not kill the Congo tradition, because it's a rich one.

Despite what has been lost, I have witnessed younger practitioners preserve the dialect in the ways that Carlos suggested. This happens both outside of the performative space of the tradition as well as in the midst of it. For example, I have witnessed male friends speak in the Congo dialect in close proximity to a female visitor whom they may find attractive as they strategize the best ways to flirt with her. Likewise, I have witnessed community members switch to the dialect in the midst of our everyday interactions if they want to share gossip or information with one another that they do not necessarily wish me or another visitor to overhear and understand. Even in these mundane ways, contemporary community members maintain double-consciousness as strategy in the ways in which they actualize the dialect.

## Congo "Like-Local": From Performative Mastery to Decency

Two weeks after I arrived for my extended field research in 2003, Sarabi, one of my young friends, yelled from the street toward my bedroom window, "¡Los gringos vienen!" By the time I reached my balcony to descend the stairs, I looked out at the largest ship I had ever seen in Portobelo. During the dry season, January through early May, small cruise ships carrying fifty to sixty passengers enter the Portobelo Bay twice a week for one-hour tours of the area. Larger vessels, such as those from Princess Cruise Line, Carnival, and Sun Cruises, dock in Colón, the northern port city of the Panama Canal, and host bus tours to Portobelo. According to statistics provided by the Instituto Panameño de Turismo on its website in 2006, approximately one-fourth of visitors to Panama came from the United States in 2003, about the same as the combined numbers from Central American, Caribbean, and European regions. This ratio has been fairly consistent for over a decade.[8]

Global trade and tourism are not new to Portobelo. The Spanish explorer Christopher Columbus made it his initial point of disembarkation for his fourth voyage to the "New World" in 1498; El Nazareno ("The Black Christ") has attracted pilgrims since the sixteenth century; the Portobelo Fairs made the town the nexus of trade in the Spanish colonial world in the seventeenth and well into the eighteenth century; the Panama Canal construction project brought workers to the area in the early twentieth century; and UNESCO declared the town a World Heritage site in 1980. However, the volume and type of tourism have shifted since the December 31, 1999, turnover of the Panama Canal. When the U.S. military controlled the waterway, it limited the amount of tourist traffic as a matter of security because of the Canal's strategic importance. In the absence of the currency generated by U.S. military personnel and the annuity that the U.S. government paid to lease the Canal Zone—

Figure 4.5 Cruise ships in Portobelo (Photo by Renée A. Craft)

which was always significantly less than the loan debt that the United States collected from Panama (Pearcy 1998, 75)—the Republic has greatly increased its emphasis on tourism to generate additional economic revenue. The cruise port, Colón 2000, located in Colón City, has been seminal in this growth; almost all Portobelo dry-season international cruise ships and bus tours pass through it. In addition to the services it provides to independent cruise lines, it also partners with local tour groups to offer excursions to Portobelo. Like the descriptions provided by international guides, local tour groups like Aventuras 2000 as well as governmental agencies such as the National Institute of Art and Culture and the Panamanian Institute of Tourism market Portobelo's Black cultural heritage. Tourists, therefore, come to the town to experience the rain forest, the colonial forts, the "Black" Christ, and the Congos—all unique markers of Black resistance culture in the region. Two popular travel guides, *Panama: The Bradt Travel Guide* and *Lonely Planet Panama,* for example, feature highlighted narrative boxes focused on the the "Black Christ." Both also include narratives that render the Congos as quaint, primitive, and foolish. The *Bradt Travel Guide* (Woods 2005) refers to the tradition as "an expres-

sive tribal dance ritual" with practitioners "feigning lunacy through movement and screams" (288). *Lonely Planet Panama* is much more egregious. The
author, Scott Doggett (2001), writes:

> The Congos, a festivity in which black people assume the role of escaped
> slaves and run around taking "captives," is held in Portobelo and some-
> times elsewhere in the province during Carnival [. . .] The celebrants are
> generally dressed in outlandish outfits that include tattered clothes and
> hats that resemble crowns [. . .] All are so animated that they look like
> they've just come from an insane asylum [. . .] Sound bizarre? It is. If you
> ever find yourself an innocent "victim" of this tradition, try not to freak
> out and kill someone. They are just harmless Congos. (315–19)

Visitors who have read these guides enter Portobelo expecting laughable
Black antics rather than a sophisticated cultural performance. As in colonial
times, the Congos render a like-local performance that shields as much as it
reveals and uses its audiences' expectations as fodder for their own amusement. As tourists prepare to witness Portobelo and its Congos, the Congos
and other Portobeleño spectators gather to be entertained by "*los gringos*"
and "*las turistas.*" On the day Sarabi summoned me downstairs to see the
first Congo like-local presentation of 2003, Carnival season was just a week
away and excitement was starting to build. When I arrived at the Customs
House, the exhibition awaiting me caught me off-guard. Taking their seats on
stone steps in the shade of an awning was the quintessential spectacle of the
North American tourist. Most of the visitors were middle-aged or older White
men and women fully clad in Bermuda shorts, Hawaiian shirts, oversized sun-
glasses, baseball caps (men), and hats with big floppy rims (women). Some
cupped small digital or disposable cameras in their palms; others wore the
shiny silver or black devices around their necks like medallions. Congo men
sometimes parody tourists by carrying plastic toy cameras. The toy-camera
holder often passes his camera to another Congo and poses with a tourist
while his Congo companion pretends to take his picture.

Whereas the Congo drama features a full spectrum of characters, tourist presentations are an abbreviated form of the tradition that includes only
the drummers, chorus, primary singer, and dancers. Although the Queen,
King, Pajarito, or someone standing in for them, may appear in like-local performances, the Devil does not. The drumming and call-and-response singing
function as the musical backbone of local and like-local performances, while
the social dance component functions as their core. Reminiscent of the local
congadas that Congo communities throughout Panama hold every Friday and

Figure 4.6 Tourists gathering for presentation (Photo by Renée A. Craft)

Saturday evening from January 20 until Lent, each Wednesday and Saturday morning throughout the tourist season the Congos of Portobelo perform like-local congadas for their international visitors.

Compared with the camaraderie, virtuosity, competition, and play that mark "respectable" female Congo local performances, female practitioners perform pristine, dispassionate respectability before their like-local spectators. While the men's Congo embodiment for tourists is just as bold and playful as their evening performances, women perform with stoic faces, glances uncharacteristically aimed downward, and with more subdued hip movements. Even when they leave their places in the chorus to dance with Congo partners, the female performers maintain neutral expressions except for moments when a Congo man or boy succeeds in stealing a kiss, which produces a smirk and gentle shove from his female counterpart.

In Congo local performance, the game of flirtation between female and male practitioners frames them metaphorically as matadora and bull, each performatively antagonizing the other with bold gestures. In tourist like-local performances, however, female practitioners enact a more demure performance, resisting rather than tempting their partners. The movement vocabulary of female Congo local performance includes direct eye contact; slightly rounded, outstretched arms near level with the chest; and pronounced side-to-side hip swings. Comparatively, Congo like-local presentations feature more distant down-turned eyes; lower, more angular arms that lift from the elbows

Figure 4.7 Elsa Molinar de la Fuentes dancing Congo with her grandson (Renée A. Craft)

at hip-level; and more compact hip swings. In this way, "respectable" like-local female performance relies on strategies of double-consciousness to combat any preconceived notions that outside spectators may have brought with them about the dance as "erotic," "raunchy," or "obscene," class- and racially laden criticisms that caused earlier generations of Congos to keep the tradition hidden and which haunt Black vernacular performance traditions throughout the Black Diaspora.[9] Although Congo social dance may be familial and innocent, as in a grandson dancing with his grandmother or friends dancing with one another, the Congos give themselves room for moderate sexual flirtation and teasing within the performative boundaries of the local tradition. Unlike their more passive, prim performances during their like-local presentations, women more than men lead the game of flirtation in local performances, both within the tradition's ritual space (as illustrated in this chapter's opening anecdote) and in its more spontaneous local iterations. In January 2003, for example, the Congos began a spontaneous congada on a chartered bus en route from Portobelo to a presentation in Panama City. Male Congos sat toward the back of the bus while women sat at the front. Each group gossiped among themselves, raising their voices at strategic points to facilitate eavesdropping. The nature of their flirtation was consistent with some forms of local Congo social dance. One of the younger Congo women, a woman in her early twenties who would wear the Queen's crown in that evening's performance, had brought a long tubular balloon on the bus with her. She laughed and joked as she twisted the balloon into a dildo, which made the women howl with laughter. Pretending to ignore the men, she sang into the balloon dildo and passed it like a microphone among the women until one of the elders playfully snatched it and bopped her on the head with it. All the while, the men were catcalling, "Chupa! Chupa!" ("Suck it! Suck it!"), joking and laughing among themselves. When one of the younger men attempted to traverse the space between the two groups (like a Congo dancer attempting to steal a kiss), several women pushed him back toward the rear of the bus and taunted him (like a Congo female dancer averting her partner's advances). He smiled coyly, acquiesced, turned as if heading back to his seat and then charged forward for one final attempt. Two Congo women pushed him back hard enough to set him off balance and leave him at the mercy of the other Congo men who caught him, setting the entire bus ablaze with laughter and taunts. The bus, in this circum-local context, functioned as "a living, micro-cultural, micro-political system in motion" (Gilroy 1993a, 4), extending the space in which to understand local Congo performances of gender and sexuality.

With scarce overnight lodging options for outsiders with no ties to Portobelo, and with bus service to the town stopping at 9:00 p.m., the number of tourist spectators for evening local Congo performances is limited.[10] Nonetheless, in the ritual space and place of Congo local performance, the Congo game has rules for "playing" with outsiders. According to Congo Queen Melba Esquina in our 2000 interview, and as discussed in chapter 2, "When an *outsider*, a strange man, tries to participate in the dance without permission from the Queen, the drummers throw down the drums and refuse to play." In contemporary Congo performance, Congo men often choreograph this part of the spectacle by pulling eager tourists into the center of the palacio to dance. When the tourist reaches the center, his Congo escort motions the drummers to drop their drums. The visitor is then asked to pay a token ransom to the Congo Queen, which may be a few coins or liquor. Once the transgressor's "tax" has been paid, Congo men walk him over to the drums and manipulate his hands to grab the drums and to place them once again between the drummers' knees. At this point, the visitor is encouraged to dance with a Congo partner or another female visitor.

As in Congo local performance when visitors are present, Congo men orchestrate the community's like-local interaction with tourists by playing with them and leading them into the dance space. Just as they do in the evening local performances, male tourists sometimes interpret the attempted kiss of the dance as an opportunity to get too close to female Congo partners. Congo women help to police such deviant male tourist interaction within the space of local Congo performance by using the movement vocabularies advocated by the tradition. Congo men, on the other hand, use the mask of buffoonery to police male transgressors during like-local performances. At the first sign of inappropriate closeness, Congo men swoop in on male tourist transgressors, aggressively blow their whistles, and good naturedly dance-walk them back to the periphery of the performance space. Connecting the Black Diaspora tricksters Eshu Elegba (Yoruba of Nigeria), Anansi the Spider (Akan of Ghana), Brother Nanci (Anansi's Caribbean name), and Brer Rabbit (United States), Arturo Lindsay (2003) asserts that such buffoonery "is simply a retention of the ruse enslaved Africans employed in order to be perceived as non-threatening" (138). While Congo social dance is generally a dance between one man and one woman, multiple people are invited forward at the end of tourist presentations in the spirit of fun and inclusion. At that moment, the faces of Congo women open up with smiles and laughter, as do those of other Congo spectators. Repeatedly, I have noticed that the pleasure of presentations for the Congos comes in large part from watching their spectators attempt the dance. With only physical clues to guide them, some female spectators inevitably end up mistakenly mimicking the male dance movements and vice versa. The Congo chorus smiles and claps encouragingly while giggling and gossiping among them. For spectators who try in earnest to do the dance, Congo men often approach them, shake their heads disapprovingly, and mimic the correct movement repeatedly until the visitor catches on. At least one flamboyantly clumsy dancer generally endears himself or herself to the Congo community. Bold and awkward tourists are just as likely as if not more likely than talented or industrious ones to win approving smiles and nods from the female chorus. In effect, each group performs for the other. Speaking during our 2003 interview about the rise of tourism in Portobelo and these "like local" experiences, Simona Esquina said:

> Tourism is coming more into Portobelo now. [. . .] It's helping rescue the tradition. [. . .] [Tourists] enjoy themselves, so much so that they carry their pictures outside of the country so that Congo is even abroad. The Congo is happening and it has a new boom [in popularity]. Yes, that's how it is.

Figure 4.8 Congos posing for pictures after tourist presentation (Photo by Oronike Odeleye)

Congo tourist presentations are "like-local mementoes" that visitors can pack away alongside handcrafts from indigenous communities and "My Name is Panamá"¹¹ t-shirts. The Congos take "like-local snapshots," too, when they travel outside their community. These mental pictures become the "gringo" anecdotes that they swap like trading cards on the way home and with their families once they arrive there. With few economic resources for travel and costly bureaucratic hurdles in the travel process, the Congo communities' primary means to "tour" gringos through face-to-face encounters are like-local presentations. Panamanians interested in traveling to the United States, for example, must pay a one-hundred-dollar nonrefundable visa application fee and set up a visa appointment. If the applicant arrives late or misses her appointment, she must pay the fee again in order to schedule a new appointment (Embassy 2006). In contrast, travelers with U.S. passports enter Portobelo with five-dollar visas that can be obtained at the departure airport hours before takeoff or upon landing in Panama. For U.S. citizens, then, traveling to Panama is often cheaper than travel across their own country and only slightly less convenient.

In packaging its tradition for tourist consumption, the Congo community has transformed the female-dominated space of Congo performance into a male-dominated and regulated space, thereby masking the gender dynamics of the local performance. Rather than bold matadors that drive the performance, female Congo performers become muted and restrained. During the temporal space of Carnival season, the palacio functions as the Congos' local domain while the steps of the Customs House serves as the tourists' domain. Whereas respectability as performative mastery guides female Congo performance in the space of the palacio, respectability as female "decency" guides female Congo performance for tourists. This more demure means of performance represents a Congo consciousness aware of the expectations of wild exoticism that tourists bring with them mixed with the practitioners' greater interest in witnessing tourists than in performing in line with their expectations. Just as the Black restaurant patrons in Gwendolyn Brooks's (1944) poem "VII. I love those little booths at Benvenuti's" amuse themselves by performing contrary to White patrons' expectations of them, Congos anticipate tourists' expectations and turn them inside out. The poem concludes:

The colored people will not "clown"

The colored people arrive, sit firmly down,
Eat their Express Spaghetti, their T-Bone steak
Handling their steel and crockery with no clatter,
Laugh punily, rise, go firmly out the door. (59–60)

In place of Brooks's "the colored people will not 'clown,'" I would pen, "the Congo women will not 'perform exotic.'" However, should the curious tourist linger in Portobelo late into the evening, she will witness a performance of female respectability that teases, controls, commands attention, and dominates.

**Figure** 5.1  Carnival "Diablito" (Photo by Elaine Eversley)

# 5

# Dancing with the Devil at the Crossroads

## Performance Ethnography and Staging Thresholds of Difference

In the winter of 2001, I staged my first work of critical/performance ethnography based on my initial research with the Congo community of Portobelo, Panama. Having read dissertations by Ronald Smith (1976) and Patricia Drolet (1980), shared email and telephone conversations with the scholar-artist Arturo Lindsay for over a year, and conducted initial interviews with key practitioners regarding the Congo tradition in Panama, I found myself adrift in competing currents surrounding its ritual form. What I had read, heard, and sensed was not lining up properly, partially because I had not yet witnessed the tradition for myself. I had seen video footage of previous Carnivals and "packaged" tourist presentations, but I had not yet experienced it during Carnival season. Attempting to gain clarity through written work alone fell short of my needs. My strongest lessons about the tradition in Panama had come through my body. I had listened to the drums, watched the women dance, and mimicked their movements. The women would clap their hands and shake their heads when I got it right, or put their hands on my hips to teach me how to move them when I got it wrong. During my first trip, most of my conversations had to be filtered through a translator because I spoke very little Spanish. The only time there was no filtering was when I danced. Congo practitioners and I communicated directly, body to body. Men and boys would dance with me gently to lull me into comfort and then overpower me with more complicated movements. They would laugh and the women would furrow their eyebrows, raise their voices, shout things I did not understand at the men, push me back into the circle, and encourage me to stand my ground and do it again. When I overpowered the men, the women would roar with claps and laughter. I understood their tones, facial expressions, the tug of a hand on my arm, the comfort of another patting my back, and the affirmation of head-shakes and winks.

After one of these events, Arturo told me that Marta, a Congo ritual specialist who later gave me the Congo name "Mariposa" ("Butterfly"), had teased, "Are you sure she isn't Portobeleña?" My body understood things that my speaking/hearing, writing/reading self could not yet know. Scripting and staging a solo performance allowed me to wrestle with these issues. I created the script and put it on my body—not to tidy up the slippages, but to get inside and better understand them. Not only did I use performance "as a complement, alternative, supplement, and critique of inscribed texts" (Conquergood 1991, 191), but also scripting the performance offered me an alternative textual mode through which to analyze it. This chapter examines the contributions that the process of creating and publicly staging four of these critically engaged performances made to this study and to my understanding of the complexity of Congo traditions.

## La historia de los congos de Portobelo: Translating History Through the Body

*La historia de los congos de Portobelo: Translating History Through the Body* was a forty-minute solo performance staged in the Mussetter-Struble Theatre in the Theatre and Interpretation Center (TIC) at Northwestern University. As I stated in the program notes, the performance was "part of an on-going conversation between my African-American southern female body, the Congo dance tradition, and those who view both." During my first visit to Portobelo, I met with representatives of several prominent Congo families: Melba Esquina and Delia Barrera Clifundo, two former Congo Queens; Virgilio "Yaneca" Esquina and Ariel "Pajarito" Jiménez, two Congo practitioners and founding members of Taller Portobelo, the workshop of the Congo artists; one of the three contemporary Major Devils, Carlos Chavarría; and Simona Esquina, one of the current Cantalantes (primary singers).

In creating *La historia de los congos*, I sought an opportunity to better understand the tradition through an embodied exploration of its central characters and metaphoric use of crossings and crosses. I staged the performance in six sections: two to introduce the audience to the material and four to delve into each of the primary Congo characters (Devil, Queen, King, and Pajarito). Wearing a loose-fitting, hibiscus-colored A-line dress with a brightly painted wind instrument dangling from my neck, and ankle bells, I stepped my bare feet onto a stage populated by two props: a six-foot wooden frame in the shape of a Christian cross, which I had painted in the pointillist style for which Congo art is known,[1] and a plastic dressmaker's form cloaked under a veil of black fabric. The cross lay center-stage, stuffed with red, orange, and yellow confetti and rose petals. Hidden beneath the colorful fluff were leg irons and wrist shackles. Upstage left, the plastic dressmaker's form stood clothed as a Congo woman beneath black fabric. I entered from the center aisle of the audience and approached the stage, the symbolic "location" I had created for the tradition, performing two original "first impression" poems. The first painted Portobelo as "exotic" to me; the second rendered me as "exotic" to Portobelo. I also used these poems and the reflexive opportunity they engendered to reflect on my initial ethnographic presence in Portobelo, when I was still very much learning what and how to "do" and "be."

During my early experiences in Portobelo, I crisscrossed the town several times each day with a clumsy video recorder, a tape recorder, a notebook, Spanish dictionary, and two other U.S. students as awkward as I was. One was a film student; the other was a dancer. Not yet trusting each other to share, we carried three of everything. Not wanting to admit that we did not know exactly what we were doing, we overdid everything. Thankfully, Portobeleños were extremely patient with us. Arturo Lindsay, who was well known in the community, had introduced us, and we looked even younger than we were, which won us extra patience. For the most part, people seemed intrigued by how interested three young Black women from the United States were in their tradition. We also amused them. Most days we were slightly more entertaining than some of the local eccentrics because we were new and our quirks were still revealing themselves. Looking back now, I see clearly the spectacle we were—and smell it too (we traveled everywhere thickly perfumed with Deep Woods Off). Ironically, when I tried to be less conspicuous during later trips, my lack of equipment was often a cause of disappointment. "Oh," a Congo member told me, "you didn't bring your recorder. You don't want to tape me like you did Simona?" Even when I just intended casual visits with Congo friends during my research year, people often interrupted their own stories to say "This is important; you might want to go get your recorder."

After performing the first two introductory sections of *La historia de los congos*, I entered the stage, which was separated into quadrants by the cross.

As I approached, two coperformers came on stage, grabbed the cross by its shorter arms, and hung it from hooks at the back of the space, leaving in place the rose petals and confetti. The cross became the backdrop for the remaining performance, and its colorful innards became a crossroads. I explored each character in the physical space of a quadrant. I started with the Devil upstage left, stepped upstage right over the imaginary dividing line and transitioned into the Queen, traversed "the line" again by stepping forward to explore the King, and crossed "the line" a final time to analyze Pajarito. This physical embodiment allowed me to explore the characters not only through their histories but also through the variations in the way they move. As I told the story of each character, I simultaneously story-talked the ritual drama of the Congo tradition as it is enacted during Carnival season.

In keeping with the movement vocabulary of the Devil character, I bent low, jumped high, keeping the heel of one foot perpendicular to the arch of the other, and kept my arms spread wide in the quadrant dedicated to "Devil." My red dress was meant to signify his red costume. The jingles punctuating my steps represented the thick cuff of bells that the Devil characters wear around their ankles to alert the Congos of their proximity. As Devil, my movements were choppy, decisive, and quick.

My movements softened and became fluid as "Queen." In the Congo tradition, she is the seat of power that the Devil attempts to capture. Because the only elements that distinguish the Queen's costume from that of other female Congo characters are her crown and large wooden cross, I used the space of her story to explore the dress and dance of Congo women as well. It was important to me to stress my movements as metonymic rather than metaphoric, especially because I had not had enough experience with the movements to translate them confidently onto my body. Also, I wanted to keep my "Black" identity and Congo "Black" identity in productive tension. I approached the black-covered dressmaker's form with the same sense of curiosity with which I continually press my Blackness up against Congo Blackness. After taking a few beats to explore the material and its girth, I unveiled the form to reveal a torso of my size and shape but dressed very differently than I was. As I pressed my body into the back of the model, grabbing up the sides of the pollera in which it was dressed, the audience witnessed my head, arms, and feet animating the wide Congo skirt through story and dance.

As I had done in the space of "Queen," I used the King's quadrant to explore his identity as well as other Congo male identities. Like the Queen, the King is distinguished from other Congo males by his crown. Because the male Congo stance is wide, I stood in a wide warrior pose to introduce the King, whose primary role is as a strategist who sends other Congos to distract the Devil in order to protect the Queen. Of all the primary characters, the King's contemporary role is least active. It is the only primary role often played in Portobelo by teen and preteen boys.

My last crossing was into the space of Pajarito, the son of the King and Queen and an interlocutor between Congos and the Devil. Pajarito always carries a whistle to alert the Congos of the Devil's approach and a black and white flag symbolizing the peace struck between the Congos and their former enslavers. Like those of the Devil, his movements are quick, but he dances like other Congos. Thus, I placed Pajarito and the Devil stage right in red light; the King and Queen, stage left in blue.

Coming full circle, my last gesture in the performance was to interrogate my space as researcher at the end of this first encounter with Portobelo just as I had done at the beginning. While I began the performance with my reflexive space neatly off the stage, I now sat onstage, facing the audience and straddling the base of the cross. Digging beneath the beautiful roses and festive confetti, I shared with the audience the warning that Yaneca Esquina had given me. He had told me that not everyone may mean me well, that I should be very careful not to leave my food or drink unattended, and that I should wear some form of clothing inside out, even in the shower, for protection. He shared this with me and the other two young scholars who were with me after one of our interviews with him. Walking home from the interview, we teased each other in private, letting quiet laughter smother our undeniable trepidation. Later that night, though, questions and uncertainty energized the air around us; sleep would not come. Then, in the darkened room we shared, one by one we lifted our bottoms beneath the mosquito nets that helped inoculate us against one danger and quietly turned our night shorts inside out to help protect us from another. We never talked about it. Through our nonverbal act of compliance, we had acknowledged the boundaries of our existential commitment. After we did so, we calmed; we quieted; we slept. Some curiosities were beyond the thresholds we cared to cross even if all that lay beyond them were open rooms or other thresholds.

In recounting this story onstage, I searched through the rose pedals and confetti to unearth shackles and placed them on my wrists. Then, I spoke the Lord's Prayer in Spanish and English while still straddling the cross/crossroads. The critique at the heart of the Congo tradition is the way Christian ideology was wielded by the Catholic Church and Spanish Crown to promote and protect the institution of slavery. Yet, many contemporary Congo practitioners are Catholic. Celedonio, we may recall, was Major Devil in the Congo tradition and a deacon in the Catholic Church. The Congo tradition's decolonial stance embodies an insider–outsider as well as an inside-out relationship not only to its Spanish colonial history but also to aspects of contemporary Panamanian historical narratives and Catholic religious praxis. The tradition exceeds the boundaries of folklore in its persistent acts of "doing," "making," and "becoming."

As the lights dimmed, I spoke the final lines of the performance: "I returned 'home' with the embodied knowledge that, for better *and* for worse, this research would, as engaged ethnographic practice must, put my body, my understandings of myself, and my understandings of the world on the line." Creating and staging *La historia de los congos de Portobelo: Translating History Through the Body* made me more conscious of the ways in which my Catholic school education and Protestant Christian upbringing helped to guide my attention and influence the socio-ethical-critical lens through which I engaged my research. My choice to engage in the research through embodied praxis also had the potential of unhinging some of the surety of these epistemologies and challenging me to "know" otherwise.

## Making the Sign of the Cross

*Making the Sign of the Cross* (2001b) was a performance installation that gave me more questions to pack in my luggage for subsequent visits to Portobelo and to stuff in my backpack to take to the archives. The ones that captured my most immediate attention were those regarding the political economy of crosses in Panama. A strip of land parceling the Pacific from the Atlantic, Panama has a geopolitical history defined by its position as a crossroad. It is, as the title of Canal historian David McCullough's (1977) monograph makes explicit, "The Path between the Seas." For the first three centuries after colonization, the Spanish used it as a bridge to transport gold from Peru (in the Pacific) to Spain (in the Atlantic) via the Río Chargres (Chargres River) and the Camino Real (the Royal Road). By partnering with English pirates and privateers to cripple the Spanish enterprise, the Cimarrones used the Camino Real to help transition themselves from criminalized runaway slaves to freed persons. By the middle of the seventeenth century, Portobelo was *the* crossroads of the colonial Caribbean world, as traders descended on it each year for up to sixty days to buy and sell merchandise from Peru and South America in the famous Ferias de Portobelo (Portobelo Fairs).[2] By the nineteenth century, the Panama Railroad traced the path of the Camino Real, transporting gold-rush traffic from the eastern United States and Europe to California.[3] Created at the dawn of the twentieth century, the Panama Canal eliminated the need to round the tip of South America in order to pass from one ocean into the other. In addition to these geographic and economic incarnations of crosses and crossroads, the Congo tradition incorporates Christian representations of crosses as well as those apparent throughout the Kongo-Atlantic world.[4] I created *Making the Sign of the Cross* as a performance installation project and altar, as a crossroads of these various, often overlapping meanings. Further, I used the project to pay homage to the youngest African-descended victims who died while their parents were enslaved, as their parents were running for freedom, and while their parents struggled for survival as Cimarrones.

I debuted the work as my final project in Dwight Conquergood's Field Methods course in the spring of 2002. The landscape of the piece consisted of two seven-by-three-foot strips of cloth placed on the ground to resemble an "X." Lit tea candles and an illuminated string of white Christmas lights traced the cross. At the start of the performance, three performers, including myself, stood at three of the four endpoints of the cross holding black lanterns. The only light in the room came from the candles, Christmas lights, and lanterns. Small hand-crocheted baby shoes, bibs, and glass bottles formed an altar of absence at the fourth point of the cross. Alongside the bottles were copies of the Lord's Prayer in Spanish and the first prayer learned by most English-speaking Christian children in the United States:

Now I lay me down to sleep,
I pray the Lord my soul to keep,
If I shall die before I wake,
I pray the Lord my soul to take.
Amen.

Opened to Genesis 9:25, a King James Bible presided over the area directly across from the altar at the opposite endpoint behind one of the performers. In front of the Bible and performer, two parallel dark-brown footprints were imprinted on the fabric, on top of which lay ankle irons reminiscent of the shackles likely used on enslaved Africans. The shackles were open and ajar, as if the feet had broken free. Snaking from the prints toward the altar was an orange leather whip. Two more thick brown footprints led away from the originals as if running in a wide stride. As the prints neared the little altar, they became fainter until they ended in a final footprint followed by the blunt print of a knee and two heavy handprints. I had achieved the effect days earlier, standing on the cloth in my living room in brown body-paint before running and falling on the other side. Like the Congo tradition, I wanted to draw attention not only to those who had survived to tell the story but also to those who had fallen along the way.

Framed by the Catholic prayer invocation and practice of crossing one-self, the performance was separated into four parts. The section names corresponded to the words of the invocation and were therefore entitled "In the Name of the Father," "The Son (Sun)," "And the Holy," "Spirit." Sections one and three examined two of the spiritual worldviews reflected in the Congo tradition. The first, "In the Name of the Father: The Kongo Cosmogram,"[5] looked at the use of crosses in pre-Christian Kongo cosmology, while the third, "And the Holy: The Church and Slavery," examined the "double cross" of colonial interpretations of the Bible, which justified the exploitation of Africans through the curse of Noah's son, Ham. It further examined the role of the Christian Church and the Spanish Crown in authorizing the transatlantic slave trade. The second section, "The Son (Sun): Panama is a Crossroads," explored the physical location of the country in relationship to geopolitics and economics. The last part, "Spirit: Meditation for Those Left and Lost," was a homage to the young spirits who embodied the defiance of cimarronaje even though their bodies were enslaved.

Performers One and Two stood facing one another on the unmarked strip of cloth, while Performer Three stood between the Bible and painted footprints on the marked/altar cloth. Slowly speaking her "In the Name of the Father" script, Performer One walked meditatively toward Performer Two and reached her by the end of the first portion of her script. Speaking "The Son (Sun)" portion of the script, Performer Two slowly walked toward the position that Performer One had vacated on the other side. Then the three performers spoke in unison, "Panama is a crossroads." Performer Three turned to face the Bible behind her, knelt, and read the passage commonly cited as "The Curse of Ham" or "The Curse of Canaan." Afterward, she arose, began her slow walk across the cloth, and delivered her portion of the script, "And the Holy: The Church and Slavery." Once to the other side, she knelt before the altar in silence. Three beats later, the other two performers left their positions on the endpoints to join her. After Performer Three spoke a meditation, the three bowed, remained silent for another few beats, returned to their starting positions on the cross, placed their lanterns in front of them, and exited the performance space. Members of the audience, who had been standing around the cross, were then invited to explore the installation at their own pace and in their own time.

During the final days of my second three-week visit to Portobelo in May 2002, I restaged *Making the Sign of the Cross* in the middle of the street in front of Taller Portobelo, the Congo workshop. I replaced the Christmas lights with an entire border of tea lights, eliminated the Bible, and re-envisioned the altar. Because I had decided to stage the performance outside, the

Christmas lights were impractical. I adjusted the script to critique the church by connecting the whip of slavery to the Devil's use of whips in Congo performance. Because Congo Devils parody brutal enslavers, who often appropriated the Christian devil trope to help maintain power over their enslaved populations, the transition was an organic one. Finally, I spent the weeks prior to the performance creating a three-foot-tall rectangular house frame with a triangular roof that would serve as the structure for my revised altar. I painted the structure blue and dotted it with gold and bronze specks in the pointillist style of the Congo tradition. I stuffed the baby shoes with tissue and suspended them from the roof of the structure with transparent fishing line so that they appeared to float six inches above the ground. I suspended the bibs such that each of the three pairs of shoes had its own bib, as if worn by "spirit" infants. El Padre Nuestro (The Lord's Prayer) and the prayer "Now I Lay Me Down to Sleep" were painted on a canvas suspended from the back wall of the structure. The glass baby bottles and plastic nipples littered the building's floor.

I staged the performance on June 6, 2001, several days before the end of that year's Spelman College Summer Art Colony. I had invited members of the Congo community and the community at large and was nervously excited to share this piece with them. While setting up, I noticed my neighbors placing folding chairs outside their house; I felt flattered. Later, two male members of the household, Juan and his nephew, moved the television from the living room to the top of the concrete terrace railing facing out toward the street and chairs. Strange, I thought. Several of the Congo painters and Art Colony participants helped me to set up my materials and light the candles. Two colony participants performed the piece with me, and Arturo simultaneously translated the performance, line by line, into Spanish. The wind was high that evening and extinguished most of the candles before we started. It was not a good sign. By the time we began, the row of chairs outside my neighbor's house was full, with more neighbors forming uneven rows behind them, all fixed on the television. I had not realized that my performance coincided precisely with the start of the NBA Championship game pitting Shaquille O'Neal of the Los Angeles Lakers against Allen Iverson of the Philadelphia 76ers. Amid live cheers and televised commentary, the performance went on. Later, I would be grateful that friends and spectators from next door peeked in at the start of the performance and during the commercials. A crowd of about ten people had come primarily for the performance, although many often visited with other game-watchers.

The performance ended and several peopled lingered to inspect the space. With Lindsay's help, I invited anyone interested to join me inside the Taller to talk about the piece. Only my friends from the Taller came. When they looked at me encouragingly but did not offer questions or comments, Lindsay helped me to explain some of my intentions in the piece. Afterward, several friends offered encouraging comments, but then, more silence. I thanked them and suggested we go watch the game. Philadelphia beat the Lakers 107 to 101 in overtime. I am told it was a great game. I looked toward the television but was more focused on what I viewed as my failure. After cleaning up the space, I stayed a while to fellowship with my friends before retreating to my room. The performance, I thought, had failed. No one could have convinced me otherwise.

Lindsay had scheduled an exhibition for all of the Art Colony participants, including the Congo artists, several days later at a small gallery in Panama City. I altered my piece a final time to fit the exhibition space and staged it as an installation without the live performance. The gallery was in the old part of Panama City called Casco Viejo and stood beside Café de Assis, a restaurant and bar known for its support of the arts. Toward the end of the evening, one of the exhibition attendees pulled up a chair beside me in the café and, with Lindsay's help, introduced himself. He was Raul Jiménez, el Diablo Segundo (the Secondary Devil), who was being groomed by Celedonio, el Diablo Mayor, to take his place. Raul congratulated me on the exhibition as well as on my June 6 performance and told me that some of the information I had shared about crosses in the Kongolese Kingdom reminded him of things his father had told him when he was a child. He wanted to know more about my research and sources. He wanted to learn more about the Kongo cosmology and possible links with his tradition. And to think, I had not even noticed him on June 6! I shared my sources with him and promised to continue to do so. He offered me an interview the following day. My interview with Raul began at the house of the artist Sandra Eleta and ended with him walking with me to Celedonio's house with the scene that began chapter 3. *Making the Sign of the Cross* not only attracted Raul's interest, it also led to productive conversations and interviews with two generations of Congo Devils. Those encounters planted the seed for my second performance project, *Dancing with the Devil at the Crossroads: La historia de los congos de Portobelo.*

## *Dancing with the Devil at the Crossroads*: La historia de los congos de Portobelo

Performed in the Wallis Theatre of Northwestern University's Theatre and Interpretation Center in February 2002, *Dancing with the Devil at the Cross-*

*roads* (2002) was a sixty-minute intertextual ensemble performance that created a dialectic between two Black Diaspora representations of "devil." The performance created a dialogue between the multiple, sometimes competing voices of two legends rumored to have made pacts with the "devil" in order to master their crafts. The first was Celedonio, the oldest living Diablo Mayor in Portobelo, Panama, who introduced the character of Diablo Mayor to the town's Congo performance tradition. The second was Robert Johnson, one of the most famous musicians of the U.S. Delta blues tradition. Born in 1911 and 1916 respectively, Johnson and Celedonio were contemporaries carrying out two distinct forms of Black cultural performance in rural areas of the Americas. Robert Johnson's musical talents as a blues guitarist are legendary. So is the mytholgy that he sold his soul to the devil at the crossroad of Highways 49 and 61 in exchange for his talent. Placing their stories, histories, musical environments, and movement vocabularies in conversation to acquire better experiential and participatory understandings of both, the performance sought to mine similarities and differences between ideologies of "crossroads" and "devil" as they circulated in the cultural contexts of these two men.

Five members made up the cast, three women and two men. The women narrated the performance through a bifurcated choreopoem. They served as an omnipotent female trinity that bridged the spatiotemporal gaps separating Johnson, Celedonio, and the audience. The male cast members performed the roles of Celedonio and Johnson. I created the script as a work in progress, organic enough for us to workshop and mold collectively. Each of the performers was chosen not only because of his or her acting ability but also because of what his or her life experiences brought to the workshop process and the performance. Through the process of scripting and performing this piece, I wanted to get a sense of how bodies steeped in different movement/musical vocabularies interpret Congo dance. I also was fascinated by Celedonio's passion for both his participation in the church and his role as Devil, both of which lit his eyes and animated his body in story-talking.

Two of the three women who joined me in the project were Latina; the other was African American. All had training in ballet and danced hip-hop socially; both Latina women also danced salsa socially. Tatiana relocated from Brazil to the United States as an adolescent and was trained in flamenco as well as belly dancing. Diana, who was born in Puerto Rico, had training in modern dance. Courtney, a U.S.-born African American woman, had training in jazz dance. Because of my movement background, I knew that my body had originally approached Congo performance through a mix of salsa, meringue, reggae, hip-hop, and ballet. The first four affected my hips and shoulders; the latter was a memory my arms knew. My body encountered dancing to blues music the same year it encountered Congo. On the rare occasions I danced to blues music, I did so with male partners who led me in Chicago-style stepping, which my body registered as a hip-hop form of what my mother refers to as "hand-dancing" with meringue turns. I wanted to know how the bodies and consciousnesses of my female performers would embrace Congo and blues. Of the three, Tatiana's dance movements most closely approached those I had seen on Congo matrons. It was not just the controlled fluidity that belly dancing brought to her hips but also the confident tenacity with which she approached the movement. She knew how to make herself big and take up space. She knew how to make her body a dare.

I chose a blues bassist to play the role of Robert Johnson and a seminary student with a passion for acting to play the role of Celedonio. The bassist, Charles, the son of a blues guitarist and younger brother of a blues drummer, had grown up with Johnson's music and lore. William, the son of a Baptist minister who was following his own calling in the faith, played Celedonio. In one of the most powerful moments of our workshops and subsequent performances, William transgressed the space between his preacher-self and performer-self to deliver the adapted transcript of one of my interviews with Celedonio. In so doing, he released the same type of energy that I had witnessed during the original interview. As the writer-director of the piece, I had been pushing William to let the words fill up his body, to almost overflow with an excitement in what he was saying. What he ultimately delivered was akin to a southern Baptist preacher at the apex of his sermon. Standing in the middle of two of the narrators as the third knelt facing him, he started as if making a point, "It is about the PUJIDO / The pujido / From the verb pujar: To raise / To raise up." Transitioning into an adaptation of Celedonio's interview text, he began to shuffle his feet a bit and let the energy work up through his thighs and torso:

It is like a possession—
But it doesn't let an outside something in,
It just amplifies what's inside.
When you're Diablo
Once you put the clothes on—
The Diablo costume—
What comes out
Is
Is an arrogance
That you don't realize

you have
The moment that you put the costume on
All that stuff comes out
All this arrogance
comes out (Alexander 2002, 21–22)

By the time he reached the second "arrogance," William's whole body was alive with energy. He elongated the word to make it "a-A-A-rogance" and added a syllable to "out" to make it "owe-ta." He continued: "It's like a possession / When it happens / I can actually fly / When it happens." His feet were moving as though he were walking, although he stayed in the same place, and his arms shot out from his body on the word "fly" as he fluttered his hands like wings. "I know I'm the one who's moving," he said, calming back down a little, "I know it's me / But I can't explain or control it" (22).

When Celedonio spoke similar words to me in Panama in June of 2000, he transitioned from a small, delicate man taking up only part of himself to a vibrant presence that seemed to extend beyond the bounds of his own flesh. His back, which had been slightly slouched during the earlier part of the interview, woke up and became perfectly erect. His brows danced and his eyes shone. The muscles of his face tightened to push out each of his words with focus and force. He placed his hands firmly on his lap, then made big elegant gestures with them in the air as his feet tapped and danced in place. At the time, I had difficulty understanding how this man who had just come from Catholic mass could get so excited, so animated about the type of energy released in him during the Devil performance. People had told me stories in private about how Celedonio would get possessed and not be himself. You could see it in his eye, the people said. He would open a door at the crossroads and let the devil step through, they had told me. Whether or not that is true, I cannot say, just as I will never know whether Robert Johnson really made a deal with the devil at the crossroad of Highways 49 and 61. The mystical and mysterious stories surrounding him led me to filter my perception of Celedonio through a lens of wonder tinged slightly with fear. That was how I had missed in 2000 what William's 2002 performance clarified for me—the fluidity of spirituality and art, the fluidity of identity. Participating in the Congo tradition is just as much a part of Celedonio's identity as participating in the Catholic faith. He has done both since his youth. An elder parishioner from William's church asked during one of the talkback sessions after a performance, "How did it feel to play the Devil, and were you afraid of what your church members might think?" William answered that it felt great, that he was an actor who loved to perform, and that his spirit had been just as active on the stage as it is in the pulpit. Hearing his explanation gave me a nuanced perspective through which to understand Celedonio's embodiment of Christian beliefs and ideologies as complementary rather than contradictory to his ability to embody the Congo Major Devil character.

## El museo congo

My final staged ethnographic performance represented my first completely collaborative project with the Congo artists of Portobelo, and it reinforced some of the complex ways in which identity politics affect ethnographic research. While I have documented my other performance projects primarily through narrative analysis, I have incorporated photographs of this culminating project in this chapter because they show how members of the Congo community of Portobelo represent the most salient parts of their tradition on their own terms.

On Saturday, July 12, 2003, I co-curated and participated in *El museo congo* at San Jerónimo Fort in Portobelo. The project was a collaboration between the Taller artists Virgilio "Yaneca" Esquina, Virgilio "Tito" Esquina, Reynaldo "Rey" Esquina, Gustavo Esquina de la Espada, Ariel Jiménez, Jose "Moraitho" Angulo, Manuel "Tatu" Golden, and Jerónimo "Jero" Chiari—all of whom are active participants in the Congo performance tradition. Almost all of these artists also have at least one relative who either relocated to Portobelo from the interior during Omar Torrijos's 1970s road contruction and land reform projects or who is of West Indian descent. The other *El museo congo* artists included Hector Jiménez, an Archangel in the Congo tradition; Danilo Barrera, a local resident related to many of the Congo artists; Jenny Arribu, a visual artist from the United States who initiated a children's art class in Portobelo; Carla Escoffery, a Panamanian visual artist who assisted with Jenny's class; Pamela Sunstrum, a visiting Botswanan artist from the University of North Carolina at Chapel Hill; and Michelle Lanier, an independent artist from the United States and previous participant of the Spelman Summer Art Colony.

A month in the planning, the project was initiated by a presentation of my work for the Fulbright Scholars' conference of grantees in the Central American Region. When one of my Congo friends asked how the presentation went, I responded by offering to do the presentation in the Taller for whoever wanted to witness it. This was a spontaneous dialogical performance that I hoped would help to better explain my project to the people so intimately involved in it as well as to raise questions I might not have anticipated.

All of the artists listed above were present, except Michelle Lanier, who had not yet arrived for her third visit to Portobelo. Until the presentation, I had never really explained my rationale of performance ethnography to the group. They had witnessed me making art but had not known how I was attempting to use it. I had incorporated various photos of them into the presentation, and they responded with pride at having been included and at how seriously I was taking what they saw as my contribution to the tradition's historical preservation. In the discussion that followed, different artists started to talk about what they might do if they were to create an installation project about their tradition. I thought that they had offered marvelous ideas and asked if they might be interested in collaborating on a performative "Congo museum" that would be based on the parts of the tradition to which each individual artist or artistic team was most attracted. They enthusiastically agreed. My brief elation quickly turned to panic when I realized that, while we had all worked on different projects with Arturo Lindsay over the years regarding various aspects of the tradition, I had never attempted to lead visual artists in such an endeavor. I have training as a performer and director, but I am primarily a self-taught installation artist. "No problem," one of the artists, Ariel, assured me; they were all self-taught artists, too.

In addition to the installations we would create, we invited Congo elders to participate by offering a congada. When they agreed, Sandra Eleta volunteered to host a lunch at her home for all the participants and their guests. Doña Cecilia (Ceci) and Soledad, two Portobeleños who assisted Sandra with the cooking and management of her home, made *fufu,* a fish stew served over coconut rice with yellow plantains, Doña Ceci's signature dish.

Roberto Enrique King, of the Asociación Cultural Alterarte in Panama City, and the U.S. Embassy helped us to publicize the event in the Panamanian press. Unfortunately, we could not have chosen a more inopportune date for our project. *El museo congo* was scheduled to take place just hours after Hurricane Claudette entered the coast as a strong tropical storm, flooding some chambers of the fort, creating a muddy mess in others, and providing us all with what Sandra would later call "a good test of character." By the 2:00 p.m. opening time, the weather had not yet allowed us to complete our setup. To improvise, Sandra invited all of the loyal enthusiasts who had come to experience our "museo" into her home for lunch. When the rain stopped and the floodwaters receded, we began. Because Sandra's land was less muddy than the fort, we relocated the congada to there and saved it as a finale. Although we had not intended it as such, our on-the-ground maneuvering and tactical "making do" created its own performative installations of the Congo tradition.

The events surrounding the creation and exhibition of Pamela Sunstrum's installation "I'll Fly Away" ("Volaré") gave us the conditions for our first productive meta-performance. Inspired by a similar ritual that Sandra and several students from the first Spelman Art Colony had initiated, Pamela decided to create a healing ritual and altar space in the area in the back of the fort where enslaved people are believed to have been held. The official purpose of the dungeon-like chamber was to hold munitions, but the stories that have passed down about it and the "feeling" one gets while in the space suggest that it also stored humans. It had the same aesthetic quality and sensual feel as similar spaces in Elmina slave castle in Ghana, West Africa, which I had experienced years prior. It was a dank, square space with one door, no window, and a small square space in the ceiling for air. At Pamela's request, Ariel collected white chicken feathers for her, which she planned to hang, one by one, from the ceiling opening by a thin white string. Inspired by the Congos' use of broken mirrors on their hats and in their artwork, she attached a small piece of glass to each feather in order to capture and reflect light. The effect would be that of a ghostly chandelier. She also planned to place dozens of candles in a flowering pinwheel design and to light them for the opening.

On July 11, the day before *El museo congo* was to be held, Sandra enlisted the help of one of the local gravediggers to clean out the fort's holding area, which was located down a flight of stone stairs at the far end of the rectangular building. The interior space was less than 800 square feet and had a dirt floor. Before the gravedigger's intervention, the smell of urine, excrement, and rot made it difficult to enter. Afterward, it smelled mostly of damp earth and the bleach he had used on the walls, and Pamela placed the candles and feathers in the room in preparation for the following day's event.

Now that the space had been literally cleansed, Pamela invited Carmelita and Angelica (two members of the Spanish Heritage Group),[6] Sandra, Doña Ceci, Soledad, Jenny, and me to join her in a ritual spiritual cleansing, which we would invent according to whatever we felt we could offer to the space. Sandra had given us several bottles of Agua de Florida, a sweet- smelling, inexpensive perfume water, to carry with us, and I offered us each a stick of jasmine incense. As we stood in the space sharing silence, some meditating, others praying, still others patiently observing, we poured our Agua de Florida as a libation to the ancestors, and Pamela invited us to speak aloud anything we wished to share. The memory that remains most distinct for me is when Doña Ceci closed her eyes and began to sing a sweet, melancholy song. I was too overwhelmed to tune my ears to the Spanish lyrics, but the emotion in her voice made me cry. When I wiped my eyes, I noticed that many of us were crying and had reached out to touch each other's hands for comfort. It was the first of several moments of communitas that the experience would yield for us. In that instance, class, nationality, and age faded into something more ephemeral and tender. A full moon had lit the sky by the time we exited. Wanting a normative communitas to sustain our spontaneous one (Turner 1982, 47), we walked away in groups of two or three locked at the elbow. By the time we reached the house, the moment had already passed. Doña Ceci and Soledad went back to work in the kitchen and teased the rest of us as "brujas" ("witches") when we decided to take the motorboat across the bay to end our cleansing ritual with a late-night swim.

On the day of the exhibition/performance, we were all devastated to learn that someone had stolen Pamela's candles and destroyed her feathers during the night. At the time, we were unsure whether this was in response to a perceived act of "brujería" ("witchcraft") or whether it was meanness, mischievous thievery, thievery for necessity, or something more random. Regardless, we were all deeply hurt. This was our second experience of communitas. The Congo artists were even more concerned because they did not want this to be the memory that Pamela would pack with her later that day to take back to the States. As we waited for the rain to subside that morning, we worked frantically to rebuild Pamela's piece. Because we wanted a better ending for our story than the one the hurricane and vandalism were offering us, we all decided to sacrifice elements of our individual pieces to ensure her project's success. Pamela's project became ours, too. Arial collected more feathers; Sandra purchased candles in small glass vases, the type sold outside the church to be lit for ancestors and blessings, to replace the long thin candles that had been stolen; Rey, Gustavo, and I offered the one hundred sticks of jasmine incense we had amassed for our project; Michelle offered a string of Tibetan prayer beads and three bowls; Danilo collected flowers; and Pamela worked to reassemble one of the most powerful pieces of our collaborative project. It was powerful not only because of its artistic value, but also because it initiated another moment of communitas that pulled us out of the slump and worry the weather had created and gave us even more incentive to rise above it.

On each of the stairs leading down to her space, Pamela placed small clay vessels created on top of plastic bottle caps. Each vessel contained Agua de Florida. At Michelle's suggestion, Pamela placed eggs, sugar, and flour in separate bowls to help nourish the ancestors' spirits. Once lit, the incense and candles gave the space a sacred, ghostly feel.

Having learned the art of Devil mask-making from Jerónimo and Raul, Jenny decided to work with several local young children on an installation

Figure 5.2  Entrance to "I'll Fly Away" (Photo by Renée A. Craft)

entitled "Caras de Portobelo: Un taller de mascaras" ("Faces of Portobelo: A Mask Workshop"). All of the participants were siblings, children, or extended family members of the participating Congo artists. The mask-making process, which lasted several weeks, involved excavating clay from the jungle, using it to create a mold, drying the mold in the sun, applying a layer of papier-mâché, and allowing it to thoroughly dry before adding a new layer. Jenny charged each of the children with creating any type of mask they chose as long as it

Figure 5.3 View from the back of "I'll Fly Away," looking out (Photo by Renée A. Craft)

represented some aspect of the tradition. At the end of the process, each child painted his or her own mask. The children created masks of the Congo Queen as well as of the Devil. On the day of the "museo," Jenny and Carla installed the masks one by one in small window slits along the back wall of the fort. Figures 5.4–5.8 are photographs of five of the thirteen masks they helped the children make. One child, my little friend Sarabi, could not decide whether to make a Devil or a Queen, so she made a Devil Queen.

Figure 5.4 Brown Congo Queen with blond rope hair and painted blue eyes (Photo by Renée A. Craft)

Figure 5.5 Brown Congo Queen with mirror fragments in her crown (Photo by Renée A. Craft)

**Figure 5.6** Blue Devil Queen with pink lips and green eyebrows (Photo by Renée A. Craft)

**Figure 5.7** Red and black Devil mask with toothpick teeth (Photo by Renée A. Craft)

**Figure 5.8** Clay, green, yellow, and pink Devil mask (Photo by Renée A. Craft)

Congo artists Ariel and Tatu restaged an installation project that they had originally presented as a part of Ferias de Portobelo 2003, which consisted of bilingual and bicultural poetry and an exhibition of biodegradable earth-works, installations, and sculptures. As a memorial to the Cimarron ances-tors, they created "El espíritu de los ancestros de los congos" ("The Spirit of the Congo Ancestors"). Their installation consisted of a chalked path bor-dered by string leading up to a Congo jacket, which was covered with bones and small bags to which they had attached feathers. The jacket was held in place by a pole with a crossbar. The bones and feathers symbolized the kinds of talismans the Cimarrones might have carried with them into the jungles. Additionally, Ariel and Tatu hung a Congo hat between two hand-carved and painted bastones (walking sticks) on the wall behind the jacket.

Located in one of the fort's front corners, Moraitho and Hector's instal-lation was a tribute to Taller Portobelo's role in preserving the tradition by

Figure 5.9 "El espíritu de los ancestros de los congos" (Photo by Renée A. Craft)

displaying several of Moraitho's paintings alongside Congo male, female, and Archangel costumes. Their piece demonstrated the ways in which the new practice of Congo visual art not only serves as a method to reflect and preserve the Congo tradition, but also serves as a method to extend the tradition into other forms of creative expression. Economically, Moraitho also reasoned that some of the people coming to see our installation might also buy his art.

**Figure 5.10** Close-up of Congo hat hung on fort wall (Photo by Renée A. Craft)

**Figure 5.11** Close-up of Congo jacket with amulets and talismans (Photo by Renée A. Craft)

Figure 5.12 Moraitho and Hector's "Untitled" installation (Photo by Renée A. Craft)

Figure 5.13 Close-up of Moraitho's artwork (Photo by Renée A. Craft)

Jerónimo and Tito created an altar to the Devils of the Congo tradition using Jerónimo's Devil costume and incorporating decorative elements from El Festival de los Diablos y Congos, including red and black painted cattle skulls adorned with ribbons and large cardboard embellishments covered with broken mirrors. Like Moraitho, they recycled parts of a burgeoning tradition, in this case El Festival de los Diablos y Congos, into the space of an older one. Like Arial and Tatu, Jero and Tito created a path leading up to their altar space. Their walkway was marked by stones, torches, and gravel. Above the costume, they suspended Jero's elaborate Devil mask. Below the costume were his ankle bells, whip, and shoes. They chose to place their altar in a chamber that had a hole in the side wall they shared with Arial and Tatu's installation, allowing anyone in the Devil space to "spy" on the Congos.

Recycling the mirrored base of an installation that Lindsay had created for "Ferias de Portobelo 2003," Yaneca created a monument to El Pajarito. Appropriately, he chose a space between the Devil chamber and the Congo space for his project. Starting with a T-shaped tree branch, he soaked pieces of canvas in gesso and wrapped them in layers around the branch, following its natural contours. As in the papier-mâché mask-making process, Yaneca allowed each layer to dry little by little over time before proceeding with the next. After he had finished "the body," he adorned it with ribbons. He carved Pajarito's face from a coconut shell and painted it. Using cardboard and broken mirrors, he created the sculpture's crown.

Rey, Gustavo, and I created an installation entitled "El monumento de homenaje a los espíritus de los congos" ("A Monument of Homage to the Congo Spirits"). Using cardboard and mirrors, we created thirteen pairs of footprints—four pairs of male prints and nine pairs of female prints. The male footprints represented three drummers and one male dancer. The nine female prints represented a seven-member chorus, one revellín, and a female dance partner for one set of male Congo prints. Before the rain flooded our original space, we had intended to place three Congo drums behind the drummer prints. After the rain, however, we eliminated the drums because we did not want to damage them. Suspended from transparent fishing line were a Congo pollera and Congo trousers turned inside out. We used the wire to give the clothing the feeling of floating/dancing. The ghostly pair swayed back and forth as the breeze animated them. A sombrero hung as though atop a Congo male's head, and a Congo Queen's crown kept watch from the open window. We had created both the sombrero and the crown especially for the project. Crisscrossing the area above us were lines of rope covered with the tethered material that had decorated the palacio's ceiling. We created a border for the space using pieces of stone that we painted with West African Adinkra

**Figure 5.14** Jerónimo and Tito's "Untitled" Devil installation
(Photo by Renée A. Craft)

**Figure 5.15** Side wall of "Untitled" el Diablo installation (Photo by Renée A. Craft)

Figure 5.16 "Pajarito" on his recycled pedestal (Photo by Renée A. Craft)

symbols. Both Rey and Gustavo use various Adinkra symbols in their visual artwork, and I use them in my poetry.

Before the storm, we had chosen a square chamber without a ceiling for our installation. The shape of the room and the absence of a ceiling would have allowed us to tie weights to the ends of our fishing wire and toss them over the walls in order to suspend the tethered cloth and clothing. Our new space did not afford us the same luxury. Between the tropical storm, having to reorganize spaces, and the theft of Pamela's materials, I was not thinking about the preservation of the four-hundred-year-old fort when Gustavo located nails and began hanging our materials in the new space. Our project

Figure 5.17 "El monumento de homenaje a los espíritus de los congos" (Photo by Renée A. Craft)

Figure 5.18 Adinkra stone border and mirror footprints (Photo by Renée A. Craft)

was not intended to create controversy, but it did. Hours behind schedule, we all were focused on getting the project mounted when Carmelita, one of the women from the Spanish Heritage Group, expressed her outrage. While I was trying to locate materials to help Pamela rebuild her installation and brainstorming with Rey and Gustavo to reimagine ours, Carmelita pulled me aside and chastised me for "allowing" Gustavo to "damage" the fort. With my nerves more than strained, I pulled away from her without a word, shared her concern with my collaborators, and asked what alternatives we might have. But Gustavo was furious. "*Dañe el fuerte* [Damage the fort]?" he wondered aloud. "*Su nuestro hacer con lo que queremos* [It's ours to do with what we want]!" Gustavo reminded me that the Spanish Heritage Group had not complained when artists from Panama City had put the same kinds of nails in the fort during the Festival de los Diablos y Congo, which it had co-sponsored. At that, he continued hanging our piece, and I went to deal with other issues. The truth of the matter was that, although I had understood Carmelita's point, I agreed with Gustavo. When she returned to see that I had not "made" Gustavo stop nailing, she stormed away.

Later that evening, Carmelita referred to me as "an imperialist American who thinks she can do whatever she pleases" and chastised the Taller artists for their lack of concern for their cultural heritage. Gustavo asked why he should revere something that was used against his ancestors and why he should have to attend to the concerns of an *extranjero* (foreigner) like her from Spain. This was our final moment of communitas that caused us to coalesce in camps around different feelings of rage and entitlement. The Congo artists felt the fort was theirs to use; the Spanish Heritage Group felt it was theirs to protect.

The brief feeling of fluid connectedness that Carmelita and I had shared the day before had evaporated. The nails in the fort did not cause the fissures; they simply aggravated them. For months, Carmelita had been frustrated by what she perceived as Portobeleños' lack of investment in their community as made evident to her in their disinterest in participating in cultural heritage, health and wellness, and community beautification projects initiated by her organization. For example, one project was a plan to purify the town's drinking water. The aqueducts that supplied the town's water were contaminated by dead frogs and in a state of disrepair. If the community would agree to pay for water treatment, the problem could be solved, but many people refused to pay. Carmelita read their refusal as apathy in improving their quality of life; I had a different understanding. In informal conversations with townspeople, I learned that they had never paid for water and the thought of doing so was completely outside of their experience. As it stood, the water sometimes made someone sick but not horribly so, and inexpensive medicine was available when it did. Also, there was no infrastructure that would be able to enforce payment if the aqueducts were cleaned, thus, no way to ensure that those who paid would have any privileges separate from those who did not pay. So, those who could afford to do so solved the problem by installing tanks on their roofs or using other methods of filtration. Carmelita thought the majority of townspeople were being unreasonable, but many townspeople thought the Spanish Heritage Group's plan was untenable.

Carmelita's reaction to me was also fueled by her anger over what she saw as the U.S. government's arrogance in going to war against Iraq. She "read" me within the frame of my nationality. To Carmelita, a woman of Spanish heritage and an employee of a Spanish cultural preservation group, I represented a selfish U.S. agent more interested in completing my own project than protecting the cultural heritage in the region. However, while she interpreted my resistance as arrogance based on nationality, I interpreted her insistence as arrogance based on race. When she insisted twice that I "make" Gustavo stop nailing, I did not hear her as the director of a project receiving a grievance from a fellow preservationist; I remain unsure that her intentions were that transparent. Rather, from my perspective, a foreign White woman was asking me, a foreign Black woman, to tell a local Black man what he could and could not do in his own hometown. She had known Gustavo as long as I had, and had come into the Taller numerous times to ask a favor, share a grievance, and lend a helping hand, yet she had approached me twice and ordered me to make him stop. Sandra offered the last words I remember on the subject: "There they go. It's like the Cimarrones and the españoles all over again!"

In an essay published in *Performance Research* (Alexander Craft et al. 2007), I shared an analysis on this event with reference to the types of useful opportunities performance ethnography offers, even in the midst of misunderstandings and missteps. It bears repeating here:

> In London, at the 2006 Performance Studies international conference, [three colleagues] and I relished riding the tube. With child-like glee, we anticipated the recorded female voice warning, "Mind the Gap" as the train doors yawned in sync. The caution meant that one should be careful of the space between the more stable platform and the moving cultural conduit that imbues it with meaning. From my first visit to Portobelo, Panamá in 2000, performance ethnography as a mode of critical ethnographic research has served as that type of productive warning in the dangerous hollows between what the community says, what I hear, and vice versa. Through its reliance on dialogism, performance ethnography serves as a steady reminder of the gap and a method to traverse it. It calls us to engage

its presence not as a wound to be healed or hole to be filled but rather a critical contour of discontinuity between the researcher and the communities within which she works. (70)

Performance ethnography has the potential to open a space for dialogues around race, gender, ethnicity, class, and nation that may unveil the ideological investments of the ethnographer no less than those of the communities with which s/he works. According to Conquergood (1985a), dialogical performances "bring self and Other together so that they can question, debate, and challenge one another" (9). As a mode of critical analysis, it serves as both an engaged practice to increase understandings across various boundaries of "otherness" as well as a method of meta-analysis (Madison 2005, 167–68; E. Johnson 2003a, 8).

The *El museo congo* installation received generous positive feedback from visitors and community members. The Congo artists saw it as another act of cultural preservation. The fragments of the tradition we chose to uplift can be grouped along the three strands that I find at the core of the Congo tradition's ability to have survived since the colonial period and to press on toward the future: 1) tradition as related to the ancestors; 2) tradition as related to contemporary practitioners and practices; and 3) tradition as transformative, able to absorb new elements without sacrificing salient older ones.

## Conclusion: Toward Sankofa

The history of the Americas starts with colonization and cimarronaje. Enslaved Africans "danced with the devils" and survived, but did not win. It was a dance toward decolonization and self-determination that continues. Citizens of the Americas remain entangled in violent struggles over resources, representation, and social justice that reflect the structural asymmetrical race relations on which the countries of the Americas were founded. The concept of "Sankofa" is derived from the Akan people of Ghana, West Africa, and is represented in an Asante Adinkra symbol as a bird with an egg in its beak, looking backward. The egg is said to represent the future. The concept teaches us the necessity to "look back" or reflectively engage with the past in order to move forward. Toward that end, this section is a Sankofa, a kinesthetic conclusion to a study that reflects on its progress as it steadily marches toward new horizons.

This study has engaged questions related to contemporary Congo traditions and twentieth-century Panamanian Blackness through five principle performative "scenes": Performance of/as Ethnoracial Identity; Cultural and Ritual Performance; Performance as/is the (Re)making of Culture; and Duality, Double-Consciousness, and the Trick of Performing for "Others." In the first, Performance of/as Ethnoracial Identity, I analyzed the evolution of "etnia negra" racial discourses over the arc of the twentieth century to understand how an African-descended community that enacts a performative tradition steeped in the history of Black presence in Panama self-identified as Black at the beginning of the century, as Mestizo at mid-century, and as Black again at the end of the century. To understand the community's discursive trajectory, I analyzed its twentieth-century sociopolitical history as an African-descended community that entered Panama during the colonial period as enslaved people in dialogue with West Indian communities that entered Panama during the neocolonial period as laborers on the U.S.-owned and controlled Panama Canal. Doing so illuminated how "Black" in the mid-century came to mean non-Panamanian, non-Spanish-speaking, and foreign in ways that threatened rights of citizenship and failed to allow space for hispanicized African-descended populations that had fought battles over citizenship and belonging centuries before without risking claims to their cultural and national identities. The dismantling of the Panama Canal Zone and the U.S. turnover of the Canal to Panama at the end of the twentieth century began an era in which the term Afro-Panamanian allowed Afro-Colonials and Afro-Antilleans a shared platform from which to demand acknowledgment of their differential ethnoracial histories and the value of their labor in building the current Republic.

Chapter 2 focused on Congo traditions through the lens of cultural performance and ritual performance. In part 1 of the chapter, I analyzed the productive friction between what Raymond Williams (1977) would refer to as the tradition's "official consciousness" and "practical consciousness" to gain a better understanding of the difference between the ways practitioners explain its meaning and purpose through third-person narratives (e.g., "This is the way it is done.") compared with the ways in which they discuss it informally and enact their contemporary participation (e.g., "This is the way we did it this year."). As Stuart Hall (2003) would argue, idealized narratives of the traditions exist in an ahistorical bubble, whereas those situated in first-person narratives constuct the tradition as "subject to the continuous 'play' of history, culture and power" (225).

For elders and ritual specialists, the road that the government built serves as a persistent marker that shifted the centrality of Congo cultural performance and interrupted an intercommunity feature of the tradition that had been key to the Congo game—war play. Before the 1960s when the road that connects Portobelo and other Atlantic coast communities to the broader Republic was constructed, isolated Afro-Colonial towns immersed themselves in Congo performances throughout Carnival season. "Playing Congo" meant living in communal relationship to other Congo practitioners, especially during the apex of Carnival season, without "breaking character" to do or be otherwise. The road brought greater access to resources and opportunities, but it also made practicing Congo something one might do intermittently between other forms of work or play. Without the immersive experience that facilitated the prolonged embodied transfer of cultural knowledge, some nuances were lost and others risked being flattened to spectacle. Part 2 of the chapter examined the notion of cultural change in the tradition as "new." Through repeated interviews and reflection, I began to understand that elements of the tradition that now form its official consciousness such as the Major Devil, Angels, Priest, and the practice of blessing or baptizing the Devils are twentieth-century additions. Although the pace of globalization dramatically increased in the latter half of the twentieth century and the construction of the road created a clear point of rupture, Congo traditions in the current form are a bricolage of elements from the colonial to the present period. They are cultural performances that maintain their relevance by a contentious process of incorporation and adaptation. More than the presentation of folkloric performances that present some seemingly sealed past, Congo performances maintain their subversive ability by moving with their practitioners—by commemorating the past and actively reflecting the present.

Taking the Devil character as its central focus, chapter 3 served as a case study to explore in greater detail some of the claims made in the previous chapter. Focused on the three practitioners who have played the Major Devil role in the living memory of local practitioners, it exercised a circum-local paradigm to analyze the ways in which this twentieth-century addition was incorporated into the Congo tradition of Portobelo, Panama, such that it now serves as a pivotal part of the official narrative. The Major Devil tradition was created through micro processes of diaspora—through the migration and return of practitioners within a narrow radius with new and different ways of doing the tradition. The community's decision to incorporate the Major Devil character and the ripples of change that this evinced, including the act of blessing the Devil and the additional characters needed to do so, involved an active embodied negotiation between the ways in which Celedonio Molinar Ávila envisioned the trajectory of his cultural intervention and the ways in which the community chose to accept it. When he served as Major Devil, Celedonio could direct the character's purpose and embodiment based his authority as the only one in the community directly trained in how the character was to be performed and the most experienced in doing so. When the time for his retirement neared, the Congo Royal Court and community exerted a greater role in how they imagined the tradition continuing. Equally important, mentees like Carlos Chavarría, the current Major Devil, exercised their right to make different existential choices regarding the parts of the Devil tradition they chose to embody and the parts they chose to ignore. I ended the chapter focused on the El Festival de los Diablos y Congos, a twenty-first-century cultural intervention that reimagines and reinstates circum-local intercommunity "visits" by creating an opportunity for Major Devils and Congo communities from throughout the Republic to share aspects of their cultural performances with one another in Portobelo outside of Carnival season while opening a dedicated space for ritual specialists to mentor and educate younger practitioners. It also serves as an act of cultural preservation and promotes the relevance and importance of the Congo tradition to the broader Republic.

Chapter 4 focused on the "scene" of Duality, Double-Consciousness, and the Trick of Performing for "Others." Portobelo and Congo traditions exist as an exotized Black cultural space and performance in the imaginaries of most external visitors. In this chapter, I analyzed the ways in which Congo consciousness about these external perceptions helps to frame tourists' presentations of the tradition in ways that shift female practitioners' embodiment from audacious and daring in the local space of ritual performance to restrained and pristine for tourist audiences. Congo male practitioners also alter their role to police aggressive or otherwise inappropriate tourist interaction with female practitioners more actively in tourist presentations, whereas Congo women often police such interactions in the ritual space of performance through movement vocabularies endemic to and expected of female practitioners' performative mastery. Finally, I examined the ways in which Congo performance allows practitioners to consume their audiences for the purposes of amusement and entertainment just as their audiences actively consume them.

My method of critical/performance ethnography has involved a continuous praxis of Sankofa—of physically returning to Portobelo as well as intellectually revising the cultural performances and texts that have emerged out of my praxis in order to correct misconceptions, fill in absences, engage in critical reflexivity, and move this study forward. For the past fourteen years, I have maintained a consistent pattern of fieldwork and homework. These "fields" have included personal and official archives in Panama and in the United States as well as dancing between "the academy" and "the community" as sites of valuation and meaning-making. Staged dialogical performance/

performance ethnography has been one of the key ways that I have traversed these fields. Likewise, interpersonal dialogical performance has helped me to engage with coperformers related to the tradition in both spaces.

Congo traditions in Panama are rich cultural sites through which to explore how African-descended communities in various towns throughout the Atlantic coast of the Republic as well as a few scattered communities along the Pacific have recorded and revised their specific histories of colonial engagement through cultural performances. This study concludes like the figure of the egg in the Sankofa bird's mouth—with a call for the important work that remains to be done about the variety of contemporary Congo performances in Panama and how communities have come to their current point of embodiment as well as what traces of Kongo history and culture may be gleaned through them. Although official narratives of Congo performance point toward uniformity of colonial encounter and contemporary expression, the Devil, as always, is in the details.

# EPILOGUE

## Dialogical Performance, Critical Ethnography, and the "Digital Present"

In February 2013 Carlos Chavarría, Major Devil in the Congo tradition and mayor of Portobelo, signed a decree to suspend Carnival in the municipality, which includes the towns of Puerto Lindo, Isla Grande, Maria Chiquita, Cacique, and Portobelo. He made the decision to do so after consulting with the Panama National Police (PNP), the governor of Colón province, representatives from affected districts, and local residents in response to increased drug-related gun violence along the Costa Arriba. It was the first time in the living memory of Portobeleños that such an action needed to be taken. Weeks prior, two men from outside of Portobelo entered the town, shot a local resident twelve times, and fled. In the days leading up to Carnival, other residents had received threats of more violence. A national newspaper, *Crítica*, quoted Carlos as saying:

> *Desistimos de esta celebración y yo, que juego diablo, lamento aún más la situación, pero no podemos dejar que se pongan máscaras porque no sabemos quién se pueda esconder con este disfraz.*

> We stopped this celebration and I, (as a person) who plays Devil, regret the

situation even more, but we cannot let people put on masks because we do not know who could hide with this disguise. (Cortez 2013)

Panama's geographic location and transportation infrastructure make it a prime transit location for the shipment of illegal drugs from Colombia to the United States and other global markets. According to the 2008 International Narcotics Control Strategy Report, released by the Bureau of International Narcotics and Law Enforcement Affairs:

> Traffickers exploit Panama's well-developed transportation infrastructure, such as containerized seaports, the Pan-American Highway, a rapidly growing international hub airport (Tocumen), numerous uncontrolled airfields, and relatively unguarded coastlines on both the Atlantic and Pacific [. . .] Drugs transit Panama via fishing vessels, cargo ships, small aircraft, and go-fast boats. Hundreds of abandoned or unmonitored legal airstrips are used by traffickers for refueling, pickups, and deliveries.

Community members have shared anecdotes about bags of cocaine washing up along the Atlantic shoreline and being retrieved by everyday people who attempt to profit from the sale of the "found" drugs. This has led to greater violence from international traffickers as well as from local gangs in large cities like Colón, which sometimes provide traffickers protection and logistical assistance.

In light of the suspension of local Carnival activities, the 2013 El Festival de los Diablos y Congos had even greater prominence than in prior years. Although the Portobelo municipality would have been unable to amass sufficient police protection for its citizens during the Saturday and Sunday evening congadas leading up to Carnival or during each of their local Carnival Tuesday and Ash Wednesday celebrations, the Mayor could more easily acquire the necessary protection for this daytime festival centralized in a two-block radius in Portobelo.

Compared with my first experience of El Festival de los Diablos y Congos a decade prior, the 2013 festival had evolved in several striking ways. First, the festivities had been moved some years ago from San Jerónimo Fort to the large open-air park on the other side of the main road where Portobelo's Ash Wednesday Congo drama concludes with the "blessing" of the Devils. The decision to relocate the festival had been made in order to protect the fort from any damage that might accrue over time as a result of festival banners being nailed into its structure as well as the safety of the thousands of people who traversed its single entrance.[1]

Second, the town had replaced the traditional wood and thatch palenque/palacio, which Congo participants typically installed annually in its more pristine form and allowed to slowly deteriorate throughout the year until it was needed again. The new palenque was a concrete gazebolike structure. On one hand, it lacks some of the aesthetic warmth that bamboo leaves and wood had given the traditional one. On the other hand, the newer one is more durable, sustainable, and aesthetically consistent for visitors who come year-round and often encounter it out of season.

As in previous years, most of the El Festival de los Diablos y Congos spectators were national visitors who had arrived for the day via car or bus, with a sprinkling of yachtsmen and women anchored in the bay and visiting artists and scholars, like myself, renting space in local homes. The third new(er) phenomena was the presence of international tourists staying either at the local hostel high atop a hill at one end of town or at the new exclusive super-luxury resort across the bay. A decade prior, staying overnight in the central town was only possible through home-stays. The only other choice that visitors had at the time was the small hotel on the outskirts of the central town.

The final cultural changes that I witnessed occurred during the festival as Devils from throughout the country surged from behind the central podium and danced into the main staging area. It was not the Devils that captured my immediate attention but the audience. As the performance began, a dense sea of arms raised to record the spectacle on smartphones and tablets then snapped back down like waves crashing toward the shore as local and global spectators attempted to upload the images to text messages, Facebook, Instagram, YouTube, and other social media. When I began this research with the Congo community in 2000, cell phones were rare, and the town lacked the infrastructure to support cell phone reception. Further, the cost of Internet access was prohibitive, and most community members did not have local access or personal computers. Now, search the web and social media for "Congos of Portobelo" and you will find videos, photos, and commentary by local practitioners as well as dynamic websites created by local organizations. Globalization in the forms of increased technology and transportation infrastructure as well as expanded tourism is changing Portobelo. The methods ethnographers use to study it must change, too.

# Digital Portobelo: Art + Scholarship + Cultural Preservation

In 2010 one of the graduate students in my Critical/Performance Ethnography course asked me if I would talk about how my research on Portobelo was a work of "critical ethnography." The question was a fair and anticipated one. In my initial response, I talked about the ways in which I coupled critical theory with embodied field research, paid close attention to the workings of power and the circuits through which the community and I variously engaged it, and attempted to intervene in the representational politics of the area, which often frame Congo performance as narrowly folkloric and social in a way that flattens its sociopolitical history and the nuances of its contemporary practice.

As a critical/performance ethnographer, I have consistently used live performance and performance-installation projects as a means to make my research more accessible, especially to the communities reflected by and invested in its outcomes. Doing so has made the research significantly stronger. Although my work serves the Congo community of Portobelo, Panama, by addressing an absence in scholarship about their cultural contributions to the development of the Republic and the cultural history of the Americas, I felt exposed by my student's question because I knew that my work did not yet effectively respond to a call from the community for a specific type of critical intervention—cultural preservation that might be more accessible and usable within the community.

For years, I had shared my photographs and recordings on a small scale with local families, but that did not effectively contribute to a communitywide cultural preservation initiative. Originally, the idea of how I might do that baffled me and far exceeded my skills and resources. By the time the student posed the question to me, however, user-friendly, open-source digital tools and greater support—in the form of monetary resources, trained personnel, and expanding digital infrastructures within my home institution as well as in Portobelo—made more plausible the possibility of responding to the community's call through a digital intervention. So, instead of merely responding to the student's question based on where I thought the project succeeded as a work of critical/performance ethnography, I decided to talk about the horizon of possibility still open for it and how I hoped to help it to explore that horizon. In doing so, I imagined aloud, for the first time, the broad strokes of what would become Digital Portobelo: Art + Scholarship + Cultural Preservation (digitalportobelo.org).

Digital Portobelo is a collaborative, interdisciplinary, digital humanities initiative that seeks to 1) establish a dual-language (English/Spanish) digital space for researchers to return the stories, interviews, photographs, and videos we have collected to the population(s) from which they came; 2) foster a collaborative digital environment in which community members and researchers can share information, correct absences and errors, and create ongoing dialogues related to Congo traditions and culture; 3) create a mechanism for local community members to archive and share their cultural practices and memories; 4) develop skills in the local community for recording and studying oral history through a curriculum on media literacy and production; 5) contribute to the growing body of work on Afro-Latinidad and on the complexity of Afro-Panamanian history and culture; and 6) offer academic communities a new digital resource through which to study Afro-Latin history and culture in our classrooms as well as through our research experiences. Digital Portobelo represents my effort to evolve alongside the community and to create a more dynamic space for us to share and co-create using digital technologies to complement and extend the face-to-face work we do together.

After receiving an inaugural 2013 UNC Digital Innovations Lab/Institute for the Arts and Humanities (DIL/IAH) fellowship, my research team[2] and I implemented the first of several developmental stages. We concentrated on gathering existing interviews and archival materials from international researchers as well as from community members in Portobelo to establish a digital repository. To initiate this process, we began with my own research.

In January 2013 I lined up over a decade's worth of Hi8, VHS, VHSC, mini DV, and audio cassette tapes from my research in Portobelo, Panama, to digitize them.[3] The process left me feeling both liberated and nostalgic. For my work, this first step toward "becoming digital" meant trading fat and skinny material objects with texture and weight for something "other" "elsewhere"—translating present, tangible objects that live in my home into distant, hyperlinked files that live on servers and external hard drives. As plastic objects, these meaning-filled coils of qualitative "data" are limited to their containers and to my ability to access them. Translated into a universal language of zeros and ones, they offer the possibility to reach out as well as reach back—to create new networks through which the research may more easily connect with intimate community knowledge and other research in order to round out our collective view of Portobelo's past and nuance the questions we are able to ask in the future.

With $15,000 of funding and additional in-kind support, my research team and I worked in collaboration with the DIL for over a year to begin the process of not only digitizing audio- and videotaped interviews but also transcribing, translating, and digitally coding/tagging them and creating a semiflexible organizational schema that would make the material searchable in ways that honored the dynamism of cultural terms and the plurality of identity claims that help give the work its context. Moreover, we worked with digital specialists to design the website within a WordPress environment that would be more navigable to scholars, like me, with only a general knowledge of website logics with the hope of creating a digital product that collaborators in the United States and Panama could eventually be trained to access and augment without a centralized gatekeeper.

In December 2013 my research team and I launched a prototype/proof-of-concept version of Digital Portobelo that reflects the first phase of the project. Built with the Digital Innovation Lab's new Digital Humanities toolkit (DH Press), it features an online searchable repository of written and performed scholarship, including visual art, audio and video interviews with English and Spanish transcripts, and short contextual videos on the Congo community of Portobelo. In addition, it begins to pull together content from disparate sources to demonstrate the ways in which the project might become a space of collaboration among scholars and the community.

The second phase of the project focuses on community engagement. It seeks to create an opportunity for Portobelo community members and international scholars to engage with the technologies and rubrics built in phase 1 in order to open a space for intergenerational, intercultural, and interdisciplinary dialogues with the existing research as well as creating new material. This phase seeks to create a series of workshops, presentations, and dialogical encounters with and between the three communities most intimately connected to this project—scholars focused on Afro-Latin identity and culture in the Americas, cultural practitioners and preservationists interested in the potential of Digital Portobelo for this and allied projects, and educators interested in the ways that the project might serve as a pedagogical tool. It also seeks feedback on the site's usability and encourages communities to enter into documented dialogue with the material and each other.

To initialize that process within Portobelo, several team members and I will return there in 2014–15 to engage in a pilot, community-based, intergenerational oral history project that will pair a small group of four-to-five upper middle and high school students with community elders in order to prompt local engagement with Digital Portobelo as an interactive repository and collaborative tool. The intergenerational community-based oral history project will 1) provide experiential training in the ethics and praxis of conducting, preserving, and sharing oral histories; 2) create opportunities for student–elder partners to discuss the relationship between the Congo tradition as represented in their lived experiences and as represented and analyzed in scholarly research; 3) offer a platform and format for community members to enter into dialogue with existing research through Digital Portobelo's social media tools; 4) provide the methodological tools necessary for each partner pair to conceptualize and conduct two oral history projects, one initiated by the student and the other by the elder; and 5) work with participants to incorporate artifacts from their personal and communal archives into their projects as part of their process. Additionally, working with the intergenerational pairs will help to point out barriers to access and understanding that may exist with the project as well as errors in content or context. Our deeper in-person conversations may evince creative solutions that might otherwise escape my research team and me.

Our work in this second phase will reflect the digital projects created through the community-based intergenerational oral history initiative. Participants will work with team members and me to collaboratively edit, transcribe, and curate these histories. We plan to share them with the Portobelo community through two performative presentations: one at the town's middle school to an audience of students and faculty members, and another at La Casa de La Cultura Congo for an audience of local community members. The presentations will be processed and uploaded to the Digital Portobelo website for global engagement. As an ongoing process, we will continue to incorporate additional interviews, videos, and archival material into Digital Portobelo to help it achieve its purpose of serving as a dynamic collaborative space.

Expanding my performance-centered work to critically incorporate digital tools and methods has given me a way to work collaboratively with the Portobelo community to address its need to better preserve its culture while advancing scholarship about it. As a powerful complement to my critical/ performance ethnographic work, digital technologies have the potential to 1) expand opportunities for dynamic, sustainable, mutually beneficial collaborations across geographic locations; 2) narrow the ideological space between researchers and the communities within which we work, especially when we return "home" from "the field"; and 3) lower barriers to access by providing open-source, user-friendly platforms that allow for more organic co-creation, critique, and consumption.

Likewise, approaching the digital humanities with tools, methods, and analytics gleaned from my location as a performance-centered critical ethnographer opens the potential to 1) challenge and expand notions of "open-access"; 2) critically engage with digital tools and the products we make of them as nonneutral cultural artifacts that circulate within plural cultural and political economies often unwrapped from the careful contexts in which we bundle them; 3) create partnerships between computer scientists, humanities scholars, web designers, program developers, and community members to analyze the ways in which some existing digital rubrics sometimes flatten the complexity of qualitative research through the translations necessary to make the work legible within more quantitative computational systems; and 4) explore those existing limits as productive challenges that might simultaneously "grow" the technology as well as lead qualitative researchers to be more explicit about the systems of coding and categorization that guide the analytical work of our projects. In order words, working together to "teach" digital tools how to organize and render our projects with the complexity we intend demands that we critically examine and explain the micro-steps we use to make the material *mean* and *matter* in the particular ways they do in our written and embodied scholarship.

Over the past year, I've had conversations in two countries, toggling between a smartphone texting program called WhatsApp, Facebook, Tumblr, Twitter, and two email accounts in order to meet, plan, and strategize with team member in Atlanta, Georgia; Los Angeles, California; Hillsborough, North Carolina; Durham, North Carolina; and Portobelo, Panama. Digital technologies are a valuable part of my current critical ethnographic toolkit. These virtual opportunities in no way stand in for the persistent need for sustained face-to-face community engagement. However, prior to these technological advances, the gaps between in-person visits were largely filled with short, expensive telephone calls to celebrate or mourn a milestone. Now, the time in between visits is filled with active collaborations and the type of sustained, informal interpersonal contact that enriches our abilities to build meaningful relationships. That said, the global digital divide is deep and wide, especially between rural and urban areas, not to mention the Global North and the Global South. It is not just a question of access but of the quality, speed, cost, and reliability of that access. What new possibilities abound in engaging the products and processes of research through digital technologies? What new frictions arise at the multiple levels of translation when textured, fragmented surfaces can be rendered seemingly smoother? What "back stage" labor, infrastructure, resources, and proficiencies are needed to make the "front stage" visible, navigable, and engaging? What resources, technologies, and proficiencies serve as the "price" of admission? And, through what processes, using which mediums, can that "price" be significantly mitigated? Digital Portobelo aspires to serve as a public platform that might allow researchers and community members to address these questions and find answers *together.*

# NOTES

## Prologue

1. Throughout this book, I refer to the people with whom I work by their full name on first reference and by their first name or pseudonym on subsequent reference. I do so for uniformity and clarity since many interviewees are related and share the same last name.

2. The performance theorist and critical ethnographer Dwight Conquergood (2013) argued that "performance-centered research takes as both its subject matter and method the experiencing body situated in time, place, and history" (92).

3. Enslaved Africans entered Panama in the early 1500s. See Rout (1976) regarding African experiences in Spanish America. See Maria del Carmen Mena Garcia (1984) for a detailed historical account of sixteenth-century Panama including the growth of Black populations. See Archivo General de Indias (1994) for archival information regarding indigenous and African-descended populations in sixteenth- and seventeenth-century Panama. Although a precise percentage is not provided, Webster (1973) indicates that free and enslaved Blacks greatly outnumbered the Spanish in Portobelo by the end of the seventeenth century. For more general historical perspectives of Black populations in Panama, see Roberto de la Guardia (1977) and Alfredo Castillero Calvo (1969). For a brief overview of colonial and West Indian Black presences in Panama, see Luis Díez Castillo (1981).

4. For additional information on Cimarron interaction with English pirates and privateers, see Frederick Rodriguez (1979). See Peter Earle (2007) for historical analysis of English pirate and privateer activity in Panama.

5. According to Robert Ferris Thompson (1984), "Spelling Kongo with a K instead of a C, Africanists distinguish Kongo civilization and the Bakongo people from the colonial entity called the Belgian Congo (now Zaire) and the present-day People's Republic of Congo-Brazzaville, both of which include numerous non-Kongo peoples. Traditional Kongo civilization encompasses modern Bas-Zaire and neighboring territories in modern Cabinda,

Congo-Brazzaville, Gabon, and northern Angola [. . .] The slavers of the early 1500s first applied the name 'Kongo' solely to the Bakongo people. Then gradually they used the name to designate any person brought from the west coast of Central Africa to America" (103).

6. Depending on its context, the word may mean to "be" Congo, which signifies one's participation in the tradition; to "dance" Congo, which refers to the male–female partner dance at the heart of the tradition; to "play" Congo, which signifies the game between those characters dressed as Congo/Blacks and those dressed as Devils/Enslavers; or to participate in the Congo "drama," which is the narrative that the community acts out between Carnival Tuesday and Ash Wednesday.

7. Variant "Congo" and "Cimarron" communities exist in the Caribbean and along the Atlantic coast of the Americas, including Cuba, Jamaica, Venezuela, and Brazil. All have related, although distinct, Black cultural performances marking their specific colonial Black experience. I was first introduced to the Congo tradition of Portobelo, Panama, through Arturo Lindsay, Sandra Eleta, the Spelman College Portobelo Panama Summer Art Colony, and Taller Portobelo. Their generous gifts of resources, feedback, insight, community, and friendship have been invaluable.

8. Some form of Carnival took root in nearly every country colonized by the Spanish, French, and Portuguese. All celebrate the power of resistance, creativity, parody, and community. However, unlike the larger, more commercial Trinidadian or Brazilian models, Carnival in Portobelo consists primarily of homemade costumes and local celebrants.

9. According to personal interviews and my own observations over the past fouteen years, the role of the Queen is to provide central leadership to the Congo organization, to gather the group when they agree to perform for a special occasion, and to act as their main organizational contact person. In the first performance of the Congo drama, "El Diablo Tun Tun," the Devil attempts to capture the Queen, the seat of Congo power, but the Congos help her trick him and subdue him before he is able to do so. The three most important primary characters in the Congo drama are the Queen, the Major Devil, and Pajarito.

## Introduction

1. The town of Portobelo is the capital of the Portobelo district, which reported a population of 1,874 in the 2000 census. For the purpose of this study, the name "Portobelo" always refers to the town, which reported 286 residents in 2000 (Instituto Nacional 2000).

2. The term "Afro-Panamanian" is used by Van Gronigen-Warren and Lowe de Goodin in lieu of "etnia negra" or "Black ethnicity," but it does not appear in the original law. Ley No. 9 del 30 de mayo de 2000 refers to the celebration and the group it commemorates as *etnia negra*.

3. In Panama Congo traditions, male practitioners use either charcoal or indigo on their faces as camouflage.

4. Elsa's response stands alongside similar community responses, which I engage in chapter 1, that point to a mid-twentieth-century period when official discourses constructed "Black" to mean other/foreign/non-Panamanian. The material consequences of these discourses were codified in the briefly upheld 1941 constitution, which listed as "prohibited immigrants" those who did not add to the "*mejoramiento étnico*" ("ethnic improvement") of the country. Translated, this included "the black race whose native language is not Spanish, the Yellow race and the native races of India, Asia Minor and North Africa" (Constitución 1941).

5.  Ronald Smith, Patricia Lund Drolet, Arturo Lindsay, Luz Graciela Joly, John Lipski, and former Portobelo Congo Queen Maricel "Paloma" Martín Zuñigan have all conducted substantial studies of specific Congo ritual, dance, linguistic, and iconographic elements. Each contributes to a body of knowledge regarding the ways that the tradition exists in the "official consciousness" of its practitioners. Based largely on the Congo community of Colón, Panama, Smith's (1976) ethnomusicological study provides a close analysis of the Congo performance as practiced in its ritualized form during Carnival season. He examines the historical background and context of specific Congo characters as well as the instruments and songs through which the tradition is expressed. Drolet's (1980) dissertation and subsequent publication through the Instituto Nacional de Cultura in Panama resulted from her two years of ethnographic research in Costa Arriba with eight Congo communities. Like Smith, Drolet places the tradition in the context of colonization and enslavement in Panama. Whereas Smith approaches the tradition as "Afro-Panamanian," Drolet focuses on the Congo ritual as an "African-American" mode of cultural and ecological adaptation in Panama (5). As such, she focuses on the ways Congo rituals represent elements of their tropical environment as well as reinvent them (250). For the past twenty years, Lindsay (2000b, 2003, 2005) has been studying, participating in, and creating visual art and essays focused on the Congo tradition as it is enacted in Portobelo. In addition to providing a Portobelo-centered history of the tradition, his work focuses on African spiritual retentions in the tradition, Congo aesthetics, and the work of El Taller Portobelo art workshop, which he co-founded, in the process of cultural preservation and economic empowerment. Providing a narrative analysis of the tradition from an insider's perspective, Zuñigan's 2002 contribution is the first published work on the Congo tradition in Panama by a practitioner. Joly's 1981 study and Lipski (1986) focus on the Congo dialect; the latter specifically argues that "the congo [sic] dialect mode, though obviously distorted by the passing of time, is in all likelihood an indication of the prior existence of more legitimate creole Spanish" (418).

6.  Although a large migration of the West Indians arrived in Panama as Canal laborers, some arrived in the early years of Panama's history. An official census of Panama City taken in 1610 lists 548 citizens, 303 women, 156 children, 146 mulattos, 148 Antillean Blacks (West Indians), and 3,500 African slaves (Meditz and Hanratty 1987a). As a category, "citizens" includes only Spanish men, and the categories "women" and "children" refer only to Spanish women and children. It is evident that the enslaved population at the beginning of the seventeenth century was more than twice the size of all the other groups combined.

7.  David Theo Goldberg (2002) discusses this conception of race as a mark of modernity. "Race," he argues, "is imposed upon otherness, the attempt to account for it, to know it, to control it. . . . What becomes increasing racially conceived is the threat, the external, the unknown, the outsider" (23). Until 2010, the 1940 census (Instituto Nacional 1943) was the last Panamanian census to include racial classification. At that time, the terms included "*Blanca*/White," "*Negra*/Black," "*Mestiza*/Mixed," and "*Otras Razas*/Other." Although race was eliminated as a category from the Panamanian census, U.S. governmental and nongovernmental agencies continue to track and record it. According to information gathered between 1999 and 2000 by members of the American Chamber of Commerce and Industry of Panama, 65 percent of Panamanians (out of 2.7 million) were *mestiza* (European-Indian mixed), and the other 35 percent were a combination of traditional Indians, Caribbean Blacks, Europeans, and Chinese (Instituto Panameño 2006a; page discontinued). Comparatively, statistical data collected by U.S. governmental sources in 2000 claims that 70 percent of the then 2,808,268 population categorized themselves as *mestiza* (mixed Amer-

indian and White), 14 percent Amerindian and mixed (West Indian), 10 percent White, and 6 percent Amerindian (Panama 2002b). According to the same report, 85 percent of the population is Roman Catholic and 15 percent is Protestant; 86 percent speaks Spanish (the country's official language) and the remaining 14 percent speaks English. Congos exist primarily in the majority 85 to 86 percent of the population who are Roman Catholic and speak Spanish, while West Indians exist primarily in the 14 to 15 percent of the population that is Protestant and speaks English. Therefore, "hispanicized" Blacks like the Congos are likely categorized as *mestiza,* while West Indian descendants are more commonly designated as "Caribbean Black."

8. The Panama Canal Treaty ensured complete turnover of the canal to Panama by December 31, 1999.

9. In *Of Revelation and Revolution: The Dialectic of Modernity on a South African Frontier,* John L. and Jean Comaroff (1997) theorize "dialectic" as a way to engage with voices, bodies, subjectivities, and/or performatives that are always co-transformative, but often with unequal access to power, privilege, movement, voice, and agency.

## Chapter 1

1. An earlier version of this chapter was published as an essay in *Latin American and Caribbean Ethnic Studies* 3(2): 123–26.

2. In some renditions, *hombres*/men replace *blancos*/whites.

3. I am grateful to the retired University of Panama English Professor and founding president of Society of the Friends of the Afroantillean Museum of Panama, Melva Lowe de Goodin, for providing me with a copy of the report and action plan "Recognition and Total Inclusion of Black Ethnicity in Panamanian Society" and for the generosity, insight, and resources she has shared with me over the life of this project. For more information on the contributions of African-descended populations to Panama, see her 2012 publication entitled *Afrodescendientes en el Istmo de Panamá.*

4. For scholarship on the United States and Panama in the 1850s via the California Gold Rush, see Aims McGuinness (2008, 2003). For work on the 1856 Watermelon Riot, see Mercedes Chen Daley (1990). For eighteenth- and nineteenth-century population analysis in Panama, see Omar Jaén Suárez (1998).

5. I employ the term "micro-diaspora" to talk about the departure and return of Black Atlantic citizens within one local Black Atlantic location.

6. The Panama Canal building project was initiated by the French in 1880. The French construction period (1881–89) ended as a result of disease (especially malaria and yellow fever) and of underestimating the cost and labor of the project. For a comprehensive history of the Canal building project, see McCullough (1977).

7. As defined by the Commission's report, *afrohispano* refers to all persons of Black ethnicity who reside in Spain or identify with Hispanic culture.

8. As defined by the Commission's report, *afrolatino* refers to all persons of Black ethnicity who reside in Latin America or identify with Latin American culture.

9. As defined by the Commission's report, *Diaspora Africana* refers to African descendants in the Americas as well as other continents and regions of the world.

10. Introduced by the Martiniquen poet and political activist Aimé Césaire, who founded a major literary movement under its banner in the 1940s, "négritude" is "a concept that denotes the positive features of blackness among people classed as, or self-identifying as,

'black'" (Whitten and Torres 1988, 7). Haiti is the only country in the Americas wherein négritude as a state-sponsored practice of nationalism took hold (9). On the other hand, "Mestizaje, the ideology of racial intermingling, is an explicit master symbol in all Latin American countries" (7).

11. For additional scholarship related to West Indian identity, politics, and anti-racism activism in Panama and as well as broader discourses of etnia negra inclusion and exclusion, see George Priestley and Alberto S. Barrow (2008), Priestley (1986), George Maloney and Jorge Arosemena (1979), Armando Fortune (1956a, 1956b, 1967a, 1967b) Dawn Duke (2010), and Sonja Watson (2009). See also Ifeoma Nwankwo's digital history project focused in part on Afro-Panamanian history and culture entitled *Voices from Our America,* http://voicesamerica.library.vanderbilt.edu/home.php.

12. I am grateful to Northwestern University Professor of African American Studies and Professor of History Darlene Clark Hine, who offered the term "internationalization of Jim Crow" after reading an earlier version of this article.

13. In writing (in)dependence using performative syntax, I intend to mark the provisional nature of Panama's U.S.-assisted "separation" from Colombia.

14. I agree with critics of Turner's social drama model, like Drewal (1994), who argue against privileging ritual structure over human agency and improvisation. In extrapolating his model to look at moments of heightened nationalism, I have bracketed each period based on activities and actions led by agents of the U.S. government, the Panamanian government, and/or African-descended communities in Panama.

15. Although the Congo tradition exists in various Colonial Black communities along the Caribbean coast of Panama, Portobelo, the probable home of the tradition (Smith 1976, 64), is consistently the only town cited in national and international tourist literature associated with the Congos.

16. For analyses of mestizaje, Blackness, and nation see, for example, Norman Whitten and Arlene Torres (1988), Michael Hanchard (1994), Peter Wade (2003, 2004, 2000, 1997), and Lourdes Martinez-Echazabal (1998).

17. Although contemporary Congo members self-identify as "Black," demographic categories officially tracking ethnoracial background prior to the 2010 census have reserved that label for West Indians. The 1940 census was the last Panamanian census to include a range of racial classifications. At that time, the terms included "*Blanca*/White," "*Negra*/Black," "*Mestiza*/Mixed," and "*Otras Razas*/Other Races." Although the 2010 census included race, it focused exclusively on indigenous people and those of African descent. Any ethnoracial identity outside of those categories was classified as "Other" (Instituto Nacional 2010, 1943).

18. Just as the members of the Congo community of Portobelo consistently link their tradition generally to "Los Cimarrones," so, too, do they define their tradition as related to "Africa."

19. According to Meditz and Hanratty (1987a), a 1610 census lists 148 Antillean Blacks, 146 mulattos, and 3,500 African slaves in a total population of 4,801.

20. According to Mitchell (1998), the total population in the Canal in 1912 was 63,000. Brenton lists the total number of contracted West Indian workers between 1904 and 1914 at 31,071, which is corroborated by information generated by the Panama Canal Authority. The Authority also lists the number of contract workers on the Zone (excluding those recruited from the United States) at 33,270. By 1914 West Indians represented 93 percent of non-U.S. contract workers. David McCullough (1977) lists the total number of White "North Americans" living in the Canal in 1914 at approximately 6,000 (2,500 of whom were women and children) (559). Because a large number of West Indians lived in shantytowns outside the

Zone, many of which were constructed during the time of the French Canal, it is also likely that groups of West Indians and Afro-Colonials had some type of daily contact.

21. In the 1846 Mallarino–Bidland Treaty signed between Columbia and the United States, the latter agreed to guarantee the neutrality of the route that would eventually encompass both the railroad and the Canal. In 1903 the Hay–Bunau-Varilla Treaty granted the Canal Zone "in perpetuity" to the United States.

22. The resentment during the Republic's first decade directed toward the United States and, by association, English-speaking West Indians had been sharpened by fifty years of contact and confrontation with U.S. interests starting with the California Gold Rush (1850–69). The blatant racism, arrogance, ruthlessness, and lawlessness left a negative impression. See Alan McPherson (2003).

23. In the case of African American workers on the Canal, the United States elevated their race above their nationality in order to relegate them to "silver roll" status. See Patrice C. Brown (1997). For detailed studies of West Indian "silver roll" workers, see Biesanz (1949, 1950), Newton (1984), Michael Conniff (1985, 1992), R. S. Bryce-Laporte (1998), and Trevor O'Reggio (2006).

24. Until the early 1970s, Afro-Colonial communities were concentrated primarily along the Atlantic coast (Costa Arriba) and were accessible only by boat.

25. Vasco Núñez de Balboa was the first European *conquistador* on record to successfully lead an expedition from the Caribbean side of Panama to the Pacific and claim the Pacific Ocean for the Spanish crown. Subsequently, as Conniff (1994) summarizes, "Panama served as a staging area for the exploration and conquest of the entire Pacific side of South America. Europeans and Africans, equipped with boats and arms, arrived at the Atlantic harbor of Portobelo. From there they moved across the narrow Isthmus and were organized into quasi-military expeditions at the Pacific port of Panama" (113).

26. Approximately one-fourth of Portobelo District's population, for example, relocated to urban centers in search of employment. According to information generated by the Panamanian Treasury Department (Controlaría General), Portobelo's population decreased from 2,191 in 1930 to 1,704 by 1970, whereas Colón's population increased from 33,460 to 48,939 (Dirección 1998).

27. This was the Madden Dam portion of the Canal.

28. Title 2, Article 12 B specifically refers to "*la raza negra cuyo idioma originario no sea el Castellano* [the Black race whose original language is not Spanish]."

29. Arnulfo began his first presidential term in October 1940 and was deposed within the year. He would occupy the position and be deposed twice more for increasingly shorter terms: one year in his first term (October 1, 1940–October 9, 1941), eighteen months in his second (November 24 1949–May 9, 1951), and ten days in his third (October 1–11, 1968).

30. My emphasis.

31. Twenty-one martyrs are honored on a monument located in the former Canal Zone. They are Maritza Alabarca, Ascanio Arosemena, Rodolfo Benitez, Luis Bonilla, Alberto Constance, Gonzalo Crance, Teofilo de la Torre, Jose del Cid, Victor Garibaldo, Jose Gil, Ezequiel Gonzalez, Victor Iglesias, Rosa Landecho, Carlos Lara, Gustavo Lara, Ricardo Murgas, Estanislao Orobio, Jacinto Palacios, Ovidio Saldaña, Alberto Tejada, and Celestino Villarreta. However, reports vary on the exact number of Panamanian casualties. As Eric Jackson (1999) states, "Various casualty figures for the several days of fighting which became known to Panamanians as the Day of the Martyrs range from 20 to 30 dead and 200 to 579 injured. The total number of dead and wounded is disputed not only due to

political motives but also different judgments about how to attribute certain incidents. For a number of reasons, not the least of which was fear that jobs or pensions with the Panama Canal Company could be lost, many of the injured were not taken to hospitals, or injuries of those who were taken to hospitals were not officially reported."

32. *Campesinos* are small farmers generally from interior regions like that of Torrijos's birth.

33. One of the unfortunate side effects of this migratory shift was that interior populations accustomed to slash-and-burn farming unintentionally sped the rate of deforestation in rain-forest areas like Portobelo as they transplanted their agricultural traditions without understanding the land or its rate of recovery. I am grateful to the sociologist Cecilia Moreno Rojas for first bringing this to my attention.

34. D. Arroyo's (1946) account and supporting statistical data indicate that Portobelo, like the rest of Panama, experienced its first major wave of twentieth-century immigration as a result of Canal laborers. Now a lush mountain of trees with the ruins of San Felipe fort and a few modest homes, from 1907–14 the land across the Portobelo bay housed U.S. military personnel and Canal workers who transplanted gravel from the area to fortify Gatun Locks, the Atlantic mouth of the Canal (78; McCullough 1977, 594). Over the life of the project, Portobelo's population, which began at 738, more than tripled. The population fluctuated around two thousand for the next six decades until its second major wave of immigration in the 1970s (Dirección 1998). Arroyo also makes it clear that Portobeleños worked on the Nuevo Portobelo project, which built quarries to excavate rock to build the Canal, and interacted with other Canal workers socially. The annual Congo tradition probably would have been performed in its ritual form at least seven times during this building process, exposing it to this new immigrant community, some members of which undoubtedly became permanent residents whose descendants became incorporated into the community and the tradition.

35. After the Carter–Torrijos Treaty was signed in 1977, several seminal initiatives helped lay the groundwork for "Afro-Panamanian" political, cultural, and economic development. These included the Primer Congreso del Negro Panameño (First Congress of the Black Panamanian); Segundo Congreso de Cultura Negra de la América (Second Congress of Black Culture in America), which was the second of three meetings held in Columbia (1977), Panama (1980), and Brazil (1982); and the establishment of El Centro de Estudios Afropanameños (the Center for the Study of Afro-Panamanians). For more information on Black political movements and race relations in Panama, see Gerardo Maloney (1989, 1983).

36. El Chorrillo also includes a sizable Chinese population, which suffered the same types of discrimination and degradations directed against West Indians and whose communities sustained grave losses in 1964 as well as 1989.

# Chapter 2

1. For more about Cimarron history in Panama, see Rodriguez (1979).

2. Although a precise percentage is not provided, Edwin Webster (1973) indicates that free and enslaved Blacks greatly outnumbered the Spanish in Portobelo by the end of the seventeenth century (13). Baptismal records, which may have provided additional clues to the number of enslaved people living in Portobelo during this period, have long since been destroyed by fire and/or the environment. The few records that remain are likely stored in

Los Archivos de Indios in Seville, Spain. Although it is outside the scope of this study, future researchers will likely find crucial keys to the Black experience in colonial Portobelo located within those archives.

3. This is a 6.92 percent increase from the 2000 census, which recorded 3,867 inhabitants of the town but did not provide additional ethnoracial data.

4. For the ways in which Panama's 2010 census model relates with reckonings about race in other parts of Latin America, see Katie Zien (2009).

5. This initiative, often referred to as the "Colonization of the Atlantic," is explained in chapter 1.

6. See Lok Siu (2005) regarding the ways in which small Chinese communities, anchored to family-owned groceries and markets, are part of the current ethnoracial landscape of Portobelo and other Congo coastal communities like it.

7. For an analysis of the popular artwork that adorns Panama's "Diablo Rojo" buses, see Peter Szok (2012).

8. Homes in Portobelo have no addresses. Mail is collected at the post office in Sabanitas, a neighboring town approximately forty-five minutes away by bus, or in Colón city, which is approximately an hour-and-a-half bus trip.

9. All of the interviews in this chapter and throughout the book took place in Portobelo unless otherwise noted. They were transcribed by Gustavo Esquina and translated into English by Oronike Odeleye. The original Spanish transcriptions can be found in the archives section of digitalportobelo.org. Because of the pace at which digital infrastructure changes, I have listed the permanent site URL rather than a link to the specific page.

10. Sebastian is the patron saint of athletes, warriors, and sufferers of plague. In Brazil and some Latin American countries, there is a syncretism between this Christian saint and Oshosi, the Yoruba patron or orisha of hunters. Additional research needs to be done exploring the relationship and relevance of this syncretism to the temporal frame of the Panama Congo traditions.

11. According to personal interviews and my own observations over the past fourteen years, the role of the Queen is to provide central leadership to the Congo organization, to gather the group when they agree to perform for a special occasion, and to act as their main organizational contact person. In the first performance of the Congo drama, "El Diablo Tun Tun," the Devil attempts to capture the Queen, the seat of Congo power, but the Congos help her trick him and subdue him before he is able to do so. The three most important characters in the Congo drama are the Queen, the Major Devil, and Pajarito.

12. Lindsay (2005) expands upon this meaning and purpose of the Angels and Souls in the Congo tradition by arguing that "the archangel represents a benevolent spirit being who is charged with the responsibility of leading the *ánimas* in a quest to capture all of the Devils in town during the Carnival celebrations and have them blessed. . . . They are tortured souls of Africans who have not yet found eternal peace" (6).

13. Zuñigan spells this as "Rebellín" in the text, but "Revellín" is consistent with spellings in other interviews and sources in her book's glossary of terms. I translated this section of Zuñigan's text.

14. The Spanish text was adapted from a dissertation entitled *La danza de los negros congos en la costa arriba de Colón* by José Domingo Olmos (1980) and translated by me.

15. Although Tatu is a visual artist of Congo performance and moved to Portobelo from Colón as a child, he is not a ritual specialist. At this early stage in my research, I did not yet understand that.

16. Translated by Alexander Craft.

# Chapter 3

1. See also Todorov (1984). Mikhail Bakhtin introduces the term to literary studies from mathematics. In Todorov's translation, Bakhtin explains chronotope as a spatial-temporal model similar to a metaphor but not the same (14). Gilroy (1993a) defines it as "an optic for reading texts as x-rays of the forces at work in the cultural system from which they spring" (4).

2. Roach (1996) defines "surrogation" as the never-ending process by which communities attempt to fill a perceived loss (2).

3. "Viudo Ceballos" is a phonetic spelling based on our taperecorded interview, which was transcribed by the Congo practitioner and project collaborator Gustavo Esquina.

4. This interview was transcribed by Gustavo Esquina and translated by Arturo Lindsay and Oronike Odeleye.

# Chapter 4

1. See Alexander Craft (2008a) for an earlier version of this chapter as an essay that was published in *Transforming Anthropology: Journal of the Association of Black Anthropologists*.

2. As Besson (1993) makes clear, the gendered separation between respectability and reputation is much more complicated than Wilson's binary allows. Elements of male culture may fit under the rubric of "respectability" just as easily as those of female culture fit under "reputation" (Besson 1993; Burton 1997). Likewise, Douglass (1992) and Karen Fog Olwig (1993) have used cultural hybridity arguments to critique the relationship that Wilson establishes linking respectability almost exclusively to foreign values.

3. Elsa is the daughter of Celedonio Molinar Ávila, the most renowned twentieth-century Major Devil in the Congo tradition of Portobelo, Panama.

4. In the Black Diaspora, using the guise of complicity has often been strongly related to what Toni Morrison (1997) refers to as a "strategy" of Du Bois's double consciousness—as method rather than as state-of-being. De Certeau (1984) discusses the ways consumers/users undermine the power of producers/makers through procedures of consumption that subvert dominant rites, rituals, and representations (18). I am also borrowing the notion of "trick back" posited by Marta E. Savigliano (1995).

5. For an analysis of the continuity between colonial and contemporary modes of Caribbean consumption and their relationship to tourism, see Mimi Sheller (2003).

6. See also Patricia Ann Schechter (2001), E. Frances White (2001), and Victoria Wolcott (2001).

7. The Congo dialect is a form of creolized Spanish that relies on reversals of meaning as a form of linguistic play. For research on the Congo dialect, see Luz Graciela Joly (1981) and John Lipski (1992). Maricel Martín Zuñigan (2002) includes a glossary with the Spanish equivalent of various words and phrases in the Congo dialect of Portobelo.

8. A total of 119,024 tourists visited Panama from the United States in 2003, compared with 49,045 from Central America, 30,425 from the Caribbean, and 38,845 from Europe—a combined total of 118,315. With the exception of Colombia, which provided 90,159 visitors in 2003, U.S. citizens traveled to Panama five times more than those of any of other country (Instituto Panameño 2006b; page discontinued).

9. There is a body of scholarship on this subject related to Jamaican dancehall. See, for example, Carolyn Cooper (1995, 2004), and Norman C. Stolzoff (2000).

10. In the last decade, a small constellation of homes has been converted to a villa-style hotel, and an exclusive luxury resort has been constructed on the opposite side of the bay, which is accessible by helicopter or boat. A hostel has also been constructed at the far end of one local neighborhood.

11. "My Name is Panamá" is a clothing brand in Panama.

## Chapter 5

1. According to Lindsay (2005), "all of the artists in the Taller have used dot patterns in their work at different times in their careers" (5). In informal conversations, Lindsay has shared that he was working in this style when he first began painting in Portobelo. He hypothesizes that some of the early Congo artists picked it up, in the spirit of workshop sharing, as they began developing their individual artistic talent and style.

2. The Portobelo Fairs took place between 1574 and 1702.

3. The alternative routes were a cross-country trip across the wilderness of the United States or a trip by sea around the tip of South America.

4. Following Robert Farris Thompson (1984), I use "Kongo Atlantic World" to mean the "new world" created as a result of the dispersal of enslaved Africans from the former "Kongo" kingdoms throughout the Americas. As he states, "Kongo civilization and art were not obliterated in the New World: they resurfaced in the coming together, here and there, of numerous slaves from Kongo and Angola. Kongo presence unexpectedly emerges in the Americas in many places and in many ways" (104).

5. As Robert Farris Thompson (1984) states, the Kongo Cosmogram served as "the Kongo sign of cosmos and the continuity of human life" (109). Depicted in the form of a cross (*yowa*) with four equal arms, "the Kongo *yowa* cross does not signify the crucifixion of Jesus for the salvation of mankind; it signifies the equally compelling vision of the circular motion of human souls about the circumference of its intersecting lines. The Kongo cross refers therefore to the everlasting continuity of *all* righteous men and women" (108; emphasis in original).

6. The names of the women and the organization are pseudonyms. Neither the women nor the organization are the intended focus of the anecdote. I include them because of what our dialogical encounter revealed about our interpretations of ownership, agency, and difference, which were anchored to ideological perspectives gleaned from inhabiting the world in bodies with different relationships to colonialism, neocolonialism, and racism. Our unintended *El museo congo* meta-performance exposed the real and imagined power dynamics tugging at our everyday interactions and cultural perceptions of one another.

## Epilogue

1. Portobelo is a UNESCO World Heritage Site. Following a meeting of its 36th Convention in St. Petersburg, Russia, in 2012, the World Heritage Committee mandated that Portobelo put additional protective measures in place in order to maintain its listing as such (UNESCO 2012).

2. My team members include Oronike Odeleye (transcription, translation, and Creative Currents collaborative partner), Gustavo Esquina (transcription, translation), Roni Nicole (photographer and videographer), Andrew Synowiez, (photographer, videographer),

Michelle Lanier (curriculum development for pilot community oral history project), Rachel Cotterman (preliminary oral history curriculum design), Lindsay Foster Thomas (audio processing, audio editing, external social media), Pam Lach (UNC DH Press and Digital Integration Project manager), Sandra Davidson (formatting and processing transcripts data), Mishio Yamanaka (processing and formatting transcript data), Joe Hope (DH Press developer), and the infrastructure provided by the Carolina Digital Humanities Initiative and UNC Digital Innovations Lab.

3. I want to offer a special thanks to UNC–CH Digital Innovation Lab undergraduate students for their contributions to the project. Charlotte Fryar performed the initial digitization of the interviews. Anna Faison assisted with final revisions to the interactive project.

# REFERENCES

Abrahams, Roger D. 1983. *The Man-of-Words in the West Indies: Performance and the Emergence of Creole Culture*. Baltimore: Johns Hopkins University Press.

Acosta-Belén, Edna. 1993. *Researching Women in Latin America and the Caribbean*. Boulder, CO: Westview.

Alexander, Bryant Keith. 2006. *Performing Black Masculinity: Race, Culture, and Queer Identity*. Lanham, MD: AltaMira.

Alexander, Bryant Keith, and Omi Osun Joni L. Jones. 2013. "A Poetic and Performative Synthesis." *Text and Performance Quarterly* 33 (3): 251–57.

Alexander, Renée Jacqueline. 2006. *Art as Survival: The Congo Tradition of Portobelo, Panama*. PhD diss., Northwestern University.

———. 2003. *Mojonga: A Performative Altar to Former Congo Queens*. Installation performance directed by Renée Jacqueline Alexander. Taller Portobelo, Panama.

———. 2002. *Dancing with the Devil at the Crossroads: La historia de los congos de Portobelo*. Directed by Renée Jacqueline Alexander. Hal and Martha Hyer Wallis Theatre, Northwestern University, Evanston.

———. 2001a. *La historia de los congos de Portobelo: Translating History Through the Body*. Directed by Renée Jacqueline Alexander. Mussetter-Struble Theatre, Northwestern University, Evanston.

———. 2001b. *Making the Sign of the Cross*. Installation performance directed by Renée Jacqueline Alexander. Taller Portobelo, Panama.

Alexander, Renée Jacqueline, Virgilio "Yaneca" Esquina, Virgilio "Tito" Esquina, Reynaldo Esquina, Ariel Jimenez, Hector Jimenez, Gustavo Esquina de la Espada, José "Moraitho" Angúlo, et al. 2003. *El museo congo*. Curated by Renée Jacqueline Alexander. Taller Portobelo, Panama.

Alexander Craft, Renée. 2008a. "'¡Los gringos vienen!' ('The Gringos Are Coming!'): Female

Respectability and the Politics of Congo Tourist Presentations in Portobelo, Panama." *Transforming Anthropology: Journal of the Association of Black Anthropologists* 16 (1): 20–31.

———. 2008b. "'Una Raza, Dos Etnias': The Politics of Be(com)ing/Performing 'Afropanameño.'" *Latin American and Caribbean Ethnic Studies* 3 (2): 123–26.

Alexander Craft, Renée, Meida McNeal, Mshaï S. Mwangola, and Queen Meccasia E. Zabriskie. 2007. "The Quilt: Towards a Twenty-First Century Black Feminist Ethnography." *Performance Research* 12 (3): 55–73.

Anzaldúa, Gloria. 1987. *Borderlands/La Frontera: The New Mestiza.* San Francisco: Aunt Lute.

Archivo General de Indias. 1994. *Indios y negros en Panamá en los siglos XVI y XVII: Selecciones de los documentos del Archivo General de Indias.* Antigua, Guatemala: Centro de Investigaciones Regionales de Mesoamérica.

Arroyo, D. 1946. *A Portobelo.* Panamá: Impr. Nacional.

Arroyo, Justo. 1995. "Race Relations in Panama." In *African Presence in the Americas,* edited by Carlos Moore, 155–57. Trenton, NJ: Africa World.

Asamblea Legislativa de la República de Panamá. 2000. *Ley por la cual se crea el día de la etnia negra nacional. LEY No. 9.*

Barnes, Natasha. 1999. "Reluctant Matriarch: Sylvia Wynter and the Problematics of Caribbean Feminism." *Small Axe: A Journal of Caribbean Criticism* 5 (March): 34–47.

Bederman, Gail. 1995. *Manliness & Civilization: A Cultural History of Gender and Race in the United States, 1880–1917.* Chicago: University of Chicago Press.

Behar, Ruth. 2013. *Traveling Heavy: A Memoir in between Journeys.* Durham, NC: Duke University Press.

———. 2003. *Translated Woman: Crossing the Border with Esperanza's Story.* 2nd ed. Boston: Beacon.

———. 1997. *The Vulnerable Observer: Anthropology That Breaks Your Heart.* Boston: Beacon.

Béliz, A. 1959. "Los Congos: Afro-Panamanian Dance-Drama." *Américas* 11 (11): 31–3.

Berger, Maurice, ed. 1999. *Adrian Piper—A Retrospective, 1965–2000: Issues in Cultural Theory.* Baltimore: University of Maryland Baltimore County, Fine Arts Gallery.

Besson, Jean. 1993. "Reputation & Respectability Reconsidered: A New Perspective on Afro-Caribbean Peasant Women." In *Women and Change in the Caribbean: A Pan Caribbean Perspective,* edited by Janet Momsen, 15–37. Bloomington: Indiana University Press.

Bhabha, Homi K. 1996. "Day by Day . . . with Frantz Fanon." In *The Fact of Blackness: Frantz Fanon and Visual Representation,* edited by Allen Read, 186–203. Seattle: Bay Press.

———. 1994a. "Interrogating Identity: Frantz Fanon and the Postcolonial Prerogative." In *The Location of Culture,* 40–65. London: Routledge.

———. 1994b. "Introduction: Locations of Culture." In *The Location of Culture,* 1–18. London: Routledge.

Biesanz, John. 1950. "Race Relations in the Canal Zone." *Phylon (1940–1956)* 11 (1): 23–30.

———. 1949. "Cultural and Economic Factors in Panamanian Race Relations." *American Sociological Review* 14 (6): 772–79.

Boyce Davies, Carole. 1999a. "Beyond Unicentricity: Transcultural Black Presences." *Research in African Literatures* 30 (Summer): 96–109.

———. 1999b. "Talking Space: Carnival, Freedom, and Self-Articulation." *Supplement to Caribbean Today,* April, p. 13.

———. 1994. *Black Women, Writing and Identity: Migrations of the Subject.* London: Routledge.

Brecher, John, Beth Nissen, and Joyce Barnathan. 1981. "Panama: Life after Torrijos." *Newsweek*, August 17, p. 46.

Brenton, L. C. T. 2001. "Afro-Antillean Language and Culture in Panama." In *Afro-American Cultural Identity in Language and Literature*, edited by V. Gronigen-Warren, B. Lowe de Goodin, and M. Lowe de Goodin, 74–77. Panamá: Editora Sibauste.

Brooks, Gwendolyn. 1944. *Selected Poems*. New York: Harper & Row.

Brown, Patrice C. 1997. "The Panama Canal: The African American Experience." *Prologue Magazine* 29 (Summer). http://www.archives.gov/publications/prologue/1997/summer/panama-canal.html.

Bruner, Edward. 2004. *Culture on Tour: Ethnographies of Travel*. Chicago: University of Chicago Press.

Bryce-Laporte, R. S. 1988. "Crisis, Contraculture, and Religion among West Indians in the Panama Canal Zone." In *Blackness in Latin America and the Caribbean: Social Dynamics and Cultural Transformations*, edited by N. E. Whitten Jr. and A. Torres, 100–18. Bloomington: Indiana University Press.

Bureau of International Narcotics and Law Enforcement Affairs. 2008. "International Narcotics Control Strategy Report—2008." *Panama News*. March 9–22. http://www.thepanamanews.com/pn/v_14/issue_05/news_07.html.

Burton, Richard D. 1997. *Afro/Creole: Power, Opposition, and Play in the Caribbean*. Ithaca, NY: Cornell University Press.

Butler, Judith. 1990. "Performative Acts and Gender Constitution: An Essay in Phenomenology and Feminist Theory." In *Performing Feminisms: Feminist Critical Theory and Theatre*, edited by Sue-Ellen Case, 270–82. Baltimore: Johns Hopkins University Press.

Calvo, Alfredo Castillero. 1969. *Los negros y mulatos libres en la historia social panameña*. Panamá: s.n.

Castro, Fidel. 1990. "The Resistance of Panama's People Is of Truly Historic Significance." In *Panama: The Truth about the U.S. Invasion*, 30–44. New York: Pathfinder.

Castro, Nils. 1990. "Panama's Only Sin Is Refusing to Go Down on Its Knees." In *Panama: The Truth about the U.S. Invasion*, 22–29. New York: Pathfinder.

Certeau, Michel de. 1988. *The Writing of History*. New York: Columbia University Press.

———. 1984. *The Practice of Everyday Life*. Berkeley: University of California Press.

Césaire, Aimé. 2001. *Discourse on Colonialism*. New York: Monthly Review.

———. 1995. "What Negritude Means to Me." In *African Presence in the Americas*, ed. Carlos Moore, 13–21. Trenton, NJ: Africa World.

Cheville, Lila R. 1965. *Folk Dances of Panama*. PhD diss., University of Iowa.

Cheville, Lila R., and Richard A. Cheville. 1977. *Festivals and Dances of Panamá*. Panamá: Litho-Impresora Panamá.

Clarke, Kamari Maxine, and Deborah A. Thomas. 2006. *Globalization and Race: Transformations in the Cultural Production of Blackness*. Durham, NC: Duke University Press.

Clifford, J., and G. E. Marcus, eds. 1986. *Writing Culture: The Poetics and Politics of Ethnography*. Berkeley: University of California Press.

Clifford, James. 1997. *Routes: Travel and Translation in the Late Twentieth Century*. Cambridge, MA: Harvard University Press.

———. 1988. *The Predicament of Culture: Twentieth-Century Ethnography, Literature, and Art*. Cambridge, MA: Harvard University Press.

Coates, Rodney D. 2004. *Race and Ethnicity: Across Time, Space, and Discipline*. Leiden: Brill.

Collins, Patricia Hill. 2000. *Black Feminist Thought: Knowledge, Consciousness, and the Politics of Empowerment*. 2nd ed. New York: Routledge.

———. 1998. *Fighting Words: Black Women and the Search for Justice*. Minneapolis: University of Minnesota Press.

Comaroff, John L., and Jean Comaroff. 1991. *Of Revelation and Revolution, Volume 1: Christianity, Colonialism, and Consciousness in South Africa*. Chicago: University of Chicago Press.

———. 1997. *Of Revelation and Revolution, Volume 2: The Dialectic of Modernity on a South African Frontier*. Chicago: University of Chicago Press.

"Comisión especial entrega al presidente el plan de acción para la inclusión plena de la etnia negra panameña." 2006. *Etnia negra panameña*. Panamá City: Ministerio de Desarrollo Agropecuario.

Connerton, Paul 1989. *How Societies Remember*. Cambridge: Cambridge University Press.

Conniff, Michael L. 1994. *Africans in the Americas: A History of the Black Diaspora*. New York: St. Martin's.

———. 1992. *Panama and the United States: The Forced Alliance*. Athens: University of Georgia Press.

———. 1985. *Black Labor on a White Canal: Panama, 1904–1981*. Pittsburgh: University of Pittsburgh Press.

Conquergood, Dwight. 2013. *Cultural Struggles: Performance, Ethnography, Praxis*. Edited by E. Patrick Johnson. Ann Arbor: University of Michigan Press.

———. 2002. "Performance Studies, Interventions and Radical Research." *TDR/The Drama Review* 46 (2): 145–56.

———. 2000. "Rethinking Elocution: The Trope of the Talking Book and Other Figures of Speech." *TPQ* 20 (Fall): 325–41.

———. 1995. "Of Caravans and Carnivals: Performance Studies in Motion." *TDR/The Drama Review* 39 (Winter): 137–41.

———. 1994. "Life in Big Red: Struggles and Accommodations in a Chicago Polyethnic Tenement." In *Structuring Diversity*, edited by Louise Lamphere, 95–144. Chicago: University of Chicago Press.

———. 1991. "Rethinking Ethnography: Towards a Critical Cultural Politics." *Communication Monographs* 58: 179–94.

———. 1988. "Health Theatre in a Hmong Refugee Camp: Performance, Communications, and Culture." *TDR/The Drama Review* 32 (3): 174–208.

———. 1987. "Between Experience and Expression: The Performed Myth." In *Festschrift for Isabel Crouch: Essays on the Theory, Practice, and Criticism of Performance*, edited by W. A. Bacon, 33–57. Las Cruces: New Mexico State University Press.

———. 1985a. "Performance as a Moral Act: Ethical Dimensions of the Ethnography of Performance." *Literature in Performance* 5 (2): 1–13.

Constitución de la República de Panamá de 1946.

Constitución de la República de Panamá de 1941. art. 23.

Cooper, Carolyn. 2004. *Sound Clash: Jamaican Dancehall Culture At Large*. New York: Palgrave Macmillan.

———. 1995. *Noises in the Blood: Orality, Gender, and the "Vulgar" Body of Jamaican Popular Culture*. 1st U.S. ed. Durham, NC: Duke University Press.

Cortez, Delfia. 2013. "Suspenden el carnaval en Portobelo por violencia." *Crítica*, February 9. http://www.critica.com.pa/notas/1423639-suspenden-el-carnaval-en-portobelo-violencia.

Crenshaw, Kimberlé. 1995. *Critical Race Theory: The Key Writings That Formed the Movement.* New York: Norton.

Cutter, Barbara. 2003. *Domestic Devils, Battlefield Angels: The Radicalism of American Womanhood, 1830–1865.* DeKalb: Northern Illinois University Press.

Daley, Mercedes Chen. 1990. "The Watermelon Riot: Cultural Encounters in Panama City, April 15, 1856." *The Hispanic American Historical Review* 70 (1): 85–108.

"Death of a Strongman." 1981. *Newsweek,* August 10, p. 33.

Denzin, Norman K. 2003. *Performance Ethnography: Critical Pedagogy and the Politics of Culture.* Thousand Oaks, CA: Sage.

Deren, Maya. 1984. *Divine Horsemen: The Living Gods of Haiti.* New Paltz, NY: McPherson.

Desmond, Jane. 2001. *Staging Tourism: Bodies on Display from Waikiki to Sea World.* Chicago: University of Chicago Press.

———. 1997. *Meaning in Motion: New Cultural Studies of Dance (Post-Contemporary Interventions).* Durham, NC: Duke University Press.

di Leonardo, Micaela. 1998. *Exotics at Home: Anthropologies, Others, American Modernity.* Chicago: University of Chicago Press.

———. 1993. "What a Difference Political Economy Makes: Feminist Anthropology in the Postmodern Era." *Anthropological Quarterly* 68 (April): 76–80.

Díez Castillo, Luis. 1975. *Los cimarrones y la esclavitud en Panamá.* Panamá: Instituto National de Cultura.

Dilg, George Robertson. 1975. *The Collapse of the Portobelo Fairs: A Study in Spanish Commercial Reform, 1720–1740.* PhD diss., Indiana University.

Dirección de Estadística y Censo. 1998. "Población de la provincia de Colón, por distrito: Censos de 1911 a 1990." *Compendio estadístico: Provincia de Colón, años 1992–1996.*

Doggett, Scott. 2001. *Lonely Planet Panama.* 2nd ed. Victoria: Lonely Planet.

Drewal, Margaret Thompson. 2000. "Nomadic Cultural Production in African Diaspora." In *Diaspora and Visual Culture: Representing Africans and Jews,* edited by Nicholas Mirzoeff, 115–42. London: Routledge.

———. 1994. *Yoruba Ritual: Performance, Play, Agency.* Bloomington: Indiana University Press.

———. 1991. "The State of Research on Performance in Africa." *African Studies Review* 34 (December): 1–64.

Drolet, Patricia Lund. 1980. *The Congo Ritual of Northeastern Panama: An Afro-American Expressive Structure of Cultural Adaptation.* PhD diss., University of Illinois at Urbana-Champaign.

Du Bois, W. E. B. 1994. *The Souls of Black Folk.* New York: Dover.

Duke, Dawn. 2010. "Black Movement Militancy in Panama: SAMAAP's Reliance on an Identity of West Indianness." *Latin American and Caribbean Ethnic Studies (LACES)* 5 (1): 75–83.

Douglass, L. 1992. *The Power of Sentiment: Love, Hierarchy, and the Jamaican Family Elite.* Oxford: Westview.

Dunham, Katherine. 1969. *Island Possessed.* Garden City, NY: Doubleday.

Earle, Peter. 2007. *The Sack of Panama: Captain Morgan and the Battle for the Caribbean.* New York: Thomas Dunne/St. Martin's.

Edwards, Brent Hayes. 2003. *The Practice of Diaspora: Literature, Translation, and the Rise of Black Internationalism.* Cambridge, MA: Harvard University Press.

Elam, Harry J. Jr., and Kennell Jackson. 2005. *Black Cultural Traffic: Crossroads in Global Performance and Popular Culture*. Ann Arbor: University of Michigan Press.

Eleta, Sandra. 1985. *Portobelo: Fotografía de Panamá*. Buenos Aires, Argentina: La Azotea Editorial Fotográfica.

Embassy of the United States: Panama. 2006. "Visa Services." http://panama.usembassy.gov/visas.html.

Fabian, Johannes. 1990. *Power and Performance: Ethnographic Explorations through Proverbial Wisdom and Theater in Shaba, Zaire*. Madison: University of Wisconsin Press.

———. 1983. *Time and the Other: How Anthropology Makes Its Object*. New York: Columbia University Press.

Fabre, Geneviève, and Robert O'Meally, eds. 1994. *History and Memory in African-American Culture*. New York: Oxford University Press.

Fanon, Frantz. 1967. *Black Skin, White Masks*. Translated from French by Charles Lam Markmann. New York: Grove.

———. 1963. *The Wretched of the Earth*. Translated by Constance Farrington. New York: Grove.

Farrington, Lisa E. 2005. *Creating Their Own Image: The History of African-American Women Artists*. Oxford: Oxford University Press.

Fortune, Armando. 1967a. "Los primeros negros en el istmo de Panamá." *Revista Lotería* XII (144) (noviembre): 56–85.

———. 1967b. "Los primeros negros en el istmo de Panamá." *Revista Lotería* XII (143) (octubre): 41–63.

———. 1956a."Estudio sobre la insurrección de los negros esclavos, los cimarrones de Panamá." *Revista Lotería* I (6) (mayo): 46–51.

———. 1956b. "Estudio sobre la insurrección de los negros esclavos, los cimarrones de Panamá." *Revista Lotería* I (5) (abril): 61–8.

Foster, Susan Leigh. 1995. *Choreographing History*. Bloomington: University of Indiana Press.

Foucault, Michel. 1990. *The History of Sexuality*. Vol. 1, *An Introduction*. New York: Vintage.

———. 1977. *Discipline & Punish: The Birth of the Prison*. New York: Vintage.

———. 1972. *The Archeology of Knowledge and the Discourse on Language*. New York: Tavistock.

Franceschi, V. 1960. "Los negros congos en Panamá." *Lotería* 51: 93–107.

Fundación Interamericana. 2002. "Hermandad Congo: Proyecto de desarrollo turístico del municipio de Portobelo." Panamá: Fundación Interamericana.

Fusco, Coco. 1994. "Other History of Intercultural Performance." *TDR/The Drama Review* 38 (1): 143–67.

Gates, Henry Louis. 1998. *The Signifying Monkey*. New York: Oxford University Press.

Genovese, Eugene. 1979. *From Rebellion to Revolution: Afro-American Slave Revolts in the Making of the New World*. Baton Rouge: Louisiana State University Press.

Geyelin, Philip. 1964. "Problems in Panama: Officials Cautiously Hopeful on Canal Zone Crisis: Closing Waterway would Cripple Many U.S. Firms." *Wall Street Journal*. Jan. 13. http://search.proquest.com/docview/59244702?accountid=14244.

Gilroy, Paul. 2000. *Against Race: Imagining Political Culture beyond the Color Line*. Cambridge, MA: Belknap Press of Harvard University Press.

———. 1995a. "'. . . to be Real': The Dissident Forms of Black Expressive Culture." In *Let's Get It On: The Politics of Black Performance*, edited by Catherine Ugwu, 12–33. Seattle: Bay Press.

————. 1995b. "Roots and Routes: Black Identity as an Outernational Project." In *Racial and Ethnic Identity: Psychological Development and Creative Expression*, edited by Herbert W. Harris, Howard C. Blue, and Ezra E. H. Griffith, 15–30. New York: Routledge.

————. 1993a. *The Black Atlantic: Modernity and Double Consciousness.* Cambridge, MA: Harvard University Press.

————. 1993b. *Small Acts: Thoughts on the Politics of Black Cultures.* London: Serpent's Tail.

————. 1991. *There Ain't No Black in the Union Jack: The Cultural Politics of Race and Nation.* Chicago: University of Chicago Press.

Glissant, Edouard. 1989. *Caribbean Discourse: Selected Essays.* Charlottesville: University Press of Virginia.

Goldberg, David Theo. 2002. *The Racial State.* Malden, MA: Blackwell.

Goodin de Lowe, Melva. 2012. *Afrodescendientes en el istmo de Panamá.* Panama City: la Sociedad de Amigos del Museo Afroantillano de Panama (SAMAAP).

Gómez-Peña, Guillermo. 2005. *Ethno-techno: Writings on Performance, Activism, and Pedagogy.* New York: Routledge.

Gonzalez, Anita. 2011. *Afro-Mexico: Dancing between Myth and Reality.* Austin: University of Texas Press.

Gordon, Avery F. 1997. *Ghostly Matters: Hauntings and the Sociological Imagination.* Minneapolis: University of Minnesota Press.

Grosz, Elizabeth. 1994. *Volatile Bodies: Toward a Corporeal Feminism.* Bloomington: Indiana University Press.

Guardia, Roberto de la. 1977. *Los negros del istmo de Panamá.* Panamá: Ediciones INAC.

Guss, David. 2000. *The Festive State: Race, Ethnicity and Nationalism as Cultural Performance.* Berkeley: University of California Press.

Hall, Stuart. 2003. "Cultural Identity and Diaspora." In *Theorizing Diaspora: A Reader*, edited by Jana Evans Braziel and Anita Mannur, 233–46. Malden, MA: Blackwell.

————. 1997. "Subjects in History: Making Diasporic Identities." In *The House That Race Built: Black Americans, U.S. Terrain*, edited by Wahneema Lubiano, 289–300. New York: Pantheon.

————. 1988. "The Toad in the Garden: Thatcherism among the Theorists." In *Marxism and the Interpretation of Culture*, edited by C. Nelson and L. Grossberg, 35–57. Urbana: University of Illinois Press.

Hamera, Judith. 2007. *Dancing Communities: Performance, Difference, and Connection in the Global City.* New York: Palgrave Macmillan.

Hanchard, Michael. n.d. "Four Faces of Race." Photocopy, Department of Political Science, Northwestern University.

————. 1999. *Racial Politics in Contemporary Brazil.* Durham, NC: Duke University Press.

————. 1994. *Orpheus and Power: The Movimento Negro of Rio de Janeiro and São Paulo, Brazil, 1945–1988.* Princeton, NJ: Princeton University Press.

————. 1991. "Racial Consciousness and Afro-Diasporic Experiences: Antonio Gramsci Reconsidered." *Socialism and Democracy* 14: 83–106.

Haraway, Donna. 1991. *Simians, Cyborgs, and Women: The Reinvention of Nature.* New York: Routledge.

Harding, Earl. 1959. *The Untold Story.* New York: Athene.

Higginbotham, Evelyn Brooks. 1993. *Righteous Discontent: The Women's Movement in the Black Baptist Church, 1880–1920.* Cambridge, MA: Harvard University Press.

Hill, Lynda Marion. 1996. *Social Rituals and the Verbal Arts of Zora Neale Hurston.* Washington, DC: Howard University Press.

Hoetink, Harry. 1973. *Slavery and Race Relations.* New York: Harper & Row.

Holloway, Joseph E., ed. 1990. *Africanisms in American Culture.* Bloomington: Indiana University Press.

hooks, bell. 1995. "Performance Practice as a Site of Opposition." In *Let's Get It On: The Politics of Black Performance,* edited by Catherine Ugwu, 210–21. Seattle: Bay Press.

———. 1990a. "Homeplace: A Site of Resistance." In *Yearning: Race, Gender, and Cultural Politics,* 57–64. Boston: South End.

———. 1990b. "Postmodern Blackness." In *Yearning: Race, Gender, and Cultural Politics,* 23–31. Boston: South End.

Hurston, Zora Neale. 1995. *Folklore, Memory and Other Writing.* Edited by Cheryl A. Wall. New York: Library of America.

Hutcheon, Linda. 1985. *A Theory of Parody: The Teachings of Twentieth-Century Art Forms.* New York: Methuen.

Instituto Nacional de Estadística y Censo. 2010. *Censos nacionales de población y vivienda 2010.*

———. 2000. *Censos nacionales de población y vivienda 2000.*

———. 1966. *Censos nacionales de 1960.*

———. 1943. *Censo de población, 1940.*

———. 1922. *Censo demográfico de la Provincia de Panamá, 1920.*

Instituto Panameño de Turismo. 2006a. "People and Culture." http://www.visitpanama.com/eng/page.php?page=people_and_culture (page discontinued).

Instituto Panameño de Turismo. 2006b. "Tourism Statistics." http://www.visitpanama.com/eng/page.php?page=tourism_statistics (page discontinued).

Jackson, Eric. 2004. "Panama's Chinese Community Celebrates a Birthday, Meets New Challenges." *Panama News* 10 (9). http://www.thepanamanews.com/pn/v_10/issue_09/community_01.html.

———. 2003. "Festival of the Black Christ." *Panama News* 9 (19). http://www.thepanamanews.com/pn/v_09/issue_19/travel_01.html.

———. 1999. "The Beginning of the End of the Panama Canal Zone." *Panama News,* December 28. http://www.hartford-hwp.com/archives/47/354.html.

Jackson, John L. 2001. *Harlemworld: Doing Race and Class in Contemporary Black America.* Chicago: University of Chicago Press.

Jackson, Shannon. 2000. *Lines of Activity: Performance, Historiography, Hull-House Domesticity.* Ann Arbor: University of Michigan Press.

Jaén Suárez, Omar. 1998. *La población del istmo de Panamá: Estudio de geohistoria.* 3a ed. Madrid: Ediciones de Cultura Hispánica.

James, C. L. R. 1995. *A History of Pan-African Revolt.* Chicago: C. H. Kerr.

———. 1989. *The Black Jacobins: Toussaint L'Ouverture and the San Domingo Revolution.* New York: Vintage.

———. 1953. *Mariners, Renegades and Castaways: The Story of Herman Melville and the World We Live In.* New York: C. L. R. James.

Jaquith, Cindy. 1990. "Why the Panamanian People are Fighting for National Dignity." In *Panama: The Truth about the U.S. Invasion,* 5–11. New York: Pathfinder.

"JASON XV: Rainforests at the Crossroads: The JASON Foundation for Education." 2003. *The Free Library,* October 1. http://www.thefreelibrary.com/JASON+XV%3A+Rainforests+at+the+Crossroads%3A+The+JASON+Foundation+for...-a0108790648.

Jiménez, José. *La Iglesia de San Felipe Portobelo: El Cristo de Nazareno/El Cristo Negro.* Panamá.

Johnson, E. Patrick. 2003a. *Appropriating Blackness: Performance and the Politics of Authenticity.* Durham, NC: Duke University Press.

———. 2003b. "Strange Fruit: A Performance about Identity Politics." *TDR/The Drama Review* 47 (Summer): 88–111.

———. 2000. "From Black Quare Studies or Almost Everything I Know about Queer Studies I Learned from My Grandmother." *Callaloo* 23 (1): 399.

———. 1998. "Feeling the Spirit in the Dark: Expanding Notions of the Sacred in the African-American Gay Community." *Callaloo* 21 (2): 120.

Johnson, John. 1980. *Latin America in Caricature.* Austin: University of Texas Press.

Joly, Luz Graciela. 1981. *The Ritual "Play of the Congos" of North-Central Panama: Its Sociolinguistic Implications* (Sociolinguistic Working Paper). Austin: Southwest Educational Development Laboratory.

Kelley, Robin D. 1994. *Imagining Home: Class, Culture, and Nationalism in the African Diaspora.* London: Verso.

Kemp, Amanda Denise. 1998. "This Black Body in Question." In *The Ends of Performance,* edited by Peggy Phelan and Jill Lane, 116–30. New York: New York University Press.

Kymlicka, Will. 2000. *Politics in the Vernacular: Nationalism, Multiculturalism and Citizenship.* Oxford: Oxford University Press.

LaFeber, Walter. 1979. *The Panama Canal: The Crisis in Historical Perspective.* Rev. ed. New York: Oxford University Press.

Lancaster, Roger. 1993. *Life Is Hard: Machismo, Danger, and the Intimacy of Power in Nicaragua.* Berkeley: University of California Press.

Lander, J., and R. Robinson. 2006. *Slaves, Subjects, and Subversives: Blacks in Colonial Latin America.* Albuquerque: University of New Mexico Press.

Landry, Bart. 2007. *Race, Gender and Class: Theory and Methods of Analysis.* Upper Saddle River, NJ: Pearson Prentice Hall.

Lane, Jill. 2005. *Blackface Cuba, 1840–1895.* Philadelphia: University of Pennsylvania Press.

Langley, Lester D. 2002. *The Banana Wars: United States Intervention in the Caribbean, 1898–1934.* Wilmington: Scholarly Resources.

Larson, Leslie F. 2002. *Panama's Caribbean Treasure: The San Lorenzo Protected Area.* Panamá: Centro de Estudios y Acción Social Panameño.

Leis, Raúl. 2003. "About Invasions and Memory Lapses. *Panama News* 9 (24). http://www.thepanamanews.com/pn/v_09/issue_24/opinion_02.html.

Lewis, Lancelot. 1994. *The West Indian in Panama: Black Labor in Panama, 1850–1914.* Madison: University of Wisconsin Press.

Lindsay, Arturo. 2005. *Como Se Cuenta El Cuento = How The Story Is Told.* Chapel Hill: University of North Carolina at Chapel Hill, Sonja Haynes Stone Center for Black Culture and History.

———. 2003. "The Research Methods of an Artist-Ethnographer on the Congo Coast of Panama." In *Breaking the Disciplines: Reconceptions in Knowledge, Art and Culture,* edited by Martin L. Davies and Marsha Meskimmon, 129–62. London: I. B. Tauris.

————. 2000a. "Bio Sketch." http://www.arturolindsay.com/bio.htm (page discontinued).

————. 2000b. "Preserving Old While Creating New Traditions on the Congo Coast of Panama." http://www.arturolindsay.com/preserving.htm.

Linebaugh, Peter, and Marcus Rediker. 2000. *The Many-Headed Hydra: The Hidden History of the Revolutionary Atlantic.* Boston: Beacon.

Lipski, John M. 2005. *A History of Afro-Hispanic Language: Five Centuries/Five Continents.* Cambridge: Cambridge University Press.

————. 1992. "The Speech of the Negros Congos of Panama." *Hispanic Review* 60 (Summer): 347–49.

————. 1989. *The Speech of the Negros Congos of Panama.* Amsterdam: J. Benjamins.

————. 1986. "The Negros Congos of Panama: An Afro-Hispanic Creole Language and Culture." *Journal of Black Studies* 16 (June): 409–19.

Liss, Sheldon B. 1967. *The Canal: Aspects of United States–Panamanian Relations.* Notre Dame: University of Notre Dame Press.

Madison, D. Soyini. 2005. *Critical Ethnography: Method, Ethics, and Performance.* Thousand Oaks, CA: Sage.

————. 2002. "Is It a Human Being or a Girl?" *Director's Notes.* Playbill, Department of Communication Studies, University of North Carolina at Chapel Hill.

————. 1999. "Performing Theory/Embodied Writing." *TPQ* 19 (April): 107–24.

————. 1998. "That Was My Occupation: Oral Narratives, Performance, and Black Feminist Thought." In *Exceptional Spaces: Essays in Performance and History,* edited by Della Pollock, 319–42. Chapel Hill: University of North Carolina Press.

————. 1994. "Story, History, and Performance: Interpreting Oral History through Black Performance Traditions." *Journal of Black Sacred Music* 8 (Fall): 43–63.

Maloney, Gerardo. 1989. "El movimiento negro en Panama. VI congreso nacional de sociología. Panama, agosto 1988." *Revista panameña de sociología* 5: 145–58.

————. 1983. Ideológia, nación y negros en Panamá: Primer encuentro de política cultural-memorias. Panamá: INAC.

Maloney, Gerardo, and Jorge Arosemena. 1979. *The African Negro Presence in Panama.* http://unesdoc.unesco.org/images/0003/000387/038734eb.pdf.

Mankekar, Purnima. 1999. *Screening Culture, Viewing Politics: An Ethnography of Television, Womanhood, and Nation in Postcolonial India.* Durham, NC: Duke University Press.

Márquez, Gabriel Garcia. 1970. *One Hundred Years of Solitude.* Translated by Gregory Rabbasa. New York: Harper & Row.

Martinez-Echazabal, Lourdes. 1998. "Mestizaje and the Discourse of National/Cultural Identity in Latin America, 1845–1959." *Latin American Perspectives* 25 (100): 21–42.

McAlister, Elizabeth A. 2002. *Rara!: Vodou, Power, and Performance in Haiti and its Diaspora.* Berkeley: University of California Press.

McCain, William D. 1965. *The United States and the Republic of Panama.* New York: Russell & Russell.

McCullough, David G. 1977. *The Path between the Seas: The Creation of the Panama Canal, 1870–1914.* New York: Simon & Schuster.

McGuinness, Aims. 2008. *Path of Empire: Panama and the California Gold Rush.* Ithaca, NY: Cornell University Press.

———. 2003. "Searching for 'Latin America': Race and Sovereignty in the Americas in the 1850s." In *Race and Nation in Modern Latin America,* edited by Nancy Appelbaum, Anne S. MacPherson, and Karin Alejandra Rosemblatt, 87–107. Chapel Hill: University of North Carolina Press.

McPherson, Alan. 2003. *Yankee No!: Anti-Americanism in U.S.-Latin American Relations.* Cambridge, MA: Harvard University Press.

Meditz, Sandra W., and Dennis M. Hanratty, eds. 1987a. "The Conquest." In *Panama: A Country Study.* http://countrystudies.us/panama/3.htm.

———. 1987b. "The Government of Torrijos." In *Panama: A Country Study.* http://countrystudies.us/panama/17.htm.

Mena Garcia, Maria del. 1984. *La sociedad de Panamá en el siglo XVI.* Sevilla: Excma. Diputación Provincial de Sevilla.

Meneses, Alvaro Samiento. 2003. "Portobelo está de festival." *La Prensa,* March 7: 58–60.

Mercer, Kobena. 1994. *Welcome to the Jungle: New Positions in Black Cultural Studies.* New York: Routledge.

Mignolo, Walter D. 1995. *The Darker Side of the Renaissance.* Ann Arbor: University of Michigan Press.

Minh-Ha, Trinh. 1991. *When the Moon Waxes Red: Representation, Gender, and Cultural Politics.* New York. Routledge.

Mitchell, B. 1998. *International Historical Statistics: The Americas, 1750–1993.* 4th ed. New York: Stockton.

Mohanty, Chandra Talpade. 1991. "Under Western Eyes: Feminist Scholarship and Colonial Discourse." In *Third World Women and the Politics of Feminism,* 51–81. Bloomington: Indiana University Press.

Moraga, Cherrie, and Gloria Anzaldúa, eds. 1983. *This Bridge Called My Back: Writings by Radical Women of Color.* New York: Kitchen Table, Women of Color.

Morrison, Toni. 2000. "Unspeakable Things Unspoken." In *The Black Feminist Reader,* edited by Joy James and T. Denean Sharpley-Whiting, 24–56. Malden, MA: Blackwell.

———. 1998. "Home." In House That Race Built: Original Essays by Toni Morrison, Angela Y. Davis, Cornel West, and Others on Black Americans and Politics in America Today, edited by Wahneema Lubianoo. 1st Vintage Books ed., 3–12. New York: Vintage Books.

———. 1992. *Playing in the Dark: Whiteness and the Literary Imagination.* Cambridge, MA: Harvard University Press.

Munro, Dana. 1964. *Intervention and Dollar Diplomacy in the Caribbean: 1900–1921.* Princeton, NJ: Princeton University Press.

National Lawyers Guild. 1990. *Report on Panama.* New York: National Lawyers Guild.

Ness, Sally Ann. 1992. *Body, Movement and Culture: Kinesthetic and Visual Symbolism in a Philippine Community.* Philadelphia: University of Pennsylvania Press.

Newton, Velma. 1984. *The Silver Men: West Indian Labor Migration to Panama, 1850–1914.* Kingston, Jamaica: University of the West Indies.

Ngũgĩ wa Thiong'o. 1986. *Decolonizing the Mind: The Politics of Language in African Literature.* London: J. Currey.

Nwankwo, Ifeoma. *Voices from Our America.* http://voicesamerica.library.vanderbilt.edu/home.php.

Olmos, José Domingo. 1980. *La danza de los negros congos en la costa arriba de Colón.* Panamá: Universidad de Panamá.

Olwig, Karen Fog. 1993. *Global Culture, Island Identity: Continuity and Change in the Afro-Caribbean Community of Nevis.* Philadelphia: Harwood Academic.

O'Reggio, Trevor. 2006. *Between Alienation and Citizenship: The Evolution of Black West Indian Society in Panama 1914–1964.* Lanham, MD: University Press of America.

Palmié, Stephen. 2002. *Wizards & Scientists: Explorations in Afro-Cuban Modernity and Tradition.* Durham, NC: Duke University Press.

Panama Canal Authority. 2002a. "APC Overview." http://www.pancanal.com/eng/acp/acp-overview.html.

———. 2002b. "Workforce." http://www.pancanal.com/eng/history/history/work.html.

———. 2001. "Canal History." http://www.pancanal.com/eng/history.

Panama Canal Society of Florida. 2002. "About." http://www.pancanalsociety.org/about.html.

"Panama Prepares to Act Out Trauma of U.S. Invasion." 1999. *Reuters,* December 18. http://www.latinamericanstudies.org/Panama/chorrillo.htm.

Patraka, Vivian. 1996. "Spectacles of Suffering: Performing Presence, Absence, and Historical Memory at U.S. Holocaust Museums." In *Performance and Cultural Politics,* edited by Elin Diamond, 89–107. London: Routledge.

Pavis, Patrice. 2013. *La mise en scène contemporaine.* London: Routledge.

Pearcy, Thomas L. 2005. *The History of Central America.* Westport, CT: Greenwood.

———. 1998. *We Answer Only to God: Politics and the Military in Panama, 1903–1947.* Albuquerque: University of New Mexico Press.

Piper, Adrian. 1996. *Out of Order, Out of Sight.* Cambridge, MA: MIT Press.

Pollock, Della. 2005. *Remembering: Oral History Performance.* New York: Palgrave Macmillan.

———. 1998a. "Introduction: Making History Go." In *Exceptional Spaces: Essays in Performance and History,* 1–45. Chapel Hill: University of North Carolina Press.

———. 1998b. "Performing Writing." In *The Ends of Performance,* edited by Peggy Phelan and Jill Lane, 73–103. New York: New York University Press.

Poole, Deborah. 1997. *Vision, Race, and Modernity: A Visual Economy of the Andean Image World.* Princeton, NJ: Princeton University Press.

Pratt, Mary Louise. 1989. *Women, Culture, and Politics in Latin America.* Berkeley: University of California.

Price, Richard, ed. 1996. *Maroon Societies: Rebel Slave Communities in the Americas.* New York: Anchor.

Priestley, George. 1986. *Military Government and Popular Participation in Panama: The Torrijos Regime, 1968–75.* Boulder, CO: Westview.

Priestley, George, and Alberto Barrow. 2008. "The Black Movement in Panamá: A Historical and Political Interpretation, 1994–2004." *Souls: A Critical Journal of Black Politics, Culture, and Society* 10 (3): 227–55.

Prince. *Emancipation.* NPG/EMI 1518631, compact disc. Originally released in 1996.

Prince, Sally, and Sidney W. Mintz. 1985. *Caribbean Contours.* Baltimore: Johns Hopkins University Press.

Reid, Lydia. 2010. "Panama's 2010 Census Promises to be Interesting for Persons of African and Indigenous Descent." *Silver People Chronicle.* http://thesilverpeoplechronicle.com/2010/05/panamas-2010-census-promises-to-be.html.

Rivera-Servera, Ramón H., and Harvey Young. 2011. *Performance in the Borderlands.* New York: Palgrave Macmillan.

Rivera-Servera, Ramón H. 2012. *Performing Queer Latinidad: Dance, Sexuality, Politics*. Ann Arbor: University of Michigan Press.

Roach, Joseph R. 1996. *Cities of the Dead: Circum-Atlantic Performance*. New York: Columbia University Press.

Rodney, Walter. 1972. "Colonialism as a System for Underdeveloping Africa." In *How Europe Underdeveloped Africa*, 205–81. London: Bogle-L'Ouverture.

Rodriguez, Frederick. 1979. *Cimarron Revolts and Pacification in New Spain, the Isthmus of Panama and Colonial Columbia, 1503–1800*. Chicago: Loyola University of Chicago.

Rojas, Don. 1990. "Panama's Fight for Sovereignty: A History." In *Panama: The Truth about the U.S. Invasion*, 12–21. New York: Pathfinder.

Rosaldo, Renato. 1993. *Culture & Truth: The Remaking of Social Analysis*. Boston: Beacon.

Rout, Leslie B. Jr. 1976. *The African Experience in Spanish America, 1502 to the Present Day*. Cambridge: Cambridge University Press.

Savigliano, Marta E. 1995. *Tango and the Political Economy of Passion*. Boulder, CO: Westview.

Schechner, Richard. 1985. *Between Theater and Anthropology*. Philadelphia: University of Pennsylvania Press.

Schechter, Patricia Ann. 2001. *Ida B. Wells-Barnett and American Reform, 1880–1930*. Chapel Hill: University of North Carolina Press.

Scott, James. 1990. *Domination and the Acts of Resistance: Hidden Transcripts*. New Haven, CT: Yale University Press.

Sheller, Mimi. 2003. *Consuming the Caribbean: From Arawaks to Zombies*. London: Routledge.

Sheller, Mimi, and John Urry. 2004. *Tourism Mobilities: Places to Play, Places in Play*. London: Routledge.

Sinfield, Alan. 1994. *The Wilde Century: Effeminacy, Oscar Wilde and the Queer Moment*. New York: Columbia University Press.

Siu, Lok C. 2005. *Memories of a Future Home: Diasporic Citizenship of Chinese in Panama*. Stanford, CA: Stanford University Press.

Smith, Ronald R. 1994. "Arroz Colorado: Los Congos of Panama." In *Music and Black Ethnicity: The Caribbean and South America*, edited by Gerard H. Béhague, 239–66. New Brunswick, NJ: Transaction.

———. 1976. *The Society of Los Congos of Panamá: An Ethnomusicological Study of the Music and Dance-Theatre of an Afro-Panamanian Group*. PhD diss., Indiana University.

Springfield, Lopez. 1997. *Daughters of Caliban: Caribbean Women in the Twentieth Century*. Bloomington: Indiana University Press.

Sterling, Cheryl. 2012. *African Roots, Brazilian Rites: Cultural and National Identity in Brazil*. New York: Palgrave Macmillan.

Stoler, Ann Laura. 1997. "Racial Histories and Their Regimes of Truth." *Political Power and Social Theory* 2: 183–206.

Stolzoff, Norman C. 2000. *Wake the Town & Tell the People: Dancehall Culture in Jamaica*. Durham, NC: Duke University Press.

Sunstrum, Pamela Phatsimo. 2004. *Culture Speaks through Art: Preserving the Congo Tradition through Community-Based Art Projects in Portobelo, Panama*. Honors Thesis, University of North Carolina at Chapel Hill.

Sutton, Constance. 1974. "Cultural Duality in the Caribbean." *Caribbean Studies* 14 (2): 96–101.

Szok, Peter A. 2012. *Wolf Tracks: Popular Art and Re-Africanization in Twentieth-Century Panama.* Jackson: University Press of Mississippi.

Taylor, Diana. 2003. *The Archive and the Repertoire.* 2nd ed. Durham, NC: Duke University Press.

———. 1994. "Performing Gender: Las Madres de la Plaza de Mayo." In *Negotiating Performance: Gender, Sexuality, and Theatricality in Latin America,* edited by Diana Taylor and Juan Villegas, 275–305. Durham, NC: Duke University Press.

Thomas, Deborah A. 2004. *Modern Blackness: Nationalism, Globalization, and the Politics of Culture in Jamaica.* Durham, NC: Duke University Press.

Thompson, Robert Farris. 1984. In *Flash of the Spirit: African and Afro-American Art and Philosophy.* New York: Vintage.

Thornton, John. 1995. "Perspectives on African Christianity." In *Race, Discourse, and the Origin of the Americas: A New World View,* edited by Vera Lawrence Hyatt and Rex Nettleford, 169–98. Washington, DC: Smithsonian Institution.

Todorov, Tzvetan. 1984. *Mikhail Bakhtin: The Dialogical Principle.* Translated by Wlad Godzich. Minneapolis: University of Minnesota Press.

Trouillot, Michel-Rolph. 1995. *Silencing the Past: Power and the Production of History.* Boston: Beacon.

Tsing, Anna. 2004. *Friction: An Ethnography of Global Connections.* Princeton, NJ: Princeton University Press.

Turner, J. Michael. 2002. "The Road to Durban—and Back." *NACLA Report on the Americas* 35 (6): 31–35.

Turner, Victor. 1986. *Anthropology of Performance.* New York: PAJ.

———. 1982. *From Ritual to Theatre: The Human Seriousness of Play.* New York: PAJ.

Underiner, Tamara. 2004 *Contemporary Theatre in Mayan Mexico: Death-Defying Acts.* Austin: University of Texas Press.

UNESCO. 2012. *Convention Concerning the Protection of the World Cultural and Natural Heritage: State of Conservation of World Heritage Properties Inscribed on the World Heritage List.* World Heritage Committee. http://whc.unesco.org/archive/2012/whc12-36com-7BAdd-en.pdf.

Van Gronigen-Warren, B., and M. Lowe de Goodin, eds. 2001. *Afro-American Cultural Identity in Language and Literature.* Panamá: Editora Sibauste & SAMAAP.

Vasconcelos, José. 1979. *The Cosmic Race.* Translated by Didier T. Jaen. Los Angeles: California State University.

Vilar, Enriqueta Vila. 1986. "Las ferias de Portobelo: Apariencia y realidad del comercio con Indias." *Revista Lotería* 358 (January–February): 39–54.

Wade, Peter. 2004. "Images of Latin American Mestizaje and the Politics of Comparison." *Bulletin of Latin American Research* 23 (3): 355–66.

———. 2003. Afterword to *Race & Nation in Modern Latin America,* edited by Nancy Appelbaum, Anne S. MacPherson, and Karin Alejandra Rosemblatt, 263–81. Chapel Hill: University of North Carolina Press.

———. 2000. *Music, Race and Nation: Música Tropical in Colombia.* Chicago: University of Chicago Press.

———. 1997. *Race and Ethnicity in Latin America.* London: Pluto.

Ward, Christopher. 1989. "Historical Writing on Colonial Panama." *Hispanic American Historical Review* 69 (4): 691–713.

Watson, Sonja. 2009. "Are Panamanians of Caribbean Ancestry an Endangered Species? Critical Literary Debates on Panamanian Blackness in the Works of Carlos Wilson, Gerardo Maloney, and Carlos Russell." *Latin American and Caribbean Ethnic Studies* 4 (3): 231–54.

Webster, Edwin. 1973. *La defensa de Portobelo*. Panamá: Editorial Universitaria Panamá.

Weeks, John, and Phil Gunson. 1991. *Panama: Made in the USA*. London: Latin America Bureau.

Weismantel, Mary. 2001. *Cholas and Pishtacos: Stories of Race and Sex in the Andes*. Chicago: University of Chicago Press.

———. 1988. *Food, Gender, and Poverty in the Ecuadorian Andes*. Philadelphia: University of Pennsylvania.

West, Richard. 1967. *The Gringo in Latin America*. London: Trinity.

Westerman, George W. 1980. *Los inmigrantes antillanos en Panamá*. Panamá: Impresora de la Nación.

White, E. Frances. 2001. *Dark Continent of our Bodies: Black Feminism and the Politics of Respectability*. Philadelphia: Temple University Press.

Whitten, Norman E. Jr., and Arlene Torres, eds. 1988. "General Introduction: To Forge the Future in the Fires of the Past: An Interpretive Essay on Racism, Domination, Resistance and Liberation." In *Blackness in Latin America and the Caribbean: Social Dynamics and Cultural Transformations*, 3–33. Bloomington: Indiana University Press.

Williams, Raymond. 1977. *Marxism and Literature*. Oxford: Oxford University Press.

Wilson, Peter. 1973. *Crab Antics: The Social Anthropology of English-Speaking Negro Societies in the Caribbean*. London: Yale University Press.

———. 1969. "Reputation and Respectability: A Suggestion for Caribbean Ethnology." *Man* 4 (March): 70–84.

Winant, Howard. 1994. *Racial Conditions*. Minneapolis: University of Minnesota Press.

Wolcott, Victoria. 2001. *Remaking Respectability: African American Women in Interwar Detroit*. Chapel Hill: University of North Carolina Press.

Woods, Sarah. 2005. *Panama: The Bradt Travel Guide*. Guilford, CT: Bradt Travel Guides.

Wynter, Sylvia. 2000. "Beyond Miranda's Meanings: Un/Silencing the 'Demonic Ground' of Caliban's 'Woman.'" In *The Black Feminist Reader*, edited by Joy James and T. Denean Sharpley-Whiting, 109–30. Malden, MA: Blackwell.

———. 1995. "1492: A New World View." In *Race, Discourse and the Origin of the Americas: A New World View*, edited by Vera Lawrence Hyatt and Rex Nettleford, 5–57. Washington, DC: Smithsonian Institution.

Young, Robert J. 1995. *Colonial Desire: Hybridity in Theory, Culture and Race*. London: Routledge.

Zárate, Dora P. 1997. *La pollera panameña: Ensayo monográfico*. 7a ed. Panamá: Impresora Panamá.

Zien, Katie. 2009. "Black Latin Americans want to be counted." *Panama News*, December 5. http://www.thepanamanews.com/pn/v_15/issue_18/news_03.html.

Zuñigan, Maricel Martín. 2002. *Paloma, reina de los congos: El orgullo de una raza*. 2a ed. Panamá: Proyecto Desarrollo Turístico del Municipio de Portobelo.

Acción Comunal, 44

aduana (Customs House), 57, 59, 61, 143, 154

Afro-Antilleans (afroantillanos), 8, 30, 35

Afro-Colonials (afrocoloniales): Blackness
marker of, 46, 55; cultural nationalisms,
36–38; ethnic categorization of, 8; history in Panama, 8; identity formation,
39–41; identity of, 30; meaning of, 6;
as mestizos, 55; represented by Congo
tradition, 8

Afro-Colonials–West Indian communitas:
1989 invasion, 52–54; Canal Zone dismantling, 54, 55; Centennial celebrations (2003), 54; The Day of Black
Ethnicity, 5–6, 21, 30, 32; Flag Riots,
48–49; Primer Festival Afropanameño
(2006), 54

Afro-Colonials–West Indian relations:
citizenship rights and, 45–46, 47; panameñismo effects on, 45–47; race and
ethnicity in, 40–42, 46–47; socioeco-
nomics in, 37, 40–41

Afrodescendiente, 30

Afro-Hispanic (Afrohispano), 30, 204n7

afrolatino, 204n8

Afro-Panamanians (afropanemeños), 7,
8–9, 30

Akan people of Ghana, 188

Alexander, Bryant Keith, 11

Alexander Craft, Reneé: Chavarría meeting,
158; "Citizen Congo I," 34–35; "Citizen Congo II," 42–43; "Citizen Congo
III," 47–48; "Citizen Congo IV," 51–52;
Dancing with the Devil at the Crossroads
(performance), 11, 166–170; La historia
de los congos de Portobelo: Translating History Through the Body (performance), 11, 158–162; learning about
dance in the Congo drama, 157–58;
Making the Sign of the Cross (installation), 11, 162–66; "A Monument of Homage to the Congo Spirits" ("El monumento de homenaje a los espíritus de
los congos"), 182, 184, 185 figs. 5.17–5.18,
186; El museo congo (installation), 11,
170–188; as other (the outsider), 19–20.
See also When the Devil Knocks (Alexander Craft)

Amoreti, Francisco, 118

"And the Holy: The Church and Slavery"
(Making the Sign of the Cross) (Alexander Craft), 164

Angel characters, introduction of, 113

Angulo, Jose "Moraitho," 170, 178–79, 181 figs. 5.12–5.13

apartheid system, 45–46

Archangel and the six Souls (Las Ánimas), 76–77, 77 fig. 2.13, 80, 113

Arias, Arnulfo, 44–47, 50

Arias, Harmodio, 44–45, 49

Arribu, Jenny, 170, 172, 173–75

Arroyo, Justo, 29

Ash Wednesday, 3, 22, 67, 76, 80, 95, 96 fig. 2.17, 123

Aventuras 2000, 147

Ávila, Celedonio Molinar. See Celedonio (El Diablo Mayor)

Ávila, Ilusca, 102

awareness, space of, 13


Bakhtin, Mikhail, 10

Balboa, Vasco Núñez de, 206n25

baptizing the Devil, 76, 81, 103, 108 fig. 3.1, 113–14

Barnathan, Joyce, 50

Barrera, Danilo, 170, 173

bastones (walking canes), 15–16

Bederman, Gail, 41

Behar, Ruth, 9

bell hooks, 10

belonging, state-defined criteria for, 31–32

Besson, Jean, 144

The Black Atlantic (Gilroy), 23, 111

The Black Christ (El Nazareno/El Cristo Negro), 14–15, 57, 59, 61, 146–47

Black Diaspora: call-and-response traditions, 93; citizens micro-travel, 111; creative critical projects of the, 18–19. See also diaspora

Black ethnicity (etnia negra), celebration of, 5–7, 21, 29–30, 32, 54

Black identity: afropanameño category and, 30; of the author, 20; author's vs. Congo in performance, 160; Canal construction in shaping, 33–42; glossary of terms related to, 30–31; Panamanian, 6–7; slavery's influence on, 30; terminology marking, 35

Black identity, nationalism and routes to: Citizens vs. Subjects era (1926–46), 32, 42–47; Construction era (1903–14), 22, 32, 34–42; Patriots vs. Empire era (1964–79), 32, 47–51; Reconciliation era (1989–2003), 32, 51–55

Black internationalism, 36

Blackness: 2010 Census categories of, 60–61; of Afro-Colonials, 46, 55; La historia de los congos de Portobelo: Translating History Through the Body (performance) (Alexander Craft), 160; tradition in contemporary constructions of, 2; 20th century, 30–31

Black(s): duality and double-consciousness of, 37, 142; meaning of, 21, 55, 189; middle class racism, 46; as other, 8, 37

blessing the Devil, 76, 81, 103, 108 fig. 3.1, 113–14

blues (musical genre), 11, 166–170

the body: dancing with the cross in/as the body, 80; embodied knowledge of tradition, 11, 87–88, 157–162; embodiment of the Devil character, 1, 95–103, 128, 130–33, 169; La historia de los congos de Portobelo: Translating History Through the Body (performance) (Alexander Craft), 159–160, 161; theoretical orientation to, 10

The Bradt Travel Guide, 147–48

Brecher, John, 50

Brooks, Gwendolyn, 154

Burton, Richard D., 140–41

bus, circum-local space of the, 111, 150–51

Bush, George H. W., 52, 53

Bush, George W., 53

Butler, Judith, 10


Cable and Wireless, 16

call-and-response singing, 148

call-and-response traditions, 93

campesinos, 207n32

cane-whips, 99, 101

"Caras de Portobelo: Un taller de mascaras" ("Faces of Portobelo: A Mask Workshop"), 173–75, 176–75.8

Caribbean, race and gender in cartoons of, 41–42

Carnival season: community/communal sharing in, 90; dates of, 65–66, 78–79, 86–88; extending the, 123; historically, 53; raising the flag during, 65–66, 86–87, 88; suspension of, 193–94; taxing the outsider, 84–86, 85 fig. 2.16, 151. *See also* Congo drama

Carnival Tuesday (Shrove Tuesday), 3, 79–80

Carter-Torrijos Treaty, 44, 49, 51, 53

Castro, Fidel, 50

Catholic Church: drama as parody of the, 3–4, 7; *Making the Sign of the Cross* (Alexander Craft), 11, 162–66

Catholic faith: Ash Wednesday participants, 95; Celedonio's, 1, 2, 133, 161, 169

Ceballos, Viudo, 112–13, 134

Celedonio (El Diablo Mayor): on appointing the Major Devil, 118; Catholic faith, 1, 2, 133, 161, 169; circum-local cultural intervention in reinventing tradition, 110, 112–14, 133–34; community respect for, 117, 133; on Congo/Devil play, 104; costume, 75 fig. 2.12, 97 fig. 2.18, 99 fig. 2.20, 128–29, 129 fig. 3.6; *Dancing with the Devil at the Crossroads* (performance) (Alexander Craft), 11, 166–170; Devils gathered at home of, 98 fig. 2.19; embodiment of the Devil character, 1, 95–103, 128, 130–33, 169; existential compromise, 130–32; length of service, 114, 119; magical ability/mysticism of, 117, 130–32; the man, 2, 112, 133; the pujido (grunt) of, 95–96, 98, 99–101; retirement, 114, 126–28, 127 fig. 3.5; on role of the Devil, 76; sociocultural identity associated with, 2; training Major Devils, 101 fig. 2.22, 102, 104, 117–18, 120; training of, 112–13

census racial classifications, 60–61, 203n7, 205n17

Centennial celebrations (2003), 54

Certeau, Michel de, 10, 65, 142

Césaire, Aimé, 204n10

Chavarría, Carlos: on animal names, 72; on Celedonio's embodiment of the Major Devil, 131; on Celedonio's retirement, 126; on change created by opening the road, 89–90; on Congo drama, 65, 81; on the dance of the Major Devil, 80; on Major Devil role, 74–75; Major Devil role of, 76, 110, 114–19, 128, 191; Major Devil training, 101 fig. 2.22, 102, 104, 117–18; mayor of Portobelo, 53–54, 193–94; meeting the author, 158; on the tax, 84–85; on working with youth, 105–6

Cheney, Dick, 52

Chiari, Jerónimo "Jero," 170, 173, 182, 183 figs. 5.14–5.15

children: diablitos (little devils), 102, 156 fig. 5.1; embodied knowledge of tradition, 87–88; of the enslaved, homage to, 163, 164, 165; mask-making workshops for, 173–75; preparing for Carnival, 28 fig. 1.1. *See also* younger generation

Chinese in Panama, 207n36, 208n6

El Chorrillo community, destruction of, 52

chorus and singers, 77 fig. 2.13, 77–80, 78 fig. 2.14, 91–94, 137–38

Cimarron, term derivation, 36–37

Cimarrones: categories of, 37; homage to in *Making the Sign of the Cross* (installation) (Alexander Craft), 163, 164; stories of relationship with Spanish settlers, 58–59; tradition in celebrating resistance of, 3–4, 22, 36–38, 63, 65, 68–69, 74–75, 103, 109. *See also* marrons

"Circum-Atlantic" (Roach), 111

circum-local exchanges: and changes in Congo tradition, 110, 111–14, 118, 120–26, 132, 133–34; the connecting road and, 84–86, 189–190; The Festival of the Devils and Congos, 23–24, 105, 110, 120–26, 123 fig. 3.3, 124 fig. 3.4, 191, 194–95

circum-local space of the bus, 111, 150–51

*Cities of the Dead* (Roach), 23

"Citizen Congo I" (Alexander Craft), 34–35

"Citizen Congo II" (Alexander Craft), 42–43

"Citizen Congo III" (Alexander Craft), 47–48

"Citizen Congo IV" (Alexander Craft), 51–52

Citizens vs. Subjects era (1926–46), 22, 32, 42–47

class mobility, 40–41

Clifundo, Delia Barrera, 94, 158

clothing turned inside-out, 6, 71, 115, 130, 161

Collins, Patricia Hill, 19

Colón 200 cruise ship port, 147

Colonial Blacks. See Afro-Colonials (afrocoloniales)

Columbus, Christopher, 146

Comaroff, Jean, 10, 47, 57

Comaroff, John, 10, 47, 57

Comisión "Etnia Negra Panameña," 30, 54

communitas: in Afro-Colonials-West Indian relations, 5–6, 21, 30, 32, 33, 48–49, 52–55; Jim Crow policies and, 41; La Separación and, 41; meaning of, 22; during El museo congo, 173, 186; Turner's theory of, 32–33; in West Indian communities, 47

congada, 79, 89–90, 148–49, 171

Congo: meaning of, 3; origin narratives, 3, 37–38, 58–59; speaking in, 144 fig. 4.4; term usage in Portobelo, 38

Congo Carnival diaspora, 134

Congo community: ability to affect change, 53–54, 118; in Congo/Devil culture, 115; consequences of the connecting road for, 89–91, 105–6, 114, 132; local and circum-local vs. like-local performances in building, 126; performance as an act of, 2; respect for the Major Devil, 116–17, 130, 133; selecting the Major Devil character, 118; taxing visitors to the, 84–86, 85 fig. 2.16, 151

Congo/Devil culture, 115

Congo/Devil play, 103–5, 113, 120–26, 123 fig. 3.3

Congo dialect, 144–46, 209n7

Congo drama: dates of, 3, 22; functions of, 22; parodic element of, 3, 22, 63, 65, 68–69, 74–75, 103, 109; primary characters, 3; ritual elements, 22–23; scenes in the, 113–14; stories of, 7; themes of good and evil in the, 3–4, 65, 74–75, 81

Congo flag, 65–66, 86–87, 88

"El Congo: Folklore Costeño de Colón" (Esquina), 64

Congo game. See Congo drama

Congo hat (kafucula), 71–72, 180 fig. 5.10

Congo jacket, 180 fig. 5.10

Congo tradition: arts celebrating the, 14, 16–18; Cimarrones resistance celebrated through, 3–4, 22, 63, 65, 68–69, 74–75, 103, 109; as cultural nationalism, 36; embodied knowledge of, 87–88; incorporating immigrants, 50; insider-outsider element in, 161–62; national reception of, 21; official narratives of, 64–67; in- vs. out-groups in the, 142; overview, 3–4; preserving the, 87–88, 105–6; (re)inventing the, 86–89, 91, 112–14, 190–91; resilience of, 25–26; study assumptions regarding, 11; tourist guides description of, 147–48; younger generation's experience of, 89, 91, 92–93. See also cultural preservation

Congo tradition, changes in: circum-local exchanges and, 110, 111–14, 118, 120–26, 132; the connecting road and, 89–91, 105, 120–21, 132; generational shift in the interpretation of, 103–6, 110, 124–25; globalization and, 86, 90–93, 132; influences on, 23; new elements, 190; the tax, 84–85; 21st century and, 110, 195

connecting road: tax collection on the, 84, 85 fig. 2.16; Torrijos' construction of the, 32, 49–50. See also circum-local exchanges

connecting road, consequences of the: to circum-local exchanges, 84–86, 189–190; to community, 89–91, 105–6, 114, 132; to Congo tradition, 89, 120–21; to global connectivity, 90–91, 132; to internal migration, 170; job opportunities, 90–91; to tourism, 86; for young people, 90–91

Connerton, Paul, 29, 91, 109

Conniff, Michael L., 50, 52

Conquergood, Dwight, 5, 9, 10, 12, 14, 17, 163, 188

consciousness: duality of in performance, 24–25, 115–16, 126, 141–46, 150; in framing tourist presentations, 191; official-practical friction, 189; third person, 141–42. *See also* official consciousness

Constitution of 1941, 45–46

Constitution of 1946, 47

Construction era (1903–14), 22, 32, 34–42

Cooper, Carolyn, 142

co-performance: awareness, space of, 13; witnessing in, 12–13

costume: children's, 6; chorus, 137–38; clothing turned inside-out, 115, 130; Congo hat and jacket, 180 figs. 5.10–5.11; the Devil's, 76, 98, 115–17, 121 fig. 3.2, 160; face painting used as, 69, 71, 74, 202n3; of King of the Congos, 68–69, 71; *La historia de los congos de Portobelo: Translating History Through the Body* (performance) (Alexander Craft), 159, 160; in local vs. like-local performances, 91–92; the Major Devil's, 75 fig. 2.12, 76, 97 fig. 2.18, 99 fig. 2.20, 115, 128–29, 129 fig. 3.6; El Nazareno, 14–15; Pajarito's, 67, 72, 73 fig. 2.10, 74, 79, 94, 161; the pollera, 69, 72, 92, 137–38; of Queen of the Congos, 68–69, 69 fig. 2.8, 160; structuring official consciousness, 65, 68–77, 70 fig. 2.9, 73 fig. 2.10, 75 fig. 2.12, 97 fig. 2.18, 99 fig. 2.20; tourist guides description of, 147–48

Covington-Ward, Yolanda, 18

Creative Currents: Art + Culture + Collaboration (was Taller Portobelo Norte), 14, 18–19

Crenshaw, Kimberlé, 19

El Cristo Negro (El Nazareno/The Black Christ), 14–15, 57, 59, 61, 146–47

cross: of the Archangel, 77; dancing with in/as the body, 80, 129–130; *La historia de los congos de Portobelo: Translating History Through the Body* (performance) (Alexander Craft), 159–160, 161; *Making the Sign of the Cross* (installation) (Alexander Craft), 11, 162–66; of the Queen, 69, 77, 160

crossroads: *Dancing with the Devil at the Crossroads* (performance), 11, 166–170; JASON XV: Rainforests at the Crossroads, 91; "The Son (Sun): Panama is a Crossroads" (Alexander Craft), 164

Cuba-Panama relations, 48, 50

cultural nationalism, 35–40

cultural preservation: conflicts, 186–87; of Congo dialect, 145–46; Digital Portobelo: Art + Scholarship + Cultural Preservation, 13, 26, 195–200; El Festival de los Diablos y Congos, 23–24, 110, 123 fig. 3.3, 124 fig. 3.4; local and circum-local vs. like-local performances, 126; Taller Portobelo painting workshop, 14, 15–16, 158; Taller Portobelo women's cooperative, 14–15

culture, performance as/is the (re)making of, 23–24, 105, 110, 112–14, 126, 190–91

culture vs. race, effect and affects of, 41

Customs House (aduana), 57, 59, 61, 143, 154

dance in the Congo drama: author's learning about, 157–58; centrality of, 77–80, 106; congada, 79, 89–90, 148–49, 171; dancing with the cross in/as, 80, 129–130; as embodied knowledge of tradition, 157–58; *La historia de los congos de Portobelo: Translating History Through the Body* (performance) (Alexander Craft), 11, 158–162; like-local interactions with tourists, 151–52; male-female negotiations of power and will, 138–39; Molinar de la Fuentes with her grandson, 150 fig. 4.7; photograph of, 62 fig. 2.4; power and presence of the Devils established through, 104; tax collection role, 85; in two palacios, 89, 91; women's ability to control space and attention through, 93, 138–39, 152, 191

dance of the Major Devil, 80, 129–130

dancers: drummer relation, 93–95, 137–38; singer relation, 93

*Dancing with the Devil at the Crossroads* (performance) (Alexander Craft), 11, 166–170

The Day of Black Ethnicity (El Día de la Etnia Negra), 5–6, 21, 30, 32, 54

Day of the Martyrs, 206n31

decency, female, 140, 154

Delvera, Juan, 14

Denzin, Norman, 11

devil (Christian): *Dancing with the Devil at the Crossroads* (performance), 11, 166–170; enslaver's appropriation and use of, 3–4, 80, 103; trope as parody, 3–4

"The Devil Knocks" (song), 1

Devil masks: Celedonio's, 128–29, 129 fig. 3.6; Chavarría on his, 115–17; "Faces of Portobelo: A Mask Workshop," 173–75, 176–75.8; El Festival de los Diablos y Congos, 121 fig. 3.2; teenaged strategies for, 124–25

Devil Queen mask, 177 fig. 5.6

Devils: Archangel and the Ánimas capture of, 80; blessing/baptizing the, 76, 81, 103, 108 fig. 3.1, 113–14; at Celedonio's home, 97–100, 98 fig. 2.19; costume, 76, 115–17, 121 fig. 3.2, 160; dance in establishing the power and presence of, 104; enslavers cast as, 4, 80; game between the Congos and the, 103–6, 113, 120–26, 123 fig. 3.3; generational shift in the interpretation of, 110, 124–25; *La historia de los congos de Portobelo: Translating History Through the Body* (performance) (Alexander Craft), 160; in like-local presentations, 24; peaceful, 102 fig. 2.23; role of, 103; "Untitled" devil installation (Jerónimo and Tito), 182, 183 figs. 5.14–5.15; whips of, 81, 105, 165. *See also* Major Devil (El Diablo Mayor)

Devil's Den, 74 fig. 2.11

Diablitos (little devils), 102, 156 fig. 5.1

El Diablo Mayor (the Major Devil). *See* Celedonio (El Diablo Mayor); Major Devil (El Diablo Mayor)

El Diablo Segundo (Secondary Devil), 3, 76

"Diablo Tun Tun" (dance), 79–80, 94

El Día de la Etnia Negra (The Day of Black Ethnicity), 5–6, 21, 30, 32, 54

dialogical performance, 9, 10, 11, 17, 25–26, 188

diaspora: circum-local exchange and changes in tradition, 110, 111–14, 118, 120–26, 132, 191; of Congo Carnival, 134; *Rara!: Voudou, Power, and Performance in Haiti and Its Diaspora* (McAlister), 13–14. *See also* Black Diaspora; migration

Diaspora Africana, 204n9

Digital Portobelo: Art + Scholarship + Cultural Preservation, 26, 195–200

double-consciousness in performance, 24–25, 115–16, 126, 141–46, 150

Drake, Francis, 3, 59

Drewal, Margaret, 10, 88

Drolet, Patricia, 157

drug trade, 15–16, 52, 194

drummers: dancer relation, 93–94, 138; lead singer relation, 137–38

drumming, 77–79, 78 fig. 2.14

Du Bois, W. E. B., 116, 141

Durban (South Africa) Conference (2001), 54

Easter, 88

economic nationalisms, 43–45

economy, 16, 86, 146, 162

education, 6, 49, 91

Edwards, Brent, 36

Eleta, Sandra, 14–16, 18, 120, 130–32, 166, 171, 172, 187

enslaved people: buffoonery as tactic of resistance, 152; the devil used as threat against, 3–4, 80, 103; resistance through language, 144. *See also* Cimarrones (self-liberated)

enslavers, Spanish: approval of whipping tradition, 103; Cimarrones resistance to, 58–59, 162; Congo language in subverting rule of, 144; Congo tradition in celebrating resistance to, 3–4, 22, 36–38, 63, 65, 68–69, 74–75, 103, 109; devil used as threat by, 3–4, 80, 103

Escabar, Arthur, 10

Escoffery, Carla, 170

"El espíritu de los ancestros de los congos" ("The Spirit of the Congo Ancestors") (Ariel and Tatu), 178, 179 fig. 5.9, 180 figs. 5.10–5.11

Esquina, Gustavo, 18, 38, 72, 87, 170, 173, 182, 184, 185 figs. 5.17–5.18, 186–87

Esquina, Melba, 64–65, 68, 72, 77 fig. 2.13, 78, 79, 94, 158

Esquina, Reynaldo "Rey," 170, 173, 182, 184, 185 figs. 5.17–5.18, 186

Esquina, Simona, 65, 68, 71, 78, 86–89, 92, 103–4, 137, 152, 158

Esquina, Vicente, 82, 87

Esquina, Virgilio "Tito," 16, 170, 182, 183 figs. 5.14–5.15

Esquina, Virgilio "Yaneca," 15–16, 18, 70 fig. 2.9, 72, 145, 158, 161, 170, 182, 184 fig. 5.16

Esquina, Zacarias, 82

ethnicity vs. race, 46–47

ethnography: of the ears and heart, 9; performance, 10–11, 187–88

etnia negra (Black ethnicity), celebration of, 5–7, 21, 30, 32, 54

exclusion, state-defined criteria for, 31–32

Fabian, Johannes, 12, 13

face painting, 69, 71, 74, 202n3

"Faces of Portobelo: A Mask Workshop" ("Caras de Portobelo: Un taller de mascaras"), 173–75, 176–75.8

faith, performance as an act of, 2. See also Catholic faith

Fanon, Frantz, 141, 144–45

Ferias de Portobelo (Portobelo Fairs), 59, 162

Fernando VII, 5–6

Festival Afropanameño, 29–30

El Festival de las polleras Congas, 105

The Festival of the Devils and Congos (El Festival de los Diablos y Congos), 23–24, 105, 110, 120–26, 123 fig. 3.3, 124 fig. 3.4, 191, 194–95

Flag Riots, 48–49

flag(s): flown in the Zone, 48–49, 50; Pajarito's, 161; raising the, 65–66, 86–87, 88

Foucault, Michel, 10

Fusco, Coco, 11

Gates, Henry Louis, Jr., 10

Gilroy, Paul, 23, 33, 51, 111

global engagement: the connecting road and, 90–91, 132; Spelman College International Artist-in-Residence Program, 16

globalization: performance within the political economy of, 24–25; tradition and, 86, 90–93, 132

global trade, 146, 162

Goldberg, David Theo, 31, 41, 203n7

Golden, Manuel "Tatu," 86–87, 170, 178, 180 figs. 5.10–5.11

Gómez-Peña, Guillermo, 11

González de Carrera, Noel, 120

good and evil, themes in the Congo drama, 3–4, 65, 74–75, 81

Great Depression, 43–44

Grosz, Elizabeth, 10

grunt (pujido), 95–96, 98, 99–101, 130–32

El Grupo Portobelo, 14

Guss, David, 10

Hall, Stuart, 57, 189

Ham, the biblical, 164

Hamera, Judith, 10

Hay-Bunau-Varilla Treaty, 206n21

Higginbotham, Evelyn Brooks, 143

hot water, 128

Hurricane Claudette, 171

Hurston, Zora Neale, 10

identity, ethnoracial: cultural nationalisms shaping, 36–40; markers of, 33, 35–36;

performance of/as, 21–22; Portobeleños, 6. *See also* Black identity

"I'll Fly Away" ("Volaré") (Sunstrum), 172–73, 174 fig. 5.2, 175 fig. 5.3

immigrants, discrimination against: assimilated vs. non-assimilated differentiation, 33, 35–36; legislated, 45–46; non-native speakers of Spanish, 46; prohibited/undesirable immigrants category for West Indians, 8, 32, 33, 45–46

immigration, U.S. imperialism and, 39, 55

Instituto Nacional de Cultura (National Institute of Culture), 61

"In the Name of the Father: The Kongo Cosmogram" (*Making the Sign of the Cross*) (Alexander Craft), 164

Jackson, John, 10

James, Yaroka, 86

JASON XV: Rainforests at the Crossroads, 91

Jim Crow, 8, 31, 39–41

Jiménez, Andres, 67, 84–85, 89, 113, 119, 142

Jiménez, Ariel "Pajarito," 86, 158, 170, 171, 178, 180 figs. 5.10–5.11

Jiménez, Fernando, 119

Jiménez, Hector, 170, 178–79, 181 figs. 5.12–5.13

Jiménez, Melida, 115

Jiménez, Raul, 101 fig. 2.22, 102, 104, 109–10, 113, 119–126, 131, 166, 173

Jiménez, Sarabi, 86, 146, 148, 175, 177 fig. 5.6

Johnson, Dwayne "The Rock," 61

Johnson, E. Patrick, 10, 11

Johnson, John, 41–42

Johnson, Robert, 11, 166–170

Jones, Omi Osun Joni L., 11

Juan de Dioso/Juan de Dios (King of the Congos). *See* King of the Congos (Juan de Dioso/Juan de Dios)

King, Roberto Enrique, 171

King of the Congos (Juan de Dioso/Juan de Dios), 24, 68 fig. 2.7, 68–69, 69 fig. 2.8, 71, 81–82, 160–61

Kongo Cosmogram, 210n5

Kongo vs. Congo, 201n5

Kymlicka, Will, 35

LaFeber, Walter, 45, 46

*La historia de los congos de Portobelo: Translating History Through the Body* (performance), 11, 158–162

La Menina (The Princess), 3, 82–83, 83 fig. 2.15

Lancaster, Roger, 10

land distribution projects, 50

language, resistance through, 144–45

Lanier, Michelle, 17, 170, 171, 173

Las Ánimas (Archangel and the six Souls), 76–77, 77 fig. 2.13, 80, 113

Latin America, race and gender in cartoons of, 41–42

lead singer, 77–78, 78 fig. 2.14, 93–94, 137–38. *See also* singers and chorus

Lent, 80, 88

Leonardo, Micaela di, 10

like-local (tourist) performance: characters of, 24, 121; components of, 148–49; Congo women pre-, 136 fig. 4.1, 141 fig. 4.3; economics of, 21, 24–25; gathering for, 149 fig. 4.6; masking gender dynamics, 149–150, 154; watching the watchers in, 25, 143, 152. *See also* local vs. like-local performance; tourists

like-local snapshots, 153

Lindsay, Arturo, 5, 11, 15–18, 20–21, 91, 93, 152, 157, 159, 165–66, 171, 182

little bird. *See* Pajarito ("the Prince")

local performance: female respectability in, 154, 191; gender and sexuality in, 149–151; like-local interactions in, 138–39, 151–52

local vs. like-local performance: characters in, 148; costume in, 91–92; double-consciousness in, 24–25, 115–16, 126, 141–46, 150; female respectability in, 140, 149–150, 154, 191; masking gender dynamics, 149–151; of singers and chorus, 91–92

*Lonely Planet Panama,* 147–48

Lord's Prayer (El Padre Nuestro), 161, 163, 165

Madison, D. Soyini, 10, 11

Major Devil (El Diablo Mayor): appointing the, 118; baptizing/blessing the, 81, 103; community respect for, 116–17, 130; costume, 75 fig. 2.12, 76, 97 fig. 2.18, 98, 99 fig. 2.20, 115, 128–29, 129 fig. 3.6; cultural contributions of, 23–24; dance of the, 80; embodying the, 116; forming the shape of the cross, 80, 129–130; insider/outsider perspective, 115–16; length of commitment as, 114, 119; palacio visit, 79–80; as parody and metaphor, 103; performative integrity of the, 116–17; pujido (grunt) of, 95–96, 98, 99–101, 130–32; the Queen and, 93–95; role of, 74–76; selecting the, 118; young practitioners view of, 103–6. *See also* Celedonio (El Diablo Mayor)

Major Devil tradition, (re)inventing the, 110, 112–14, 133–34, 190–91

*Making the Sign of the Cross* (installation) (Alexander Craft), 11, 162–66

Mallarino-Bidland Treaty, 206n21

Mama Guardia, 82–83

Mankekar, Purnima, 10

*Maroon Societies* (Price), 36

marrons, 36, 38. *See also* Cimarrones

Mata, Juana de, 83

McAlister, Elizabeth, 13–14, 142

McCullough, David, 162

men (Congo): animal names chosen by, 72; buffoonery used by, 72; controlling deviant tourist interactions, 138–39, 191; costume, 71–72, 180 figs. 5.10–5.11; face painting used by, 69, 71, 74, 202n3; like-local interactions with tourists, 151–52

Merced/Mercedes (the Queen). *See* Queen of the Congos (Maria Merced/Mercedes)

mestizos, 6, 8, 31, 37, 55, 203n7

meta-art theory, 25

middle class racism, 46

migration: the connecting road and, 170; intra-isthmian, 50; "Nationality and Immigration" legislation effect on, 45. *See also* diaspora

mise en scène, 62–63. *See also* official consciousness; mise-en-scène elements structuring

modernity, race as a mark of, 203n7

*Mojonga: A Performative Altar to Former Congo Queens* (installation) (Alexander Craft), 11

Molinar de la Fuentes, Elsa, 7, 141–42, 150 fig. 4.7

Monroe Doctrine, 39

"A Monument of Homage to the Congo Spirits" ("El monumento de homenaje a los espíritus de los congos") (Craft, Rey, Gustavo), 182, 184, 185 figs. 5.17–5.18, 186

Morgan, Henry, 3

Moscoso, Arnulfo, 44

Moscoso, Mireya, 44

*El museo congo* (installation): artist collaborators, 170; background, 170–71; communitas, 173, 186; "Faces of Portobelo: A Mask Workshop," 173–75, 176–75.8; feedback received, 188; "I'll Fly Away" ("Volaré") (Sunstrum), 172–73, 174 fig. 5.2, 175 fig. 5.3; introduction, 11; "A Monument of Homage to the Congo Spirits" (Alexaner Craft, Rey, Gustavo), 182, 184, 185 figs. 5.17–5.18, 186; "Pajarito" (Yaneca), 182, 184 fig. 5.16; "The Spirit of the Congo Ancestors" (Ariel and Tatu), 178, 179 fig. 5.9, 180 figs. 5.10–5.11; "Untitled" Devil installation (Jerónimo and Tito), 182; "Untitled" installation (Moraitho and Hector), 178–79, 181 figs. 5.12–5.13

music, centrality of, 106

"My Name is Panamá" clothing, 153, 209n11

National institute of Art and Culture, 147

nationalism, Panamanian: Citizens vs. Subjects era (1926–46), 22, 32, 42–47; Construction era (1903–14), 22, 32, 34–42; origins of, 8, 42–45; Patriots vs. Empire era (1964–79), 22, 32, 47–51; Reconciliation era (1989–2003), 22, 32, 51–55

"Nationality and Immigration" legislation, 45

El Nazareno (El Cristo Negro/The Black Christ), 14–15, 57, 59, 61, 146–47

négritude, 31, 204n10

Nissen, Beth, 50

Nombre de Dios, 58–59, 112–13, 114, 134

Noriega, Manuel, 15, 52–53, 145

"Now I Lay Me Down to Sleep" (prayer), 165

Nuevo Portobelo project, 207n34


Odeleye, Oronike, 14, 18

official consciousness: Devil character in the, 114; like-local (tourist) performance in the, 92; narratives of Congo tradition, 64–67; new elements in the, 190; official-practical friction, 189; Williams', 23, 63. See also consciousness

official consciousness, mise-en-scène elements structuring: Archangel and the six Souls, 76–77, 77 fig. 2.13, 80; cast of characters, 65; costume, 65, 68–77, 70 fig. 2.9, 73 fig. 2.10, 75 fig. 2.12, 97 fig. 2.18, 99 fig. 2.20; dance and drumming, 77–80, 78 fig. 2.14; drumming, 77–79; Major Devil character, 74–76; narrative meaning, 66 fig. 2.5; props, 65, 69, 74; ritual space, 65–66, 66 fig. 2.5; ritual time, 65–66, 67, 76, 78–80, 96 fig. 2.17; royal court, 68 fig. 2.7, 68–69, 69 fig. 2.8, 71–74; singers and chorus, 77, 78 fig. 2.14

Operation Just Cause (U.S. invasion), 15–16, 52–54

Oshosi, 208n10. See also Sebastian, feast day of St.

other (the outsider): author as, 19–20; Blacks as, 8, 37; positionality and dialectics of difference, 19–21; state-defined criteria

for belonging, 31–32; taxation of, 84–86, 85 fig. 2.16, 151. See also tourists


El Padre Nuestro (Lord's Prayer), 161, 163, 165

Pajarito ("the Prince" "Little Bird"): costume, 73 fig. 2.10, 74; flag carried by, 161; Jiménez, Ariel, 86, 158, 170, 171, 178, 180 figs. 5.10–5.11; La historia de los congos de Portobelo: Translating History Through the Body (performance) (Alexander Craft), 160, 161; performance, 67 fig. 2.6, 124; role of, 24, 67, 72–73, 74, 79, 84–86, 94, 161; tax collection by, 85; whistle of, 67, 72, 74, 79, 94, 161

"Pajarito" (Yaneca), 182, 184 fig. 5.16

el palacio/el palenque/el rancho, 65–67, 66 fig. 2.5, 88–91, 93, 137, 154, 194–95

Palma, Ileana Solís, 112, 129

Paloma, reina de los Congos (Zuñigan), 77–78

Panama: census racial classifications, 60–61, 203n7, 205n17; cultural nationalism, 35–36; demographics, 203n7; discrimination in 1941 Constitution, 45–46; drug trade, 15–16, 194; economic nationalisms, 43–45; Great Depression, 43–44; historically, 162; independence from Colombia, 34–42; racism, historically, 9; state-defined criteria for othering, 31–32; symbolic Blackening/feminizing, 42; travel prohibitions for citizens of, 154. See also nationalism, Panamanian; United States–Panama relations

Panama Canal construction and control: beginnings, 204n6; French period, 204n6; global effect of, 162; immigration and, 39, 55; nationalism and, 22

Panama Canal Treaty, 8–9, 32

Panama Canal workers: silver vs. gold, 39, 41; statistics, 205n20; U.S. Jim Crow policies and, 8, 31, 39–41. See also West Indian Canal workers

Panama Canal Zone: effects of dismantling, 55, 56; flags flown in the, 48–49, 50; granted in perpetuity to the US, 206n21; lease payments, 43–44, 146; turnover's effect on tourism, 21, 146; whites living in, statistics, 205n20

Panama-Cuba relations, 48, 50

Panamá for the Panamanians (Panameñismo) campaign, 32, 45–46

Panamanian flag, 48–49, 50

Panamanian Institute of Tourism, 147

*Panama: The Bradt Travel Guide,* 147–48

Panameñismo (Panamá for the Panamanians) campaign, 32, 45–46

parody element of Congo drama, 3–4, 7, 22, 63, 103, 109, 165

Patriots vs. Empire era (1964–79), 22, 32, 47–51

Pavis, Patrice, 62

performance: as an act of faith and community, 2; author engagement with, 12; circum-local exchanges in, 120–26, 191; colonial era, 142; cultural, 22–24, 63; dialogical, 9, 10, 11, 17, 25–26, 188; duality/double-consciousness in, 24–25, 115–16, 126, 141–46, 150; of/as ethnoracial identity, 21–22; (re)making of culture, 23–24, 105, 110, 112–14, 126, 190–91; subversive ability, 25, 143, 152, 190. *See also* like-local (tourist) performance; local vs. like-local performance

performance ethnography, 10–11, 187–88

"Performance Studies, Interventions and Radical Research" (Conquergood), 9

performative writing, as documentation modality, 9–10

performers: *specific groups:* audience relations, 143, 191; character-role separation, 133; names chosen by, 72; post-performance, 139 fig. 4.2, 153 fig. 4.8; pre-performance, 136 fig. 4.1, 141 fig. 4.3. *See also* like-local (tourist) performance

Perro Negro (Black Dog) prayer, 131

Philadelphia-Lakers game, 165–66

Piper, Adrian, 11, 17, 25

pollera skirt, 69, 72, 92, 137–38, 160, 182

Pollock Della, 9

Poole, Deborah, 10

Portobelo: the arts in, 14, 16–19; contempo-rary, 61–62; cruise ships to, 146, 147 fig. 4.5; described, 57–58; drug epidemic in, 15–16; economy, 16, 146, 162; ethnora-cial groups, 61; ethnoracial identity, 6; global engagement, 7–8; historically, 22, 58–59, 146, 162; intra-isthmian migrants, 50; photo of, 56 fig. 2.1, 60 fig. 2.3; popu-lation, 60–61, 207n34; street view, 58 fig. 2.2; tourism in, 21, 32, 86, 146–47

Portobelo Fairs (Ferias de Portobelo), 59, 162

*Portobelo: Fotografía de Panama* (Eleta), 15

Portobelo Foundation, 15

Powell, Colin, 52

practical consciousness: the "changing same" of Congo characters, 81–86; Devil character in the, 114; official-practical friction, 189; Williams,' 23, 63

prayer: *La historia de los congos de Portobelo: Translating History Through the Body* (performance) (Alexander Craft), 161; *Making the Sign of the Cross* (installa-tion) (Alexander Craft), 163–64, 165; "Now I Lay Me Down to Sleep," 165; El Padre Nuestro (Lord's Prayer), 161, 163, 165; Perro Negro (Black Dog) prayer, 131

Price, Richard, 36

Priest character, 76–78, 81, 103, 108 fig. 3.1, 113

Primer Festival Afropanameño (2006), 54

the Prince (Pajarito). *See* Pajarito ("the Prince")

The Princess (La Menina), 3, 82–83, 83 fig. 2.15

pujido (grunt), 95–96, 98, 99–101, 130–32

Queen of the Congos (Maria Merced/Mer-cedes): costume, 68–69, 69 fig. 2.8, 160; with her King, 68 fig. 2.7, 69 fig. 2.8; *La historia de los congos de Portobelo: Translating History Through the Body* (performance) (Alexander Craft), 160–61; the Major Devil and the, 93–95; masks, 176 fig. 5.4; *Mojonga: A Perfor-mative Altar to Former Congo Queens* (installation) (Alexander Craft), 11; physical strength, 94; power of the, 94; The Princess/La Menina and, 82; role of,

80–82, 93, 160, 202n9, 208n11; in tourist presentations, 24

race as a mark of modernity, 203n7

race vs. ethnicity, 46–47

racial nationalisms, 44–47

*Rara!: Voudou, Power, and Performance in Haiti and Its Diaspora* (McAlister), 13–14

Reagan, Ronald, administration, 52

El Real Aduana de Portobelo (The Royal Customs House), 61

Reconciliation era (1989–2003), 22, 32, 51–55

Reid, Lydia M., 60–61

Republic of Panama. *See* Panama

respectability/reputation, 140, 143–44, 149–150, 154

ritual space: structuring official consciousness, 65–66, 66 fig. 2.5; women's ability to control through dance, 93, 138–39, 152, 191. *See also* space

ritual time structuring official consciousness, 65–66, 67, 76, 78–80, 96 fig. 2.17

Rivera-Servera, Ramón H., 34

Roach, Joseph, 23, 57, 111

Robles, Ricardo, 115

Rojas, Don, 48–49

Roosevelt, Theodore, 39

Rosaldo, Renato, 61, 109

"the ruins of Santo Domingo monastery in the colonial section of the city" (installation), 17

Sankofa, 188, 191–92

Santizo, Felicia, 15

Savigliano, Marta E., 10, 142

schools, 6, 49

Scott, James, 145

Sebastian, feast day of St., 65, 86. *See also* Oshosi

Secondary Devil (El Diablo Segundo), 3, 76

Shrove Tuesday. *See* Carnival Tuesday (Shrove Tuesday)

singers and chorus, 77–80, 78 fig. 2.14, 91–94, 137–38. *See also* lead singer

slavery: influence on Black identity, 30; *Making the Sign of the Cross* (installation) (Alexander Craft), 11, 162–66; tradition in celebrating resistance to, 3–4, 22, 36–38, 63, 65, 68–69, 74–75, 103, 109. *See also* enslaved people

slave trade, 30, 164

Smith, Ronald, 37, 64, 157

social media, 195

Solio, Antonia, 115

"The Son (Sun): Panama is a Crossroads" (*Making the Sign of the Cross*) (Alexander Craft), 164

space: of awareness, 13; circum-local space of the bus, 111, 150–51. *See also* ritual space

Spanish Crown: drama as parody of, 7; settlement in Panama, 58–59; slave trade, 30, 164

Spanish enslavers: approval of whipping tradition, 103; Cimarrones resistance to, 58–59, 162; Congo language in subverting rule of, 144; Congo tradition in celebrating resistance to, 3–4, 22, 36–38, 63, 65, 68–69, 74–75, 103, 109; devil used as threat by, 3–4, 80, 103

Spanish Queen, 80

speaking Congo, 144 fig. 4.4, 144–46

Spears, Britney, 61

Spelman College International Artist-in-Residence Program, 16

Spelman College Summer Art Colony, 14, 16–18

"Spirit" (*Making the Sign of the Cross*) (Alexander Craft), 164

state-defined criteria for othering, 31–32

Stoler, Ann Laura, 22

Sunstrum, Pamela, 170, 172–73, 174 fig. 5.2, 175 fig. 5.3, 186

Taller Portobelo Norte (later Creative Currents: Art + Culture + Collaboration), 14, 18–19

Taller Portobelo painting workshop and gallery, 5, 14, 15–16, 158

Taller Portobelo women's cooperative, 14–15

taxing the outsider, 84–86, 85 fig. 2.16, 151

third-person consciousness, 141–42

Thomas, Deborah, 10, 142

Thompson, Robert Ferris, 201n5

Torres, Arlene, 31, 38

Torrijos, Martín, 30, 44

Torrijos, Omar, 44, 49–50, 52

tourism: ease of for Panamanians vs. U.S. citizens, 154; growth in, 21, 32, 86, 146–47; historically, 146; involving the younger Congo generation through, 93; performance within the political economy of, 24–25; for reviving the official Congo performance, 92; statistics, 209n8

tourist guides, 147–48

tourists: countries of origin, 146; as entertainment, 143, 148, 152, 191; like-local interactions with, 138–39, 151–52, 191; out-group status, 143, 146; taxing the, 84–86, 85 fig. 2.16, 151; watching of the watchers, 25, 143, 152. See also like-local (tourist) performance

trickster tradition, 152

trope of evil in the Congo drama, 3–4, 65, 74–75, 81

Tsing, Anna, 10

Turner, Victor, 12, 22, 32–33, 54, 63

UNESCO World Heritage Sites, 146

United States, race and gender in cartoons of, 42

United States–Panama relations: 1989 invasion (Operation Just Cause), 15–16, 52–54; Carter-Torrijos Treaty, 44, 49, 51, 53; economic, 43–44, 146; Flag Riots, 48–49; nationalism, influence on, 44–45; Panama Canal Treaty, 8–9, 32. See also Panama Canal construction and control

University of Panamá, 45, 50

"Untitled" Devil installation (Jerónimo and Tito), 182, 183 figs. 5.14–5.15

"Untitled" installation (Moraitho and Hector), 178–79, 181 figs. 5.12–5.13

"VII. I love those little booths at Benvenuiti's" (Brooks), 154

Wade, Peter, 37, 41, 51, 54

walking canes (bastones), 15–16

War on Drugs, U.S., 52

West Indian Canal workers: Citizens vs. Subjects era (1926–46), 32, 42–47; discrimination against, 8, 32, 33, 45–46; ethnoracial controls, 41; markers of national and ethnoracial identity, 35–36; Panamá for the Panamanians campaign against, 45–46; race-ethnicity-class relations, 39–42; statistics, 205n20; treatment of, 39–40

West Indian Museum of Panama, 32

West Indians: Afro-Antilleans (afroantillanos), 8, 30, 35; assimilation, 33; citizenship rights, 45–46, 47; cultural nationalisms, 35–36, 38–40; ethnoracial controls, 41; Great Depression unemployment, 44–45; identity formation, 39–41; integration tactics, 32; in Panama historically, 8; term meaning, 6; as undesirable immigrants, 8, 32, 45. See also Afro-Colonials–West Indian relations

When the Devil Knocks (Alexander Craft): performance analysis in, 21–26; performance-centered approach to, 7, 9–11

When the Devil Knocks field research (Alexander Craft): beginnings, 159; collaborative workshop approach, 13–14; collaborators, 18–19; community and outsider relationships, 19–21; Creative Currents: Art + Culture + Collaboration, 14, 18–19; dates of, 18; local interactions of the author, 159; positionality and dialectics of difference, 19–21; Sankofa praxis in, 191–92; Spelman College Summer Art Colony, 14, 16–18; Taller Portobelo painting workshop, 14, 15–16; Taller Portobelo women's cooperative, 14–15; witnessing, community and coperformance, 12–13

whipping: the Archangel and Souls, 81; intimacy of, 102; tradition, enslavers approval of, 103; young practitioners practice of, 104–5

whips: the Devil's, 81, 105, 165; the enslaver's, 74, 81, 165; the Major Devil's, 76, 99, 101, 122; *Making the Sign of the Cross* (installation) (Alexander Craft), 165; razor blades on, 105

whistles, 92, 95, 124, 152. *See also* Pajarito's whistle

Whitten, Norman, 31, 38

Williams, Raymond, 23, 63, 88, 89, 109, 189

Wilson, Peter, 140

witnessing in co-performance, 12–13

women (Congo): ability to control space and attention through dance, 93, 138–39, 151–52, 191; author relations, 20; commitment to Congo, 89; controlling deviant tourist interactions, 151–52; King of the Congos responsibility for, 82; mutiny against the mayor, 53–54; pollera skirt, 69, 72, 92, 137–38; pre-tourist presentation, 136 fig. 4.1, 141 fig. 4.3; respectability in local vs. like-local performances, 140, 149–150, 154, 191; sociocultural expectations of appearance of, 20; Taller Portobelo women's cooperative, 14–15. See also *specific women's performance roles*

*Yoruba Ritual* (Drewal), 88

Young, Harvey, 34

younger generation: Congo experience, 89, 91, 92–93; consequences of the connecting road for, 90–91; Devil masks created by, 124–25; The Festival of the Devils and Congos involvement, 122, 128; involving through tourism, 93; preserving the Congo dialect, 145–46; shifting the interpretation of tradition/Devil character, 103–6, 110, 124–25; whipping by, 104–5. *See also* children

Zuñigan, Maricel Martín, 77–78

BLACK PERFORMANCE AND CULTURAL CRITICISM SERIES
Valerie Lee and E. Patrick Johnson, Series Editors

The Black Performance and Cultural Criticism series includes monographs that draw on interdisciplinary methods to analyze, critique, and theorize black cultural production. Books in the series take as their object of intellectual inquiry the performances produced on the stage and on the page, stretching the boundaries of both black performance and literary criticism.

*When the Devil Knocks: The Congo Tradition and the Politics of Blackness in Twentieth-Century Panama*
RENÉE ALEXANDER CRAFT

*The Queer Limit of Black Memory: Black Lesbian Literature and Irresolution*
MATT RICHARDSON

*Fathers, Preachers, Rebels, Men: Black Masculinity in U.S. History and Literature, 1820–1945*
EDITED BY TIMOTHY R. BUCKNER AND PETER CASTER

*Secrecy, Magic, and the One-Act Plays of Harlem Renaissance Women Writers*
TAYLOR HAGOOD

*Beyond Lift Every Voice and Sing: The Culture of Uplift, Identity, and Politics in Black Musical Theater*
PAULA MARIE SENIORS

*Mutha' Is Half a Word: Intersections of Folklore, Vernacular, Myth, and Queerness in Black Female Culture*
L. H. STALLINGS

*Prisons, Race, and Masculinity in Twentieth-Century U.S. Literature and Film*
PETER CASTER

CPSIA information can be obtained
at www.ICGtesting.com
Printed in the USA
FFOW04n1300130516
24095FF